THE

AMERICAN LUTHERAN CHURCH,

HISTORICALLY, DOCTRINALLY, AND PRACTICALLY

DELINEATED,

IN SEVERAL OCCASIONAL DISCOURSES:

BY S. S. SCHMUCKER, D. D.,

PROFESSOR OF CHRISTIAN THEOLOGY, IN THE THEOLOGICAL SEMINARY OF THE GENERAL SYNOD, GETTYSBURG, PA.

FIFTH EDITION.

PHILADELPHIA:
E. W. MILLER, RANSTEAD PLACE.
1852.

GEO. D. EMERSON & CO.
STEREOTYPERS,
SPRINGFIELD, OHIO

PREFACE.

In offering this work to the public, it is proper that some of the considerations which have actuated the publishers, should be stated. The title itself is significant of the subject on which it treats. The true history, real character, present position, and distinctive features of the Lutheran Church in the world, are little known, often misunderstood, and sometimes grossly misrepresented in this country.

Among the causes which may be assigned for this, we mention the want of a proper knowledge of Church History in general, and of Protestantism in particular; non-acquaintance with the German language, and it is to be feared, denominational bigotry.

The Lutheran Church was the first to throw off the yoke of ecclesiastical tyranny, and break the scepter of religious despotism; to maintain the great Protestant principle, that the Bible is the only infallible rule of faith and practice;

to assert the right of private judgment in the interpretation of the Scriptures; and to proclaim the doctrine of Justification by Faith alone, as the foundation of a "standing and falling church." Her institutions are second to none on earth; and her literature, embracing every subject of religious inquiry, is the glory of Christendom, furnishing an antidote to false philosophy and rationalism on the one hand, and to vulgar infidelity on the other.

Her fundamental doctrines are those of the Reformation, found, in their essential aspects, in all the symbols of Protestantism.

Her peculiarities place her in a medium position in Church extremes—in doctrine, worship, rites, and government. Her territory of operation is extended over a large portion of the globe, embracing more than thirty millions of human beings, constituting nearly one-half of Protestantism, and the hope of much of the world.

Her history is intimately interwoven with that of the reformation of the sixteenth century, furnishing lessons of wisdom and experience to instruct and encourage, as well as of presumption and folly to warn and rebuke. All God's dealings with her should teach all her sons, that she was planted, watered, and preserved by Him.

But the volume before us treats of the "AMERICAN LUTHERAN CHURCH." This is a branch of the same vine, planted here more than a century ago, by the right hand of the Lord. Although laboring under many disadvantages, arising from the union of Church and State in Europe, the oppressions of their governments, the unsettled state of this country, and the want of a knowledge of its language, she has nevertheless overcome many of them, and extended herself far and wide over our land. The number of her ministers and membership has been doubled every fifteen years, by natural increase and immigration; so that she is already in number the third Protestant denomination in the United States.

Notwithstanding all this, the remark made at the beginning of this Preface is true, that much ignorance exists, and constant misrepresentations take place, relative to the Lutheran Church in the United States. Although information has been spread through her periodicals and publications, in this country, there is none in which so full and satisfactory an account of the Lutheran Church in America can be found as in the present volume.

The First Discourse embraces a history of the rise and progress of the Church in this country.

The Second presents her characteristic features—the peculiarities by which she is distinguished from other branches of the Protestant family.

The Third gives a biography of her founders, here, showing us the extent of their labors, the soundness of their doctrinal views, the sincerity of their piety, the profundity of their knowledge, the wisdom of their measures, and the success of their labors.

The Fourth discusses the nature of the Saviour's presence in the Lord's Supper, in which the corporal presence of Christ's human nature is denied, and his spiritual presence according to his divine nature, is maintained.

The Fifth discusses the question pertaining to her doctrinal basis and ecclesiastical position, in this country; showing that it is neither rigid symbolism, binding the conscience to the letter of every doctrine and statement contained in the whole of the symbolical books, nor loose latitudinarianism, discarding all creeds but the adoption of the Augsburg Confession and Luther's Smaller Catechism, as teaching the fundamental doctrines of the word of God, "in a manner substantially correct."

The Sixth points out her vocation, calling upon her to realize her obligations, to take warning from past errors, to guard against present dangers to develope her various resources, to advance her spiritual interests, and to extend her blessings to all her children.

The author, the Rev. Dr. S. S. Schmucker, has been, for twenty years, Professor of Theology in the Theological Seminary at Gettysburg, Pennsylvania. In the Lutheran Church he is extensively and favorably known; and no man in this country has done more than he to elevate her character, and to advance her welfare. As a writer, he is able and clear. His style is chaste and easy, and his arguments strong and convincing. His "Fraternal Appeal" to the American churches on Christian union, is a master-piece, which with his other theological and philosophical works, has made him extensively known, beyond the bounds of his own church, both in America and England. To render the work more acceptable, we have inserted the likeness, having had it engraved expressly for this volume.

In the hope that it may awaken, among Lutherans, a stronger attachment to their church, and draw forth their benevolence in supplying her wants; give correct information to all who may desire to become better acquainted with the American shoot of the trunk of Protestantism; strengthen the hands of our self-denying ministers in all their trials; and encourage the hearts of many of our people, who are yet destitute, and as sheep without a shepherd; we send it forth, praying that the Great Head of the Church, without whose favor nothing can prosper, would own and bless it to the sanctification and salvation of many souls.

D. HARBAUGH,
J. B. BUTLER.

SPRINGFIELD OHIO, August, 1851.

CONTENTS.

I. DISCOURSE.

II. DISCOURSE.

III. DISCOURSE.

IV. DISCOURSE.

V. DISCOURSE.

VI. DISCOURSE.

THE

AMERICAN LUTHERAN CHURCH.

I. DISCOURSE.

RETROSPECT OF LUTHERANISM IN THE UNITED STATES.

Remember the days of old, consider the years of many generations, ask thy father and he will show thee, thy elders and they will tell thee.—DEUT. xxxii. 7.

MAN, my brethren, we are told in the good book of God, is wonderfully and fearfully constructed. This is true not only of the tenement of clay which we inhabit, but far more illustriously true of the immortal mind, which mainly constitutes ourself. Possessed of powers of cognition, of feeling and of action, man is adapted for the high destiny marked out by the Almighty, for a sphere little lower than that of angels, encircled with honor and glory. As he journeys through life, he is surrounded on all sides by a certain extent of intellectual vision, which, like the torch of the benighted traveler, forms a circle of illumination around him, in which he can safely direct his steps. His powers of cognition embrace a knowledge of the present, some certainties commingled with many probabilities in the future, and copious reminiscences of the past. The past is our richest and most instructive teacher; and it was justly said by one of the most brilliant intellects of heathen antiquity, that not to know what happened before we were born is to remain always a child. This power of retrospection sheds its influence on every department of human life—on our social, our intellectual, and our religious interests.

It is in this field of retrospection that the Christian finds many of his dearest social enjoyments. Fond memory delights to dwell on the pleasing and interesting associations of our early years, especially associations of effort in the cause of the Redeemer. And it is here, too, that "pensive memory retraces scenes of bliss forever fled," it is here she "dwells in former times and places;" it is here she "holds communion with the dead." On this occasion, my brethren, these feelings rise commingled in my breast, when I see before me some of those beloved brethren, with whom I shared the toils of early ministerial life, and when I fail to see others, who twenty years ago were co-workers with us, but have gone to their rest.

It is in the wide field of retrospection, that we gather our richest treasures of wisdom and experience. It is memory that enables us to appropriate to ourselves the knowledge and experience of past ages; to hold communion with apostles and prophets and patriarchs, and virtually to extend our life from threescore to a thousand years. It is in the rich fields of retrospection, too, that the Christian finds the incidents, the principles, and many of the evidences of his holy religion; the glorious displays of Divine Providence, and the heavenly, the expansive power of that gospel, which, aided by the Spirit, serves in every age as the conductor of saving influences from heaven to man. In the Old Testament church, festivals were expressly appointed to cherish the memory of God's mercies to his people. And our blessed Saviour himself not only attended those festivals, instituted by Moses, but appointed a mnemonic rite in his own church, and seems not to have disregarded the feast of dedication which was of mere human appointment. John x. 22.

But it is not only in the Old Testament dispensation that the hand of Providence and the power of God's word may be recognized. They are displayed with increased lustre in the developments of the New Testament church throughout her history. They are seen in the Reformation of the sixteenth century, when, after ages of concealment beneath the dust of ignorance and superstition, the seed of the word was brought to light and scattered among the people. They are seen in the history of Pietism in Germany, of the Methodist church, the Presbyterian, the Episcopal and other churches, and, we may add, in the History of our Lutheran Zion in these United States. Here, too, the precious seed scattered abroad by a few able and faithful servants of Christ, was richly watered by the Spirit, and produced abundant fruit to the praise of his grace; and here, too, there are abundant materials for the recognition of his Providence.

More than two hundred years have rolled away since the first disciples of Christ bearing the name of Luther, traversed the mighty deep to seek a resting-place in this Western world. For more than a century has an uninterrupted stream of immigration continued to swell their numbers. Various and interesting and instructive are the incidents which have since transpired; and as the improvement of such incidents is often enjoined in scripture, it may be well for us to adopt the language of Moses, when about to bid adieu to his brethren after the flesh: "*Remember the days of old, consider the years of many generations, ask thy father and he will show thee, thy elders and they will tell thee.*" This will be the more appropriate as we are assembled to deliberate on the welfare of the church at large, and especially as we are on the eve of a centenary celebration, for which we are expected to make arrangements. It would, indeed, be more grateful to the feelings of the speaker, and we trust of those who hear him, if the contemplated celebration pertained to the body of Christ at large, and not only to one branch of it; yet if all invidious comparison be avoided, if with our reminiscences of the goodness of God to our Zion, we forget not his mercies to others, and cherish a deep sense of our unprofitableness; in short, if the spirit of sectarianism be, as I trust it will be, excluded from the celebration, it may tend to the glory of that Redeemer, who would have all his disciples regard each other as brethren, whilst they acknowledge, as their one and only Master, neither Luther, nor Zuingle, nor Calvin, nor Wesley, but Jesus Christ. With these views we invite your attention to

A RETROSPECT OF THE LUTHERAN CHURCH IN THE UNITED STATES.

We shall

I. *Glance at the history itself;* and,

II. *Consider several particular topics connected with it.*

The history of this portion of Christ's kingdom naturally divides itself into three periods. The I. may be termed the *Colonial Era,* extending from the first settlement of Lutherans in this country, (about 1626,) to the Declaration of American Independence in 1776, and embraces about one hundred and fifty years. The II. extends from that period, to the establishment of the General Synod, in 1820, including forty-four years. This may be regarded as the *middle era;* and the III. from that period to the present time, which may be styled the *era of the General Synod,* and includes twenty years.

I. THE COLONIAL ERA.

The earliest settlement of Lutherans in this country, was made by emigrants from Holland to New York, soon after the first establishment of the Dutch in that city, then called New Amsterdam, which was in 1621. This fact, which is of some historical interest, rests upon the authority of the venerable patriarch of American Lutheranism, Henry Melchior Muhlenberg. "As I was detained at New York, (says he in his Report to Halle,[1]) I took some pains to acquire correct information concerning the history of the Lutheran church in that city. This small congregation took its rise almost at the first settlement of the country. Whilst the territory yet belonged to Holland, the few Low Dutch Lutherans were compelled to hold their worship in private; but after it passed into the possession of the British, in 1664, liberty was granted them by all the successive governors to conduct their worship publicly without any obstruction."[2] The establishment of Lutherans was, therefore, made little more than a century after the re-discovery of America by

(1) Hallische Nachrichten, p. 360.

(2) The Lutheran Herald, vol. iii, No. 1, gives us the following particulars: "Indeed, so great was the number of Lutherans. even at this time, that the very next year, 1665, after the English flag had been displayed from fort Amsterdam, they petitioned for liberty to send to Germany a call for a regular pastor. This petition Governor Nicols of course granted, and in February, 1669, two years after he had left the government, the Rev. Jacobus Fabricius arrived in the colony and began his pastoral labors." "On the 13th of October, 1669, Lord Lovelace, who had succeeded Gov. Nicols publicly proclaimed his having received a letter from the Duke of York, expressing his pleasure that the Lutherans should be tolerated."

Columbus, in 1492;[1] within a few years of the landing of the Pilgrims on Plymouth rock, 1620, and whilst the Thirty Years' War[2] was raging in Germany, and threatening to exterminate Protestantism from Europe. Their first minister was Jacob Fabricius, who arrived in 1669, but after eight years' labor, left them and connected himself with the Swedish Lutherans.[3] The names of his immediate successors we have not found; but from 1703 to 1747, their pastors were the Rev. Messrs. Falkner; from 1703 till 1725, Berkenmayer, and Knoll, and subsequently Rochemdahler, Wolf, Hartwick and others. The first church (a log building,) was erected 1671,[4] and Mr. Muhlenberg says it was in a dilapidated state when it was taken down and its place supplied by one of stone,[5] in the time of Mr. Berkenmayer. The cause of the emigration from Holland we have not seen stated, but it may easily be conjectured, as the emigrants left that country a few years after the famous Synod of Dort (1618,) and whilst the government was enforcing the intolerant decrees of that body.

To this settlement succeeded that of the *Swedes on the Delaware*, in 1636, about ten or twelve years after that in New Amsterdam, and sixteen years after the arrival of the pilgrims at Plymouth. This colony was first contemplated during the reign of Gustavus Adolphus, and was sanctioned by that enlightened and illustrious king. It was delayed by the commencement of the Thirty Years' War in Germany; but after Sweden's noble-hearted monarch had poured out his life's-blood on the plains of Lutzen, it was revived and executed under the auspices of his distinguished prime min-

---

(1) It is now fully established that America was not first discovered by Columbus; but Greenland had been visited by Eirck, the Red, and New England by Biarni Heriulphson, the former in 982, the latter in 985. See Discoveries of the North Men.

(2) This most memorable of all the wars in the history of Protestantism, which deluged Germany in blood, and had it not been for the magnanimous aid of Gustavus Adolphus and his brave Swedes would perhaps have extirpated Protestantism from the earth, was commenced in 1618 and ended in 1648.

(3) Clay's Annals, &c., p. 150. Fabricius took charge of the Swedish church at Wicaco now Southwark, Philadelphia, where he labored fourteen years, during nine of which he was blind. He died 1692.

(4) Lutheran Herald, vol. iii. p. 51. (5) Halliche Nachrichten, p. 363.

ister, Oxenstiern.[1] For many years this colony prospered, but receiving no accessions from the parent country, it never increased much in numbers; the rising generation commingled with the surrounding English and Germans, and at the present day the Swedish language is entirely abandoned in their worship. For many years their ministers, who were generally men of sterling character, were in habits of the most friendly intercourse and ecclesiastical co-operation with their German Lutheran brethren; but the prevalence of the English language having early placed them under obligation to our Episcopal brethren, who supplied them with ministrations in that language, these churches, three or four in number, have successively fallen into Episcopal hands.[2]

The *third* settlement of Lutherans in this country was that of the *Germans*, which gradually spread over Pennsylvania, Maryland, Virginia and the interior of New York and the Western States. The grant of Pennsylvania was given to Penn by Charles II. in 1680, and from this date, till about twenty years afterward, many hundreds of families emigrated to Pennsylvania. The tide of German emigration, however, fairly commenced in 1710, when about three thousand Germans, chiefly Lutheran, oppressed by Romish intolerance, went from the Palatinate to England in 1709, and were sent by Queen Ann to New York the succeeding year. In 1713 one hundred and fifty families settled in Schoharie; and in 1717, we find in the Colonial Records of Pennsylvania, that the Governor of the province felt it his duty to call the attention of the "Provincial Council" to the fact, "that great numbers of foreigners from Germany, strangers to our language and constitution, had lately been imported into the province." The council enacted that every master of a vessel should report the emigrants he brought over, and that they should all repair to Philadelphia within one month to take the oath of allegiance to the government,[3] that it might be seen whether they were "friends or enemies to his majesty's

(1) Clay's Annals of the Swedes, p. 16.

(2) That these churches have dwindled away to almost nothing, would seem to appear from the fact, that when their present amiable rector, the Rev. J. C. Clay, was elected, December 5th, 1831, the entire number of votes given, was, at the Wicaco church (Philadelphia,) 16, at Upper Merion 29, and at Kingsessing 37. Clay's Annals, p. 133.

(3) Colonial Records, vol, iii, p, 18.

government." In 1727, the year memorable alike for Francke's death and the origin of the Moravians, a very large number of Germans came to Pennsylvania from the Palatinate from Wurtemberg, Darmstadt and other parts of Germany. This colony was long destitute of a regular ministry; there were however some schoolmasters and others, some of whom were probably good men, who undertook to preach; and as many of the emigrants brought with them the spirit of true piety from Germany, they brought also many devotional books, and often read Arndt's True Christianity and other similar works for mutual edification.[1] For twelve years, from 1730 till the arrival of the patriarch of American Lutheranism, Dr. Henry Melchior Muhlenberg, the Swedish ministers kindly labored among the Germans, as far as their duties to their own churches admitted. But before we pursue the history of this colony any farther, our attention is claimed by

The *fourth* settlement of Lutherans in this country, who established themselves in Georgia, in 1733, and to designate the gratitude of their hearts to the God who had protected them, styled their location Ebenezer. These emigrants were from Saltzburg, formerly belonging to Bavaria, and restored to the Austrian dominions at the peace of 1814. Persecuted at home by those enemies of all righteousness, the Jesuits,[2] and by Romish priests and Romish rulers, this band of disciples sought a resting-place in these western wilds, where they could worship God according to the dictates of their consciences, under their own vine and fig-tree, without molestation or fear. Through the instrumentality of Rev. Urlsperger, of Augsburg, who was a corresponding member of the British Society for the Promotion of Christianity, pecuniary aid was afforded by that liberal and noble-minded association, and the oppressed Saltzburgers enabled to reach the place of their destination. Happily, they were immediately supplied by two able and faithful pastors, Messrs. Bolzius and Gronau. The latter was taken away by death after twelve years labor among the emigrants, but Bolzius was spared to the church about thirty years. In 1738 these colonists erected an orphan house at Ebenezer,

(1) See Hallische Nachrichten, p. 665. (2) Heinsius' unparteiisch Kirchen historie, vol. iii. p. 291.

to which work of benevolence important aid was contributed by that distinguished man of God, George Whitefield, who also furnished the bell for one of the churches erected by them. The descendants of these colonists are still numerous, and are connected with the Lutheran synod of South Carolina and adjacent states.

Soon after the above colonization, numerous Germans coming from Pennsylvania and other states, settled in North Carolina,[1] who enjoyed the labors of many excellent servants of Christ—Nussman, Arndt, Storch, Roschen, Bernhard, Shober and others, and whose descendants constitute the present numerous churches in the Carolinas.

In 1735 a settlement of Lutherans was formed in Spottsylvania, as Virginia was then sometimes called,[2] which we suppose to be the church in Madison county of that state. Their pastor, the Rev. Stoever, visited Germany for aid, and together with several assistants obtained three thousand pounds, part of which was expended in the erection of a church, the purchase of a plantation and slaves to work it for the support of their minister, and the balance expended for a library, or consumed by the expenses of the town.[2] As might have been expected, this church seems never to have enjoyed the smiles of our Father in Heaven.

In 1739 a few Germans, emigrated to Waldoborough, Maine, to whose number an addition of fifteen hundred souls was made thirteen years afterward. But the title to the land given them by General Waldo proving unsound, many left the colony, and its numbers have never greatly increased. For many years they enjoyed the pastoral labors, successively of Rev. Schaeffer (from 1762,) Croner (from 1785,) and Ritz, and since 1811 are under the charge of Rev. Mr. Starman.[3]

Of all these colonies that which in the Providence of God has most increased, and has hitherto constituted the great body of the Lutheran church in this country, is that in the

---

(1) Shober's Luther, p. 137. (2) Hallische Nachrichten, p. 331.

(3) Heinsius speaks of a colony of Swiss Lutherans, who tired of Romish oppression, also sought refuge in this Western world. They came by way of England, under the direction of Col. Purry, who established them in a place called after himself Purrysburg. This colony, if we mistake not, was in Beaufort county, South Carolina, but we have not been able to find any account of its progress or present condition. Heinsius' Kirchengeschichte, vol. iii. p. 291.

Middle states, Pennsylvania, interior New York, Maryland, &c., whose history was traced in its proper place till 1742. This was a memorable year for the Lutheran church. It was signalized by the arrival of Henry Melchior Muhlenberg, whose high intellectual and moral qualifications, whose indefatigable zeal and long life of arduous and enlightened labor for the Master's cause, constitute a new era in the history of our American Zion, and justly entitle him to the appellation of patriarch of the American Lutheran church. There had indeed been Lutherans in Pennsylvania sixty years earlier. There had been churches built at New Hanover, and near Lebanon (the Bergkirche,) where the Rev. Stover labored in 1733, and at York in 1734. In Philadelphia also the Lutherans had worshipped jointly with their Reformed brethren in an old log house in Arch street. But in general they had enjoyed no regular ministry, until 1742. Muhlenberg came to this country with qualifications of the highest order. His education was of the very first character. In addition to his knowledge of Greek and Hebrew, he spoke English, German, Holland, French, Latin and Swedish. But what was still more important, he was educated in the school of Francke, and had imbibed a large portion of his heavenly spirit. Like Paul, he had an ardent zeal for the salvation of "his brethren, his kinsmen according to the flesh." He first landed in Georgia, and spent a week with the brethren, Bolzius and Gronau, to refresh his spirit and learn the circumstances of the country; and then pursuing his course by a dangerous coasting voyage, in a small and insecure sloop,[1] which had no accommodations for passengers, he arrived in Philadelphia, Nov. 25, 1742. Having reached his place of destination, and surmounted the opposition of Count Zinzendorf, who, under the assumed name of Thurnstein, had passed himself off as a Lutheran minister and inspector,[2] he was cordially received, and en-

(1) During this voyage all on board endured many privations; and being delayed and tossed about by contrary winds, suffered much for want of water. So great was the destitution of water that even the rats ate out the stoppers of the vinegar bottles, and by inserting their tails, extracted the cooling liquid, and drew them through their mouths. And some of these animals were also seen licking the perspiration from the foreheads of the sleeping mariners. Hallische Nachrichten, p. 9.

(2) The writer has in his library a volume of sermons published in Budingen 1746, evidently by Count Zinzendorf, in which the writer on the title

tered on his labors with comprehensive and well-directed views for the benefit of the whole church. He continued to labor for near a half a century, with indefatigable zeal. Whilst Edwards was co-operating with the extraordinary outpourings of God's spirit in New England, and the Wesleys were laboring to revive vital godliness in England; whilst Whitefield was doing the same work in England and America, and the successors of Francke were laboring to evangelize Germany; Muhlenberg was striving with similar zeal and fidelity to do the work of God among his German brethren in this Western world. Of him, as also of some of his earliest associates, it may be truly said, that, "he was in journeyings often, in perils of waters, in perils of robbers, in perils by his own countrymen, in perils by the heathen, in perils in the city, in perils in the wilderness, in perils in the sea, in perils among false brethren, in weariness and painfulness, in watchings often, in hunger and thirst, in fastings often, and in cold and nakedness." He preached in season and out of season, in churches, in dwellings, in barns and in the open air, until at last that divine Master, whom he so faithfully served, received him into the society of the apostles and prophets at his right hand.

Such was Muhlenberg. Throughout his long life he was regarded by all as the leader of the Lutheran phalanx, as the father of the Lutheran church in this country. Although we see no necessity for attaching a season of grateful acknowledgment of the Divine goodnes, to any specific date, as it is at all times proper; yet if such a date be sought, no one more appropriate could be found than the year of Muhlenberg's call to this work, (September, 1741,)[1] or his actual arrival in this country in 1742.

Muhlenberg was soon joined in the American field by other highly respectable men, of excellent education and of spirit like his own; the greater part of whom were in like manner sent from Germany, such as Brunnholtz and Lemke, 1745; Handshuh, Hartwick, the generous founder of the seminary that bears his name, and Weygand, 1748; Heinzelman and Schultz, 1751; Gerock, Hausil, Wortman, Wag-

---

page is represented to have been Lutheran Inspector and Pastor in Philadelphia in 1742.

(1) Hallische Nachrichten, p. 7.

ner, Schartlin, Shrenk and Rauss, 1753; Bager, 1758; Voigt and Krug, 1764; Helmuth and Schmidt, 1769; and Kunze, 1770. In company with Mr. Brunnholtz came also Messrs. N. Kurtz and Schaum, who were ordained in 1748 and were among the most faithful and useful of our ministers. The former was the father of the venerable servant of Christ, whom we are permitted this morning to welcome in our midst, the oldest Lutheran minister in the United States, bereft of late of the partner of his life, himself yet kindly spared amongst us as a relic of a former generation. The increase of ministers was slow. When the first Synod was held, in 1748, there were only eleven regular Lutheran ministers in the United States.[1] Three years after that time the number of congregations was rated at about forty, and the Lutheran population in America at sixty thousand.

The greater part of these men were indefatigable in their labors. Numerous and arduous were the difficulties in their way. The population was unsettled, ever tending farther into the interior;[2] intemperance had already made sad havoc in the land;[3] the semi-civilized habits so natural to pioneers in colonization, the various frolics, the celebrations in honor of Tammany, the Indian chief, &c., which were then extensively observed,[4] were formidable obstacles to religion. Inadequate ministerial support; difficulty of traveling from want of roads in many directions; and not unfrequently the tomahawk and scalping knife of the Indian impeded their progress. I cannot stop to tell the soul-stirring story of many an Indian massacre. A single instance, from the pen of father Muhlenberg himself, may teach us alike to appreciate the security of our worship and the bitter cost at which our fathers provided it; may teach us that we are reaping the fruits of their sweat and blood. The case was that of a man whose two grown daughters had attended a course of instruction by Mr. Muhlenberg, and been solemnly admitted by confirmation to the communion of the church. This man afterwards went with his family some distance into the interior to a tract of land which he purchased.

(1) In 1743, Naesseman, the Swedish minister, reported to Sweden, that there were at that time twenty German Lutheran congregations in America. Heinsius, iii, p. 687.

(2) Muhlenburg states that in five years half his congregation had changed. (3) Hal. Nach. p. 474. (4) Hall. Nach, p. 1441.

When the war with the Indians broke out, he removed his family to their former residence, and occasionally returned to his farm to attend to his grain and cattle. On one occasion he went accompanied by his two daughters to spend a few days there, and bring away some wheat. On Friday evening after the wagon had been loaded, and everything was ready for their return on the morrow, his daughters complained that they felt anxious and dejected, and were impressed with the idea that they were soon to die. They requested their father to unite with them in singing the familiar German funeral hymn: "Who knows how near my end may be,"[1] after which they commended themselves to God in prayer and retired to rest. The light of the succeeding morning beamed upon them and all was yet well. Whilst the daughters were attending to the dairy, cheered with the joyful hope of soon greeting their friends, and being out of danger, the father went to the field for the horses, to prepare for their departure home. As he was passing through the field, suddenly he saw two Indians, armed with rifles, tomahawks and scalping knives, rushing towards him at full speed. The sight so terrified him, that he lost all self-command and stood motionless and silent. When they were about twenty yards from him, he suddenly, and with all his strength, exclaimed: "Lord Jesus, living and dying I am thine." Scarcely had the Indians heard the words, "Lord Jesus," (which they probably knew as the white man's name of the "Great Spirit,") when they stopped short, and uttered a hideous yell. The man ran with almost supernatural strength into the dense forest, and by taking a serpentine course the Indians lost sight of him and relinquished the pursuit. He hastened to an adjoining farm, where two German families resided, for assistance. But on approaching near it, he heard the dying groans of the families, who were falling beneath the murderous tomahawk of some other Indians. Having providentially not been observed by them, he hastened back to learn the fate of his daughters. But, alas! on coming within sight, he found his house, barn and stable, enveloped in flames! Finding that the Indians had possession here, too, he hastened to an adjoining farm for help. Returning armed,

(1) The well known German hymn, "Wer weisz wie nahe mir mein Ende."

with several men, they found the house reduced to ashes, and the Indians gone! His eldest daughter had been almost entirely burnt up, a few remains only of her body being found! And awful to relate, the younger, though the scalp had been cut from her head, and her body was horribly mangled from head to foot with the tomahawk, was yet living! "The poor worm," says Muhlenberg, "was yet able to state all the circumstances of the dreadful scene." After having done so, she requested her father to stoop down to her that she might give him a parting kiss and then go to her dear Savior, and after she had impressed her dying lips upon his cheek, she yielded her spirit into the hands of that Redeemer,[1] who, though his judgments are often unsearchable and his ways past finding out, has nevertheless said, "I am the resurrection and the life, if any man believe in me, though he die yet shall he live."

Such were the difficulties and dangers with which our fathers had to contend, in planting the gospel in these western wilds. But we must pass on to glance at the second, or

MIDDLE ERA OF OUR CHURCH IN THIS COUNTRY.

The event selected as the division between the first and second periods of our retrospect, is one illustrious in the annals of the world. It separates between the reign of different political theories, the divine right of kings to govern the people, and the people's right to govern themselves; between the principles of liberty and slavery; between the union of church and state, which had prevailed in Europe since its establishment by Constantine about fourteen hundred years before, and absolute liberty of conscience un-

(1) Hallish. Nachr. p. 1007, 8. The case here narrated was neither extreme nor rare. The elder Mr. Kurtz on the 2d of July, 1757, states that on that day, the lifeless bodies of no less than seven members of his congregation were brought to the church for burial, they having been murdered by the Indians the evening before. Being anxious to improve this solemn scene to the spiritual welfare of his hearers, Mr. Kurtz deferred the interment until the succeeding day, and suffered the mangled bodies to remain in the church until the congregation convened; a pleasing evidence this, of his solicitude for souls.

controlled by civil governments. But the struggle by which this glorious declaration of Independence was sustained, and in which our forefathers took a distinguished part, was like every other war, detrimental to the religious prosperity of the community. Christianity is a religion of peace, and the tempest of war never fails to blast and scatter the leaves which are for the healing of nations. Hear the account of one of those venerable men, the Rev. Dr. Helmuth, just after General Gage had landed at Boston with 9000 British troops, dated Feb. 25th, 1775. "Throughout the whole country great preparations for war are making, and almost every person is under arms. The ardor is indescribable which is manifested in these melancholy circumstances. If a hundred men are required, many more immediately offer, and are dissatisfied when all are not accepted. I know of no similar case in history. Neighborhoods concerning which it would have been expected, that years would be requisite to induce themvoluntarily to take up arms, became strongly inclined for war, so soon as the battle of Lexington was known. Quakers and Menonists take part in the military exercises, and in great numbers renounce their former religious principles. The hoarse din of war is hourly heard in our streets. *The present disturbances inflict no small injury on religion.* Every body is constantly on the alert, anxious, like the ancient Athenians, to hear the news, and amid the mass of news the hearts of men are, alas! closed against the good old word of God. The Lord is chastising the people, but they do not feel it. Those who appear to be distant from danger are unconcerned; and those whom calamity has overtaken are enraged and meditating vengeance. In the American army there are many clergymen, who serve both as chaplains and as officers. I myself know two, one of whom is a Colonel and the other a Captain. The whole country is in a perfect enthusiasm for liberty. The whole population from New England to Georgia is of one mind, and determined to risk life and all things in defence of liberty. The few who think differently are not permitted to utter their sentiments. In Philadelphia the English and German students are formed into military companies, wear uniform, and are exercised like regular troops. Would to God that men would once become as zealous and unanimous in asserting their spiritual liberty, as they are in vindicating their political freedom ![1]

This melancholy state of things lasted upwards of seven years. Many of the churches were destroyed throughout the land, and especially in New England. Zion's church, the largest in Philadelphia, was occupied as a hospital[2] by the British army in 1778, and the congregation for a season wholly expelled; and their other church, St. Michaels, which had been built 1743, the year after Muhlenberg's arrival, was used by the enemy as a garrison church, half of every Lord's day, the congregation having the use of it in the afternoon. During the ravages of this war, no regular reports were forwarded to Halle, and our acquaintance with the particulars of our history is necessarily circumscribed. Many, however, of the fathers of the church survived the revolutionary struggle, and remained in the field during the earlier part of this period; yet one by one they dropped off, and were received to their eternal rest. From the (Kirchenagende) "Directory for Worship," published in 1786, three years after the Independence of these United States was acknowledged by Britain and the war closed, we learn, that at that time our ministry in the Middle States embraced the following twenty-four persons: Henry Melchior Muhlenberg, D. D., senior of the ministerium, Nicholas Kurtz, his younger brother William Kurtz, Lewis Voigt, John Andrew Krug, Christian Imanuel Schultze, John George Bager, Just Christian Henry Helmuth, D. D., John Frederick Schmidt, John Christopher Kunze, D. D., Gotthilf, Henry Ernst Muhlenberg, D. D., Conrad Wildbahn, Jacob B. Buskirk, John Friderici, Christian Streit, John George Jung, Conrad Roeller, Jacob Georing, Daniel Schroeter, Daniel Lehman, Henry Moeller, Frederick Ernst, Frederick Valentine Melsheimer, and Daniel Kurtz, D. D.

In addition to these, the following laborers among many others, entered the field during the second period, and carried forward the work of the Lord: John Frederick Weinland, Frederick David Schaeffer, D. D., Wm. Carpenter, George Lochman, D. D., John George Schmucker, D. D., Christian Endress, D. D., Ernest L. Hazelius, D. D., Philip

(1) Hallische Nachrichten, p. 1367, 8.
(2) Hallische Nachrichten p. 1408.

F. Mayer, D. D., John Bachman, D. D., John Ruthrauff, George Flohr, Paul Henkel, John Staunch, F. W. Geissenhainer, D. D., Augustus Wackerhagen, D. D., G. A. Lintner, D. D., G. B. Miller, D. D., Jno. Herbst, John Knosky, H. Muhlenberg, D. D., David F. Schaeffer, D. D., John Hecht, Jacob Miller, D. D., Ulrich, Baetis, Ernst, D. D., J. Becker, D. D., F. C. Schaeffer, D. D., J. P. Shindel, A. Reck, B. Kurtz, D. D.

The number of congregations and ministers was much increased during this period; but owing to the want of a suitable institution for their education and to other causes, the proportion of men destitute of a learned education was also augmented. Nor can it be denied, that, whether it is attributable to the unhallowed influence of the war, or to this and other causes in conjunction, the standard of piety in the churches was somewhat on the decline, especially in the latter part of this period. As the same remark is also applicable to all the other religious denominations of our land, the war of the Revolution and the war with England in 1812, were most probably its principal reason; for a general effect requires an equally general cause. With this cause co-operated another, almost as influential, the general and unprecedented facilities offered by our young and nascent country to accumulate deceitful riches, and to neglect the treasures in heaven; and also the less pious character of the late accessions made to our churches by emigration from Germany, then devastated and demoralized by the deadly poison of war.

In addition to their pastoral labors, several of our principal men occupied important posts in literary institutions. Dr. Kunze was professor of the Greek, Latin and German languages, in the University of Pennsylvania, established in 1779; in 1785 Dr. Helmuth was appointed to the same station; and they were confessedly as learned men as any connected with the institution. At this time the Academy which had previously existed, was converted into a preparatory school to prepare German youth to understand the instructions of the University.

In 1786, the Kirchenagende was published, which continued in use during nearly the whole of this period until in 1818, the one now employed in our German churches, was published.

In 1787, the Legislature out of gratitude for the revolutionary services of the Germans, and respect for their industry and excellence as citizens, endowed a college in Lancaster for their special benefit, to be forever under their control. Of this institution Dr. Muhlenberg, then pastor in Lancaster, was chosen president. And in 1791, the same body passed an act, appropriating 5000 acres of land to the flourishing free school of the Lutheran church in Philadelphia, in which at that time eighty poor children were receiving gratuitous education.

In 1796, at which time the difficulties resulting from the conflict between the German and English languages, that prolific source of endless evils to our churches, already began to appear, there was a very enlarged and enlightened plan for the establishment of a German and English school with five teachers, devised, and if we mistake not, put into operation; but for reasons which we do not find on record, it seems soon to have been abandoned.

Had this plan been persisted in, and as a necessary concomitant, suitable provision been made to have the doctrines of the gospel preached in English to those who could not understand German, the Lutheran church might at this day be as numerous as any other in Philadelphia. But in pursuance of a policy which we cannot but regard as mistaken, every effort to introduce English preaching was, until about the close of this period, met with determined opposition. Much may, however, be said on both sides of this question. Emigration[1] was still going on rapidly, and as the increasing numbers of German congregations gave full employment to all the laborers in the field, and filled up the places of those who left the church; it is perhaps less matter of surprise than regret, that the fathers of that era, made no provision for the portion of the rising generation unacquainted with the German language.

At the request of the Philadelphia church council, their

(1) In 1785, a German Society was established in New York, of which Dr. Kunze was an active member, and in which Baron Steuben, celebrated in our revolutionary struggle, took a deep interest, the object of which was alike to encourage emigration from Germany and to protect the rights of those who seek a home amongst us. Similar societies had previously existed in Philadelphia and Baltimore. Hall. Nach. p. 1508, 1518.

pastors, 1791, addressed a pamphlet to the Lutherans of that city, on the signal evidences of the divine goodness and mercy to them, calling on them, to acknowledge and evince their gratitude by upholding their German religious institutions and language. It was published on occasion of the re-opening of St. Michael's church, after a thorough repair; and amidst much most excellent religious instruction, states the fact, that three of the largest churches in the city would not contain all the descendants of the German fathers, if they were animated by the zeal which characterized their ancestors in 1742. There is one incident in the early history of our German churches in Philadelphia, affording so striking an evidence of the proverbial integrity of the German character, that it deserves to be particularly noted. The corporation paid a large debt due by the church, to some mechanics, in continental money, when that money was at par. Soon after, however, that currency depreciated to almost nothing, and of course the loss both in law and equity would have fallen on those in whose possession the notes were at the time found. But our noble hearted German fathers could not bear the thought, that any one should lose upon money received from them, and though they were not under the least obligation to do so, they actually made up the entire deficiency and paid the debt a second time in gold and silver! In that same church, there was as early as 1804 a flourishing Sabbath school of two hundred scholars and forty teachers, a conclusive evidence that the cause of God was prospering at that time.

Although the influx of ministers from Germany had diminished near the close of this middle era; the bond of Christian sympathy and union between us and the mother country, was by no means either severed or impaired. Of this a pleasing demonstration was afforded in 1814. When Halle, the mother of our central American church, the alma mater of Muhlenberg, of Handschuh, Heinzelman, Schultz, of Bager, of Voigt, of Krug, of Helmuth, of Schmidt and others, had greatly suffered by the devastation of the Buonapartean wars, collections were taken here, with great promptness, and forwarded to Halle, amounting to two thousand three hundred and thirty-four dollars, and ten cents; a specimen of Christian sympathy this, which was liberally repaid, when in 1826, Dr. Benjamin Kurtz visited Germany in behalf of the Theological Seminary of this Synod.

About the close of this period the state of piety in the American churches generally was improving, and a clearer day began to dawn also on our Lutheran Zion.

III. THE THIRD PERIOD we style the era of the GENERAL SYNOD, because the formation of this noble institution, was a starting place and a central radiating point of improvement in the church, whose influence has been uninterrupted and most propitious; and not entirely confined to the Synods which formally acceded to the union. Prior to this era the church had gradually become divided into five or six different, distant, and unconnected Synods. Having no regular intercourse with each other, these several portions became more or less estranged; and lost all the advantages of mutual consultation, confidence and co-operation. But a number of the most enlightened and active men in different portions of the church lamented its decline, and resolved on efforts for its improvement. The first of these efforts, and that which brought in its train many others of blessed influence, was the establishment of the General Synod in 1820, whose stated meeting has convened us on this occasion.

The particular circumstances attending the formation and growth of this blessed institution are known to you all, and our time will not allow us to narrate them. Nor will delicacy permit us in the presence of some of them, to speak, as they deserve, of that noble band of brethren, who were foremost to repel the onset and the outcry against this Synod and bear it onward to victory and triumph; nor of that band of younger brethren, who, when the recession of the mother Synod of Pennsylvania threatened certain dissolution to this body, stepped forward and nobly sustained it against fearful odds, until the storm was overblown, and by a course of well-doing the prejudices of some and apprehensions of others were removed.

Much might be said of the spirit of brotherly love, of union and of piety which this Synod tended to diffuse; and of the Theological Seminary established by this body, in which upwards of one hundred[1] laborers have been trained for the vineyard of the Lord.

Powerful and extensive has been the influence of this body in introducing scriptural discipline into our churches, and promoting correct views of church government.

Most salutary has doubtless been the influence of that selection of ardently pious and evangelical hymns published by this Synod, by which hundreds of thousands of souls have been aided in their devotions and taught to sing the songs of Zion in their pilgrimage toward the heavenly Jerusalem.

Much might be said of the honorable manner in which the greater part of the brethren and churches in East Pennsylvania, and elsewhere, whilst yielding to the prejudices of the weaker members, yet continued to afford their substantial and increasing aid to every good work undertaken by this Synod, so that much of the credit for what has been achieved, is justly due to their co-operation.

In other Synods not connected with the General Synod, a similar spirit of improvement characterizes this age. Upon the whole, therefore, the Lutheran portion of the Redeemer's kingdom in this country has, during the third period, been making rapid strides in improvement. This era is also distinguished by the establishment of the theological seminaries at Hartwick, which is the oldest of all, at Lexington and at Columbus; all of which are doing an important work for the church and age. The general progress of the church is demonstrated by the fact, that at the commencement of this era, there were but one hundred and forty Lutheran ministers* in the United States, and at the present day we number four hundred and six.[2] With this cursory review of our past history, we hasten in the

II. PLACE, TO GLANCE AT SOME SELECT TOPICS CONNECTED WITH IT.

Our *first topic* for observation shall be the *character of the church government and Discipline* adopted by the fathers

(1) Now, (1851,)the number of those who have been connected with the Seminary, has increased to 259.

* Synod of Pennsylvania, including Maryland and Virginia, contained 74 ministers; Synod of Ohio, 23; North Carolina, 15; South Carolina, 10; and New York 10. (2) Now, 771.

of our American branch of the church. Though coming from a country, where the union of church and state, as well as other circumstances, prevented the early Reformers from restoring church government and discipline to its primitive and apostolic form; when our fathers reached this land of liberty they at once adopted the form which Luther and Lutheran divines generally, have always regarded as the primitive one, namely parity of ministers, the co-operation of the laity[1] in church government, and the free voluntary convention of Synods. Six years after the arrival of father Muhlenberg, the first Synod was held in Philadelphia, August 14th, 1748. Even at this first Synod, lay delegates were in attendance, and regularly participated in the transaction of business.[2] The character of this and the subsequent Synods and conferences, was interesting in the extreme, and breathed a spirit truly apostolic. The time was spent in administering the affairs of the churches and in pastoral consultation; and such was the zeal and interest of the brethren, that they repeatedly during the same conference, continued their pastoral consultations till three o'clock in the morning, communing together about the things pertaining to the kingdom of God. But hear Muhlenberg himself. Speaking of a Synod held in 1760, at New Providence, a village, then the place of his residence, and now called Trap, after Rev. Gerock had preached a German sermon in the forenoon, and the excellent Provost Wrangel of the Swedish church, an English discourse in the afternoon, he says: "After the close of public worship all the ministers convened at my house, and held a biblical colloquy (colloquium biblicum) on the essential characteristics of genuine repentance, faith, and godliness; in which they endeavored to benefit each other according to the grace given them, by communicating the results of their own experience and self-examination, so that it was a cheering and delightful season. The residue of the evening was spent in singing spiritual hymns and psalms and in conversation about the spiritual condition of our churches; and so short did the time appear, that it was 3 o'clock in the morning before we retired to rest. Oh, (he adds) how delightful it is when ministers, standing aloof from all po-

(1) Hallische Nachrichten, p. 968. (2) p. 284, 286.

litical and party contests, seek to please their Lord and Master Jesus Christ, and have at heart the welfare of their churches and the souls entrusted to their care; and are willing rather to suffer reproach with the people of God, than choose the treasures of Egypt."[1]

Of their practice to require the laity to unite in the vocation of ministers, we have a decided instance in the case of that distinguished and laborious servant of God, the Rev. Nicholas Kurtz. After his examination in 1748, by Messrs. Muhlenberg, Brunnholtz, Handschuh and Hartwick, we are told, the elders and deacons of the church in which he had labored as a licentiate, were called on to sign his vocation.[2]

In matters of discipline also, the church took part. When members had been guilty of any grievous and public offense, Muhlenberg required them to appear publicly in church before the altar, and profess their penitence; after which he called on the members to decide by vote, whether the individual should be restored to the privileges of church-membership, and especially of sacramental communion.[3]

As to the character of their discipline, it was evidently scriptural and evangelical. They practiced the public excommunication of immoral members from the church. Different instances of this practice are detailed in the journals of Muhlenberg,[4] of Helmuth[5] and others. In 1772 Helmuth, in order more effectually to prevent the approach of unworthy members, introduced the practice of requiring all who desired to commune, to communicate their names to him before hand.[6] The register of names was read before the congregation, and those of immoral members publicly erased. Father Muhlenberg introduced a very scriptural discipline in the Lancaster church, of which his successor, Dr. Helmuth, speaks in terms of high commendation. One of the same character was introduced in the Philadelphia church in 1663, which gave to the pastors power to reject all immoral members from the sacramental table.[7] And in 1784 at the Synod held at Philadelphia, the resolution of a previous Synod was confirmed, requiring of certain transgressors public acknowledgment before the congregation,

(1) Hall. Nach. p. 855. (2) p. 284. (3) p. 185.
(4) p. 907. (5) p. 1347. (6) p. 1346. (7) p. 962.

as the only condition of restoration to the privileges of church members.[1] How scriptural, therefore, was the government, how spiritual, how faithful the discipline of our fathers! Well may it be said, that those amongst us, who are most zealous and active in winning souls to Christ, approximate nearest to the good old ways and example of our fathers.

The *second* topic, to which we invite your attention, is the *literary character and labors* of the founders of our church in this country. Their literary character was indisputably of the first order. The greater part of them received a full university education at Halle. Muhlenberg, Handschuh, Heinzelman, Shultz, Bager, Voigt, Krug, Helmuth, and Schmidt and others were educated in different institutions. So fully was this fact felt by the literati of that day, that the honorary degree of Doctor of Divinity, a degree then very rarely conferred, was bestowed on a goodly number of them, and their being appointed to professorships in different institutions and elected members of different learned societies, affords evidence of the same truth.

Several of them preached both in English and German, and of Muhlenberg can be said what is applicable not to one in a hundred of the ablest and best ministers and missionaries of our own age, that he statedly preached in three different languages on the same day, English, Holland and German. Overloaded as they were with missionary labor and pastoral care, these devoted men found little leisure for any other literary labor than was necessary for the worship and government of their churches. The Swedish Lutheran minister, provost Wrangle, in 1761, published an English version of Luther's catechism, which had also, as early as 1642, been translated into the language of the neighboring Indians, by Campanius, likewise a Swede. Benjamin Franklin had an edition of the same work printed in German, and also issued proposals for publishing "Arndt's True Christianity." In the year 1786 both the German hymn book and the "Kirchen Agende," or Directory for Worship, were published. Of the former, the editors were Drs. Muhlenberg, Senr. Kunze, Helmuth and Muhlenberg, jr., of Lancaster. The historical narrative of the establishment and

(1) Hall. Nach. p. 1458.

progress of the Lutheran church in this country, constituting a quarto volume of 1518 pages, was contributed chiefly by Dr. Muhlenberg, sen., (whose valuable and pious contributions would form several 8vo volumes,) Brunnholtz, Handschuh, Kunze and Helmuth. Even literary labor may be expended amiss, when performed at the expense of more active and urgent care of souls. It therefore redounds to the credit of these men, that although so well qualified, they devoted comparatively little time to literary performances. Yet did some of them, such as Dr. Kunze, Dr. Helmuth, Dr. Muhlenberg of Lancaster, make valuable and learned contributions to the literature and science of our land; and Lutheran divines in this country generally, have by no means been deficient in the labors of their pen.

But why did they fail to furnish the church with such literary and theological institutions, as had always been the glory of the Lutheran church in Europe, and one of her most successful means of extension? Not because they were insensible to their importance, or inattentive to their duty. Even in the earlier years of his ministry, Muhlenberg advocated the necessity and importance of establishing a theological and literary institution to supply the church with well qualified laborers. As early as 1765, Dr. Freylinghausen remarks: "Mr. Muhlenberg has often expressed his earnest desire, that the vast and increasing multitude of German Lutherans in North America might be better provided for in regard to religious instruction. He is convinced, that the present arrangements are insufficient; and that a Seminary ought to be established to train up laborers to publish the doctrines of the gospel. But, he adds,—and this teaches us the principal obstacle which baffled their efforts—hitherto the erection of houses of worship has caused such extensive expenditures, that the greater part of our congregations are burdened with debt, and unable to contribute to such an enterprise."[1]

In 1773 a commencement was actually made to establish such an institution, chiefly through the zeal and enterprize of Dr. Kunze, confessedly one of the most learned and enlightened divines of America, and an ornament to our church, to whom Dr. Miller, of Princeton, pays the following deserved

(1) Hall. Nach. p. 1253–4.

tribute: "The various acquirements of this gentleman, and particularly his oriental learning, have long rendered him an ornament of the American republic of letters. He has probably done more than any individual now living to promote a taste for Hebrew literature, among those intended for the clerical profession in the United States. He is doubtless entitled to the character of a benefactor of the American churches."[1] That the efforts of such a man, seconded by the co-operation of Father Muhlenberg and others, failed of eventual success, would seem to compel us to the conclusion, that the fault lay not in them, but in the peculiar condition of our congregations at that day. Six years afterward, in 1779, when the Academy in Philadelphia was erected into a University, a German professor of Latin, Greek and Hebrew, was appointed, principally through the influence of Dr. Kunze, who was one of the Trustees. Dr. Kunze himself was urged to accept the appointment, and in connection with Dr. Helmuth, labored with some success for the German portion of the community, but eventually this plan also was abandoned. In 1785 Messrs. Helmuth and Schmidt, then pastors in Philadelphia, commenced a private seminary, and for twenty years continued so far as their numerous pastoral duties would permit, to instruct candidates for the Lutheran ministry, among whom were many of the best pastors and divines of the middle era of our history; but old age and eventually death also terminated these efforts.

But in the providence of God the time seems to have arrived, when our churches are alike able and willing to accomplish that which our fathers longed and prayed for, and wished to see, but died without the sight. It is one of the glories of the present era of our church, that she has been actively employed in laying the foundations and beginning to rear the walls of such theological and literary institutions as the Providence of God so signally blessed, in founding and extending the churches of the Reformation both in Europe and America. We say beginning to rear the walls; because though we have nominally four theological seminaries in this country, they are not half endowed. None of them have funds enough to support half as many teachers as are necessary to give adequate instruction in the whole

(1) Dr. Miller on the 18th century, vol. ii. p. 56.

theological course. The entire time of three professors at least is requisite for this purpose; and the best endowed of our seminaries has in addition to its buildings, little more than a support for one professor. Is it not evident then, that we owe it to the memory of our enlightened and zealous fathers, who laid the foundation of our church, that we should rear the superstructure? When they of their *poverty* erected altars and temples to our God in this howling wilderness, ought not we of our *abundance* to finish the work they so nobly began, and make adequate provision for laborers to cultivate our vineyard, and to send forth others into the field of the world? Will not that righteous Judge, who requires much from those to whom much is given, demand it at our hands? But we cannot doubt from what we have seen and heard on the subject of our contemplated centenary, that your hearts will devise liberal things, and that your hands and those of our brethren throughout the length and breadth of our church will, by the blessing of heaven, nobly execute them.

The *third and last* topic to which we invite your attention, is the *practical piety* of our fathers, and their views of conversion and prayer meetings and revivals of religion. Muhlenberg and his early fellow laborers had been trained by the spirit of God as worthy disciples of the Frankean school. The period of their education was the age of revivals in Germany, and succeeded the era of the pietistic controversies, which grew out of them, and enlisted on one side or other, the entire theological intellect of that country. These laborers were selected by Franke the younger, and Freylinghausen, and were therefore men after their own heart, were chosen spirits of Germany. They were men not unworthy of the age in which their lot was cast, the age of Edwards, of Whitefield, of Wesley. Their own views were decidedly orthodox and evangelical, and they were careful to require evidences of genuine piety from applicants for the ministerial office. When the venerable father who is yet in our midst was licensed in 1784, among the principal questions which he was required to answer, were the following: How do you prove that Christ was not only a teacher, but also that he had made an atonement for the sins of men? What is meant by the influences and blessings of the Holy Spirit? What are the evidences of conversion?

How do you prove the propriety of pedobaptism? How do you prove the eternity of future punishment? Were the apostles infallible in their instructions? Questions having a manifest bearing on the errors prevailing, or beginning to prevail in that age. Their preaching was most evangelical and edifying, and their journals show, that they earnestly prayed and looked for the divine blessing. Muhlenberg states, that he sometimes, after sermon, added a brief paraphrase or exhortation on the closing hymn, and described the case of a young man who attributed his conversion to this practice. Those devoted men were not desirous of merely pleasing their hearers. They were none of

> Those "gentle theologues of calmer kind,
> Whose constitution dictates to their pens,
> Who cold themselves, think ardor comes from hell,'

On the contrary, all that they have written, and all that is on record of their sermons, proves, that they were anxious mainly for the glory of their Saviour and the salvation of the souls committed to their care. It was in this spirit that they plainly assailed the prevailing vices of the land, and often incurred the displeasure of the vicious. Thus, for his faithfulness towards Sabbath breakers, in Philadelphia, Dr. Kunze, in 1784, was attacked in the newspapers of the day. Soon after his settlement in New York, Dr. Kunze remarks: The souls that have been gained by the truth, are as yet few in number. Several individuals have come to me, and with tears besought me to teach them, what they must do to be saved." The reports which they statedly sent to Halle, abounded in individual narratives of conversions, and demonstrate that they watched for souls as those that must give an account.

They encouraged prayer-meetings among their church-members, and often conducted them themselves. Nor did they deem it necessary to forbid these meetings, although formalists within the church opposed them, and the ungodly world without sometimes disturbed the meetings, as was done at Lancaster in 1773, in the pastoral charge of Dr. Helmuth. Speaking of a revival of religion, then in progress, he says: "Twice or thrice a week, meetings were held in the evening, at different places by the subjects of this work of grace, and the time spent in singing, in praying, reading a chapter of the word of God, or of Arndt's True Christianity, and if no prayer-meeting was held on Sabbath evening in the church, the substance of the sermon was discussed. In some houses the number was rather large, there being sometimes as many as forty persons assembled at one place. The children of this world several times attempted to disturb their worship, by standing at the windows listening, and by throwing against the doors. But by grace they were enabled to bear it without any resistance, and even when on their way home they were assailed on the streets with various nicknames, and stigmatized as hypocrites, pietists, &c., they answered not a word. Some of their persecutors also, when they heard these men sing and pray with so much fervor and sincerity, not only ceased their opposition, but induced others to do the same."[1] The labors of the greater part of these men were extensively blessed. Speaking of a visit he paid to Tolpehocken, father Muhlenberg says he found many souls who professed the Rev. Mr. N. Kurtz as their spiritual father; and his own labors were crowned with very extensive success. In 1782 there was also a season of revival, of special interest in the church in Philadelphia. "Particularly among the young (says Dr. Kunze) there has been a fire kindled which continued to burn to our great joy about a year." And numerous other similar scenes might be detailed if our time admitted. But we must close.

Thus, my brethren, we have taken a hasty retrospect of our past history in this country, from the time when our fathers first pitched their tents in the howling wilderness, surrounded by ravenous wolves and panthers, and still more ferocious savages. The view is rich in lessons of various instruction; but our trespass on your time and attention, already too long continued, forbids us to pursue them. What Christian, in reviewing this history, does not feel, that the founders of our American church were men, whose character and works deserve to live in the hearts of posterity. Who does not feel that instead of having outstripped their zeal and fidelity, we have too often fallen short of their

(1) Hall. Nach. p. 1351-2.

bright example ? Who is not compelled to admit that their memory has been too little cherished among us ? That in the language of our text we have too seldom "remembered the days of old, and considered the years of many generations ?" That we have too seldom asked our fathers to tell us the story of God's dealings with them in the land of their pilgrimage ? Or what elder, what ruler, or pastor of the church among us, must not admit that he has too rarely from the sacred desk magnified the goodness of God to our fathers, and through them to us.

The memory of the pilgrim fathers is cherished by our New England brethren, with an interest bordering on veneration. And yet we hesitate not to affirm, that in regard to piety and zeal, father Muhlenberg, and Brunnholtz, and Handschuh, and Bolzius, were by no means inferior to Cotton, Hooker, Davenport, or the Mathers ; and in learning they were their superiors. Let then the contemplated centenary be improved as a favored season, to review the goodness of God to us and his American Zion in general. Let us bless God, not that we are better than our fathers ; but that they were so good, so faithful, so rich in blessings, which have flowed down to us. Let us thank God, not that we are better than other portions of his kingdom in our land ; but that, in common with them, we have fallen heirs to so rich a legacy of civil and political, and above all, of religious liberty, bought by the joint blood of our fathers and theirs, bestowed by the kind Providence of their God and ours.

Let us learn from the review, that if God so abundantly blessed the labors of our fathers, amid such mountains of difficulty, he will not withhold the gracious influences of his Spirit from us ; but that whenever a Paul faithfully plants, and an Apollos attentively waters, God will never withhold the increase. Let us therefore humbly and impartially contemplate our defects as watchmen on Zion's walls, and by the grace of God, purpose their removal. Let us consider attentively the various defects in some of our churches, the low state of piety, the laxity of discipline, the worldliness and indifference ; and let us humble ourselves, and pray and labor for the coming of a brighter day. Let us take to heart the pecuniary difficulties, the imperfect means of instruction afforded by our imperfectly endowed institu tions, amid which our ministers must struggle into the ministry; and let us not rest until by the blessing of God, those difficulties are removed, until our church can boast of something like a Halle in the United States, until we can offer to our students advantages equal to those which the founders of our church enjoyed in the land of their fathers. Then will our church increase in efficiency and piety; then will she be enabled to exert a more powerful and salutary influence on the future destinies of this great nation; then will she be a more worthy coadjutor with the other churches of our Lord, in spreading the triumphs of the cross, in establishing the universal reign of king Emanuel, in ushering in the day of millenial glory, when the kingdoms of this world shall have become the kingdoms of our Lord and his Christ.

II. DISCOURSE.

PORTRAITURE OF LUTHERANISM.

And after these things I saw another angel come down from heaven, having great power; and the earth was lightened with his glory. And he cried mightly with a strong voice, saying, Babylon the great is fallen, and is become the habitation of devils, (*daimonon*, deities, saints and idols,) and the hold of every foul spirit, and a cage of every unclean and hateful bird. And I heard another voice from heaven, saying, Come out of her, my people, that ye be not partakers of her sins, and that ye receive not her plagues.—Rev. xviii. 1–4.

That which we have seen and heard declare we unto you, that ye also may have fellowship with us; and truly our fellowship is with the Father, and with his Son, Jesus Christ.—1 John i. 3.

If there come any unto you and bring not this doctrine. receive him not into your house, neither bid him God speed.—2 John v. 10.

The visible church of Christ is that external kingdom, which the Son of God established upon earth. It embraces those who make a credible profession of his religion, and is designed as a nursery to train souls for that kingdom in heaven, into which no unholy thing can enter. Though at present unhappily divided, it is substantially one universal body. It embraces not the members of any one denomination alone, but all of every land, of every name, and of every complexion, who love the Lord Jesus Christ. The members of this body of Christ sustain certain mutual relations of fraternity; and however in the providence of God, they have been permitted to adopt some diversities of external form, and to entertain, as did the primitive disciples themselves, some minor differences of opinion, "they are bound to exercise holy fellowship and communion," not only towards those of their own house and denomination, but "as God offereth opportunity, unto all those in every place, who call upon the name of the Lord Jesus,"[1] and hold the cardinal doctrines of our common Christianity. At the same time, if any come, preaching another gospel; we are prohibited from "receiving them into our house, or bidding them God speed." Hence, wherever a church is established in a place where her doctrines are imperfectly known, it is due to surrounding Christians whose fellowship is invited, and to whom the hand of Christian fraternity is tendered, that such exposition be made of her views and peculiarities, as will enable others justly to appreciate her claims to recognition and regard.

In this flourishing city a large proportion of the inhabitants have, from the beginning, either immediately or by descent, belonged to the great German family, and very many of them to its Lutheran branch. The larger part of these having by the current of business, of social relations and political institutions, been led into greater familiarity with the adopted language of our land, have, in the last thirty years united with the several English churches; in which, we trust, they are doing and receiving good. Others, if we are rightly informed, who preferred to worship in the German language, erected a church about the year 1800, in union with our German Reformed brethren, and made it a united German church for both denominations, which is still flourishing at this time. Within the last few years, two other churches, entirely Lutheran, have been built by the labors of the Rev. Mr. Heyėr, the zealous missionary of our domestic missionary society, in conjunction with a little band of enterprising Lutheran laymen, one located in the city proper, and the other in Alleghanytown. To-day we are assembled within the sacred walls of a third, an English Lutheran church, erected by a portion of the same enterprising and zealous band, in conjunction with their beloved pastor, the Rev. Mr. McCron. There having heretofore been no edifice in this city, devoted to the worship of God by Lutherans in the English language, the English

---

(1) Westminster Confession, Art. xxvi. 2. See also Augsburg Confession. Art. vii. viii.

community has remained comparatively unacquainted with the precise doctrines and forms of worship of this eldest member of the Protestant family, of that church which, under God, was the first to obey the voice from heaven, and "come out from the Romish Babylon," and which, by the Divine blessing, has been extended over a wider field and larger population than any other in the entire Protestant world. In our own commonwealth, also, this church is decidedly the largest, though not in ministers, yet in the number of her churches and members.[1] Under these circumstances it is deemed alike appropriate to the occasion and respectful to this promiscuous assembly, to step aside from the ordinary topics of pulpit discussion, and spend the hour in attempting to present

A PORTRAITURE OF THE LUTHERAN CHURCH.

We invite your attention

I. To HER ORIGIN.
II. HER PRIMITIVE FEATURES.
III. HER EXTENSION. And,
IV. HER PROGRESSIVE DEVELOPMENT OR IMPROVEMENT.

The Lutheran church is indebted for her name, as is the Protestant ministry for the name preacher,[2] to the derision of the Catholics. The distinguished papal theologian, Dr. Eckius,[3] the opponent of Luther and Carlstadt, in the cele-

(1) The number of Lutheran churches in Pennsylvania is 328; the number of communicants reported, 36 516; the number of ministers, 111. of whom 64 belong to the synod of East Pennsylvania, 40 the synod of West Pennsylvania, and 7 bordering on the state of Ohio, are connected with the synod of that State. Nov. 1852, there are 200 min. 575 churches, and 5 syds.

(2) As preaching had been almost entirely neglected by the Romish priesthood, and their worship had degenerated into little else than a mere routine of ceremonies, the fact that Lutheran ministers made the preaching of God's word a prominent part of their public services, naturally arrested attention, and the Romanists stigmatized them as mere proclaimers, "prædicantes" or "prediger" (Dutch preeken, French precher, English "preach,") "*preachers*," a term of far less dignity and significance in their eyes than that of *priest*.

(3) Dr. Vater, in his Continuation of Henke's Church History, vol. ix. p. 205, attributes part of the credit of this name to Pope Adrian, as also to the anti-Melanchthonians.

brated disputation at Leipsic, in the year 1519, wishing to show his contempt for Luther and his cause, and not dreaming whereunto this matter of the reformation would grow, first stigmatized[1] the friends of the reformer as *Lutherans*, with the same feelings with which we speak of the Owenites and Fanny Wright men of our day. The term being regarded as a happy conceit, was soon spread among the enemies of the cause; and its friends, though opposed to it in principle, responded to the name, because they were not ashamed of their leader. But the name officially adopted by the Lutheran reformers was that of the Evangelical church, that is, the gospel church, in antithesis to the legal ritual of the Old Testament, the very name recently adopted by the united Lutheran and Reformed church in Prussia. Luther himself, like the great apostle of the Gentiles, protested most decidedly against the use of his name as the Shibbolet of a sect, and it is to be regretted that his advice was disregarded.

The Lutheran church in this country has, in common with that of our German Reformed brethren, also been distinctively termed the *German* church. This designation must not be understood as implying the limitation of the worship of either of these churches to the German language. It is known to the intelligent hearer, that in different countries, the services of the Lutheran church are conducted in the Swedish, the Norwegian, the Danish, the Icelandic, the Russian and the French, as well as in the English and German languages. Yet it is true, that as Germany was the cradle of the reformation, she was also the primitive seat of that church, which grew out of the reformation in the land of Luther. Germany is still the most extensive seat of Lutheranism, as she also is the land of our fathers. No other foreign country is therefore fraught with such inter-

---

(1) Koecher's Vertheidigung, &c., p. 66, 68. Thus George, the Margrave of Brandenburg, when reproached for being a Lutheran, indignantly and nobly replied: "I was not baptized in the name of Luther, he is not my God and Savior, I do not believe in him, and am not saved by him; and therefore, in this sense I am no Lutheran. But if I be asked, whether with my heart and lips I profess the doctrines which God restored to light through the instrumentality of his blessed servant, Dr. Luther, I neither hesitate nor am ashamed to call myself a Lutheran. In this sense I am, and as long as I live, will remain a Lutheran."

esting and hallowed associations to the great mass of American Lutherans as Germany, the mother of the reformation, the cradle of Lutheranism, the land where our fathers proclaimed the gospel of salvation, where Spener sowed the seed of truth, where Arndt preached and wrote and lived his "True Christianity," where Franke wrought his works of love, and where believing Luther poured his prayer of faith into the lap of God! But it is not only to Lutheran minds that Germany is encircled with interesting associations. Although the populace are too little acquainted with the fact, yet what intelligent scholar does not know that the Germans constitute one of the most distinguished branches of the human family, and that at different periods throughout the two thousand years of their national history, they have excelled in all that is truly noble and praiseworthy in heathen virtue, or interesting in the fruits of an enlightened and active Christian piety? Germany was originally inhabited by a heroic and martial people, whose origin is enveloped in some obscurity. Their language and religion point us to Asia. They certainly proceeded from the north of the Euxine sea, and known as Scythians, Teutones, Franks, &c., overspread all Western Europe. The English are both as to language and population, in part descended from two of these German tribes, the Anglos and the Saxons, who at an early day conquered Britain, and formed the Anglo-Saxon race, whose lineage is often boasted of by a portion of our citizens. When first visited by the Romans about the time of our Saviour, the Germans had already for ages inhabited the country, and had lost all traces of their earliest history. Divided into many independent tribes, and often engaged in intestine wars, each tribe acknowledged no laws but those enacted by the majority at a general council. Far removed from the refinement and literary character of the Romans, they were alike free from their licentiousness and effeminacy. Hospitality and conjugal fidelity were prominent characteristics of the Germans; and a promise given to friend or foe, they held inviolable, even at the risk of life. They cherished a firm belief of the immortality of the soul, and of future retributions. They were indeed polytheists, but their religion was of the sublimer cast. They neither bowed down to idols, nor worshipped in temples made with hands, but offered their devotions in open groves, under the broad canopy of heaven; for, says the Roman historian, they regarded their gods as too sacred and great to be confined in temples, or represented by idols of wood or stone.[1]

Of the different tribes of this numerous family which overspread all western Europe, those only retain the name of Germans, in modern history, who reside in the territory denominated Germany. Their martial spirit rendered difficult the introduction of Christianity among them, which was however effected at least in name successively among the different tribes, from the third to the eighth century. The forgiving spirit of the gospel gained a tardy victory over their warlike minds; as was strikingly illustrated in the instance of Clovis,[2] king of the Franks, a tribe that settled in Gaul. On one occasion, whilst Remigius was preaching to them and depicting in glowing colors the sufferings of the Saviour when suspended on the cross, the king, no longer able to restrain his spirit, cried out in the midst of the congregation: "Ah, if I had been there with my Franks, the Jews should not have crucified the Lord!" Unhappily the Christianity first introduced among them was strongly tinctured with the corruptions of Rome, and in the progress of ages, the Germans participated extensively in the increasing superstitions and degeneracy which reigned at the fountain head. But in the providence of God it was reserved for this heroic and undaunted people, to take the lead in breaking the bonds by which Europe had for ages been held in subjection. "Whilst," says the distinguished Lutheran historian, Dr. Mosheim, "the Roman pontiff slumbered in security at the head of the church, and saw nothing throughout the vast extent of his dominion but tranquility and submission, and while the worthy and pious professors of genuine christianity almost despaired of seeing that reformation on which their ardent desires and expectations were bent; an obscure and inconsiderable person arose, on a sudden, in the year 1517, and laid the foundation of this long-expected change, by opposing with undaunted resolution his single force to the torrent of Papal ambition and despotism. This remarkable man was MARTIN LUTHER, of Eisle-

(1) See Schroeck's Allgemeine, Weltgeschichte, vol. iii, p. 68.

(2) Clovis belonged to the German, Salian tribe. Henke, vol. i, p. 387.

ben, in Saxony,[1] an Augustinian monk, and professor of theology in the university which had been erected at Wittenberg a few years before." It was this interesting people, after they had thrown off the yoke of Rome, and through the instrumentality of their countryman, Luther, and others, received the pure and unadulterated word of God, that constituted themselves a reformed, an evangelical church, which has been denominated Lutheran. And it is from this interesting nation and this church, that the German portion of the Lutherans in this country are descended.

The incidents of this interesting revolution, which affected both church and state throughout Europe, we cannot stop even to glance at. It was a revolution not merely of outward forms, but of the elementary principles, which had for ages been the basis of all institutions, both civil and ecclesiastical. Suffice it to say, that by his ninety-five theses, by his various disputations, by his noble translation of the bible into German, (a work to which even Schiller, confessedly one of the greatest masters of the German language, has professed himself much indebted,) by his laborious preaching and teaching, and by his very numerous publications, which Seckendorf enumerates at several hundreds; Luther and his Spartan band of co-workers, Melancthon, Zwingle, Calvin, and others, accomplished the greatest and most salutary revolution which Europe has witnessed since the commencement of the Christian era; a revolution, also, to which, in the providence of God, these United States may clearly trace their liberties.

Without originally designing a separation from Rome, the increasing light which burst in upon his mind, as well as the inflexible opposition of the Papal court to all reform, taught him the necessity of entire separation from that degenerate hierarchy which had corrupted the waters of life, and refused to have them purified by the salt of the gospel.

The question here arises, was the Romish establishment still a Christian church, or was she antichrist? And was the ordination valid which Luther obtained in her? Though lamentably corrupt, we must still regard her as at that time a part of the true church of Christ, because some of the grossest corruptions which prevailed in a part of the

---

(1) Mosheim, vol. iv, p. 25.

Romish church were not general, and having not yet been received into the official standards of papacy, could not be charged on her as a whole, and did not form a necessary part of her system. Such corruptions are the denial of the cup to the laity, canonization of the vulgate version of the scriptures, the elevation of tradition to an equality with the word of God, &c. But when the Council of Trent, about twelve years after the publication of the Augsburg Confession, (1542,) enacted these abuses into integral and essential parts of Romish faith, and required them of all who desired to be members of the Romish church, the marks of antichrist were indelibly impressed upon her, and she lost her claim as a church to Christian recognition. Her ordination of Luther, therefore, in 1507,[1] was valid, and as he renounced her jurisdiction on Dec. 10, 1520, by committing the papal bull of citation to the flames, her subsequent excommunication did not reach him, and he stands as a seceder from her communion.[2] Or, if we date the origin of the Lutheran church from 1530, and suppose Luther to have remained under Romish jurisdiction till then, when the Augsburg Confession was published, the ordination of Luther and his associates still remains untouched; for the papal bull of excomunication in 1520, being wholly unrighteous and contrary to the word of God, could no more deprive them of their ministerial character, than the decision of the Jewish Sanhedrim against the apostles, commanding them to speak no more in the name of the Lord Jesus; or the excommunication of the orthodox ministry by the Arians, when they gained a temporary ascendancy in the fourth century, could divest them of their clerical character. The Lutheran and the protestant ministry generally, is therefore as valid as was that of Rome at the time of the reformation, even if we admitted the necessity of a lineal, personal succession from the apostles.

As to the doctrine of *papal* apostolic succession, it is a

(1) Luther was ordained on the fourth Sunday after Easter, called, in the old calenders, Sunday Cantate.

(2) The bull of citation to repentance and retraction within sixty days, was published June 15, 1520; and the final bull of excommunication January 3rd, 1521, twenty-five days after he publicly renounced Romanism by burning the former bull.

mere figment, and can never be proved by the Papists themselves. To say nothing of their doctrine of intention, which cardinal Bellarmine himself asserts,[1] renders doubtful the validity of every Romish sacrament; where was their papal succession when Liberius, the occupant of the holy see, professed Arianism, A. D. 357? Where was it in the fourteenth century, during the so-called great western schism, from A. D. 1378 to 1414, when two different lines of contending pontiffs reigned simultaneously, each having a portion of the church adhering to him, each excommunicating the other, and finally both deposed as heretical and perjured by the Council of Pisa in 1409?[2]

We admit, indeed, that the existing ministry of the church are ordinarily the proper agents to induct others into the sacred office, and thus the propriety of regular *ministerial* succession arises. But it is conceded by all, that such succession is found in all the Protestant churches, and therefore their ministry is valid. But the necessity of even this succession or appointment, in some extraordinary cases, it would be difficult to establish. As we learn from our text, the scripture commands us to test those who come unto us by their doctrines, before we "bid them God speed," but does it say any thing about their apostolic succession? Accordingly, Luther, and many distinguished Lutheran divines, maintain, in accordance with our brethren of the Congregational church, that whenever necessity requires it, the congregation of believers have the power to elect and constitute one of their number as pastor.[3]

Having thus glanced at the origin of the Lutheran church, we proceed to inquire,

I. What were her primitive features?

The *first feature* embraces the fundamental principle adopted by the church.

"The great and leading principle of the Lutheran church," says Dr. Mosheim,[4] "is that the holy scriptures are the only source, whence we are to draw our religious sentiments,

(1) Bellarm. Lib. Just. cap. 8. Sacramentum non conficiatur sine intentione ministri, et intentionem alterius nemo videre possit. See Waddell's Letters to editor of Catholic Miscellany, p. 13; New York, 1830.

(2) See Appendix, note A. (3) See Appendix, note G.

(4) Vol. iii. p. 208 of his Eccles. Hist.

whether they relate to faith or practice; and that these inspired writings are, in all matters that are essential to salvation, so plain, and so easy to be thoroughly understood, that their signification may be learned, without the aid of an expositor, by every person of common sense, who has a competent knowledge of the language in which they are composed. There are indeed certain formularies adopted by this church, which contain the principal points of its doctrine, ranged for the sake of method and perspicuity, in their natural order. But these books have no authority but what they derive from the scriptures of truth, whose sense and meaning they are designed to convey." This was the noble principle adopted by the Lutheran church, a principle which has the cordial assent of every Lutheran in the present day, and in regard to which our only regret is, that though it was adopted in theory by all the Protestant churches, not one of them had yet light and grace and charity enough consistently to practice it.

The principal books here referred to as subsidiary to the bible, were of two classes: first, the confessions of the primitive centuries, the so-called Apostles' Creed, the Nicene Creed, and the Athanasian Confession, by which the Lutheran church established her identity with the church of the apostolic and succeeding ages; and, secondly, the Augsburg Confession, composed by Melancthon, and presented before the Emperor Charles V., at the diet in 1530; the Apology or Defense of this Confession by the same hand; the Smalcald Articles by Luther, and also his Catechisms.

The prominent doctrines taught in these books, may be regarded as the SECOND FEATURE. They are none other than those commonly termed *the doctrines of the Reformation*, the doctrines which, with few variations, are held in common by all the so-called orthodox churches. They are among others the following:

First. The doctrine of the *trinity* of persons in one Godhead; or to use the language of the Augsburg Confession, "That there is one divine essence which is called and is God, eternal, incorporeal, indivisible, infinite in power, wisdom and goodness—and yet that there are three persons, who are of the same essence and power and are co-eternal, the Father, the Son, and the Holy Spirit."[1]

(1) Art. i. p. 44 of Popular Theology.

Secondly. These books also teach the *proper and eternal divinity of the Lord Jesus Christ* in all its amplitude. Their language is: That the Word, that is, the Son of God, assumed human nature, in the womb of the blessed virgin Mary, so that the two natures, human and divine, inseparably united into one person, constitute one Christ, who is true God and man."[1]

Thirdly. The *universal depravity of our race.* Their language is: "Since the fall of Adam, all men who are naturally engendered, are born with a depraved nature, that is, without the fear of God, or confidence towards him, but with sinful propensities."[2]

Fourthly. On the *Atonement* they teach its vicarious nature and unlimited extent. Says the Augsburg Confession: "The Son of God, truly suffered, was crucified, died, and was buried, that he might reconcile the Father to us, and be a *sacrifice* not only for original sin, but also for all the actual sins of men." He also sanctifies "those who believe in him, by sending into their hearts the Holy Spirit, who governs, consoles, quickens and defends them against the devil and the power of sin."[3]

Fifthly. On *Justification* they teach, "That men cannot be justified before God by their own strength, merits or works; but that they are justified gratuitously, for Christ's sake, through faith."[4]

Sixthly. Concerning a *Holy Life,* or *Good Works,* they teach, "That this faith must bring forth good fruits; and that it is our duty to perform those good works which God has commanded, because he has enjoined them, and not in the expectation of thereby meriting justification before him."[5]

Seventhly. Concerning *The Ministerial Office* and *the Means of Grace,* the Augsburg Confession declares: "In order that we may obtain this faith, the ministerial office has been instituted, whose members are to preach the gospel and administer the sacraments," (namely, baptism and the Lord's supper.) "For through the instrumentality of the word and sacraments, as means of grace, the Holy Spirit is given,

(1) Art. iii. p. 130
(2) Art. ii. p. 123.
(3) Aug. Confession, Art. iii. p. 131.
(4) Art. iv. p. 131.
(5) Aug. Confession, Art. vi. p. 165.

who in his own time and place, produces faith in those who hear the gospel message, namely, that God, for Christ's sake, and not on account of any merit in us, justifies those who believe in Christ."[1]

And, *finally*, of the *Future Judgment*, and *world of retribution*, the same Confession teaches,[2] that at the end of the world, Christ will appear for judgment; that he will raise all the dead; that he will give to the pious and elect eternal life and endless joys: but will condemn wicked men and devils to be punished without end." Such are the prominent doctrines avowed by the Lutheran church in the beginning, all of which are at this day received by the entire Lutheran church in this country.

The THIRD FEATURE is her government. "The Government of the Lutheran church," (in Europe,) says Dr. Mosheim ;"[3] seems equally removed trom episcopacy on the one hand and from Presbyterianism on the other, if we except the kingdoms of Sweden and Denmark, which retain the form of ecclesiastical government that preceded the Reformation, purged indeed from the superstitions and abuses that rendered it so odious.[4] The Lutherans are persuaded that there is no law of divine authority which points out a distinction between the ministers of the gospel with respect to rank, dignity or prerogatives: and therefore they recede from episcopacy"[5] On the other hand, the early reformers having been trained under the aristocratic governments of Europe, and accustomed to the imparity of Romanism, regarded some diversity in the authority, rank and duties of ministers as conducive to order and harmony. Hence, with the universal acknowledgment of the parity of ministers by *divine right*, they introduced some subordination on the

---

(1) Art. v. p. 148.

(2) Aug. Confession, Art. xvii. p. 288

(3) Eccl. History. vol. iii. p. 211, 212.

(4) On this subject. Dr. Maclaine, the distinguished translator of Mosheim's History, uses this language: "The archbishop of Upsal is primate of Sweden, and the only archbishop among the Lutherans. The luxury and licentiousness that too commonly flow from the opulence of the Roman Catholic clergy, are unknown in these two northern states; since the revenues of the prelate now mentioned, do not amount to more than four hundred pounds yearly, while those of the bishops are proportionably small." Vol. iii. p. 211.

(5) Mosheim's Eccl. History, vol. iii. p. 212.

ground of human expediency, and designated those to whom the supervision of certain districts was confided, superintendents, consistorial counsellors, inspectors, &c. In the United States entire parity is maintained, and even the nominal office of Senior Ministerii, is retained by only one out of all our synods. And as Dr. Henke very justly remarks, the assertion, that Sweden and Denmark retained the office of bishop, can be made only by special latitude of speech, by using the term bishop for an office divested of the mystic idea of higher or holier dignity, sometimes attached to the name.[1] Even in what was then the dutchy of Prussia, two of these officers were still termed bishops, fifty years after the Reformation, namely, the Pomesanisch and the Samlœndisch bishops.[2] And Frederick William, the late king of Prussia, amid other arbitrary acts of interference with ecclesiastical matters, again conferred the title of diocesan bishop on several favorites, much to the displeasure of the great mass of German divines. In this country, although our ministers are strenuous advocates of parity, they pretty extensively favor the idea of returning to the use of the word bishop in its scriptural sense, in which, according to the concession of many of the most distinguished advocates ofimparity, it was synonymous with elder, or preacher, and is applicable to every minister of the gospel; the sense in which as Luke informs us, instead of one bishop having oversight over a large district of country or diocese, there were several bishops in the one city Ephesus."[3]

In Europe, where the unhappy union between church and state, established by the emperor Constantine in the fourth century, still continues, the civil rulers exercise more or less influence in all the churches. But in this country, the Luth eran church in common with her Protestant sister churches, deprecates as unwarranted and dangerous all interference of civil government in religious affairs; excepting the mere protection of all denominations and all individuals in the unrestricted right to worship in any and every way they think proper.

---

(1) Hencke's Kirchengeschichte, B. iii. s. 303.

(2) Henke, iii. p. 364.

(3) Acts. xx. 28. To the elders, i. e. ministers of Ephesus, Paul says: "Take heed of the flock, over which the Holy Ghost hath made you overseers," or as the Greek is, *bishops*.

The FOURTH FEATURE of Lutheranism, is found in her *Liturgies* and *festivals*. In all the different countries of Europe and in America, our churches have liturgies, differing in minor points, but agreeing in essentials. These are used more or less in public worship, and serve as a directory in the performance of the different ministerial functions. These liturgies are about one-third as long as those of the Protestant Episcopal church; and, as to character and contents, very similar to them. In the United States, we have adopted a short liturgy, which it is left optional with each minister to use as often or as seldom as he may judge most conducive to edification. In regard to such forms our own impression is, that when properly constructed, they tend to give fixedness, tangibility and definiteness to christian worship in the popular mind; but they should be short, lest when frequently repeated, they tire; nor should they be exclusively used, lest they degenerate into mere instruments of formality.

As to *ecclesiastical festivals*, of human appointment, those only are observed which were instituted to commemorate the fundamental facts of the christian religion, such as the nativity, death, resurrection and ascension of the Son of God, and the outpouring of the Holy Spirit on the day of Pentecost. As christianity is a religion based upon these facts; it is important that the recollection of them, in their literal, historical import, be cherished by her professors. And as ministers rarely preach once a year on each of these topics, unless called on by some such custom; we regard the influence of these festivals as salutary in their appropriate design; and the abuses which are practiced on them in some places by the irreligious, are not necessary consequences of them, and should be obviated.

But this portraiture of Lutheranism would be incomplete, were we to omit the FIFTH FEATURE, her particular *attention to the religious instruction of the children of the church*, and habit of calling on them, when they attain years of discretion, personally to *confirm* and assume the vows made for them at their baptism. The Lutheran church, believing that God has not revoked in the New Testament, the institution of infant membership in his church, which he established in the Old, receives into her bosom both the actual and adopted children of professed believers, by the initiatory rite of baptism, according to the Saviour's command. Having thus received them, she treats them accordingly. From the days of the Reformation the Lutheran church inculcated it as a principal duty of her ministers and members to provide for the adequate instruction of the children of the church in the doctrines of our holy religion. In this country, where in most cases, each minister has charge of three or four churches, his personal instructions cannot well reach all the children with sufficient frequency; yet it is regarded as the duty of every minister, occasionally to convene the children of each congregation for instruction in the catechism; and that minister will prove most successful, and best deserve the confidence of his charge, who, by the establishment of a Sabbath School in every congregation, and the employment of the pious members of his charge, brings the lambs of his flock, and all others who are without a shepherd, and are appropriately within the sphere of his labors, under full and stated influence of the doctrines and precepts of the gospel. Annually also, and if necessary oftener, the minister holds a series of meetings with those who are applicants for admission to *sacramental communion*, or as in reference to the infant baptism of the applicant, it is called, *confirmation*. To these meetings are invited all who feel a concern for their salvation, and especially all those subjects of infant baptism, who have attained years of discretion. "Every meeting is opened by singing and prayer, and closed by an address to the throne of grace. The time of the first meeting, is chiefly occupied by the pastor in explaining the object of the contemplated course of instruction in as solemn and impressive a manner as possible. This object he states to be, not merely the acquisition of doctrinal knowledge—nor merely the admission to the Lord's table; for Paul tells us, that many eat and drink judgment to themselves. But says the zealous pastor who feels the eternal importance of this solemn occasion, the object is to show you in so plain and simple a manner, that you cannot fail to understand it, the natural depravity of your hearts, your habitual and base rebellion against your best benefactor, your father and your God, and your danger of being shut out forever from his blissful presence; to show you that you must be born again, or be eternally excluded from the kingdom of heaven, and to give you such instructions and directions from day to day, as will if faithfully pursued, sooner or later, certainly eventuate in your conversion to God.[1] Every succeeding meeting is occupied in conversational lectures on experimental religion, and in the examination of the catechumen on the fundamental doctrines and duties of religion as contained in the bible and Luther's Catechism. These meetings afford to the faithful pastor better opportunities of access to the hearts of the rising generation in his church, than are enjoyed by any denomination who neglect this practice. At the close of these meetings, which are continued through from six to twelve weeks once or twice each week, and in the last if convenient daily, the church council are convened to examine the catechumens on their qualifications for sacramental communion. It is here that our practice is sometimes less rigid than it ought to be. The council should faithfully examine every applicant, and admit none but such as give evidence of living faith in that Redeemer, whose dying love they wish to commemorate. Although in the hands of an unconverted minister this duty, like all others, will be mere formality, and attended with little profit; yet we have never met, nor do we expect to meet a pious minister, who faithfully practised this system, and did not regard it as a most blessed and successful method of bringing souls to Christ. After an experience and observation of thirty years in the ministry, we cannot but regard this practice faithfully pursued, as one of the glories of the Lutheran church.

Having occupied much time in delineating the primitive features of the Lutheran church, a few words must suffice on the subject of

III. Her extension.

After her establishment in Germany by the labors of Luther, Melancthon and others, about 1525, when the Elector John, of Saxony, first publicly adopted the amended system, the Lutheran doctrines were introduced into *Sweden*, by the instrumentality of Olaus Petri in 1527, under the sanction of king Gustavus Vasa Ericson.[2] Into *Denmark* the Lutheran doctrines were fully introduced in 1527, in the

(1) Popular Theology, p. 230, 231, ed. 2.

(2) See Appendix, note B.

reign of Frederick, after some preparatory steps by Christiern II. The Lutheran church is also established in Norway, in Lapland, Finland, and Iceland; and has some congregations in Hungary, France and Asia.

In Russia the Lutheran population amounts to 2,600,000 with 500 ministers.[1] In the United States, the first Lutheran churches were established by the Swedes, who emigrated to this country and settled on the banks of the Delaware during the reign of queen Christina, and under the sanction of her prime minister, Oxenstiern, about the year 1636, sixteen or seventeen years after the settlement of New England by the pilgrim fathers, and about thirty years after the establishment of an English colony in Virginia. As these churches were few in number, and received no accessions from the mother country, the Swedish language was soon lost by the rising generation, and preaching in the English tongue was necessary long before any of our German pastors officiated in that language. Under these circumstances recourse was had to our Episcopal brethren for English ministrations, and thus these churches gradually became connected with that denomination; though by their charter they are still styled Swedish *Lutheran* churches.[2]

The next Lutheran establishment was by Lutherans from Holland, who erected a Lutheran church in the city of New York in 1703, in which worship was conducted in the Holland, the English, and afterwards also in the German tongue.[3]

The first *German* Lutheran churches in this country, were regularly organized by Rev. Messrs. *Bolzius* and *Gronau*, in 1733; and in 1742, by *Henry Melchior Muhlenberg*, one of the patriarchs of American Lutheranism. This indefatigable and talented servant of Christ, whilst located in the city of New York, was in the habit of preaching in the German, the Holland, and the English languages, every Lord's day. Had his successors followed his noble example, and qualified themselves to preach in the English lan-

---

(1) See Reinwald's Repertorium.

(2) Annals of the Swedes on the Delaware, by Rev. J. C. Clay, p. 3, 4, 161, &c. Also Schubert's Schwedische Kirchenverfassung, vol. ii. p. 439 -442.

(3) See "Authentic Account of a Bill in Chancery," New York, p. 4, &c.

guage wherever it was necessary, the Lutheran church would at this day be twice as numerous in this country as it is.

We have, at present, (1840,) about 350 ministers and 1000 churches;[1] and amid the long catalogue of distinguished divines, who have since wielded the interests and advanced the cause of our Zion, and have entered on their celestial inheritance, what friend of the church does not delight to name a Kunze, a Schmidt, a Kurtz, another Muhlenberg, a Goring, a Helmuth, a Melsheimer, a Storch, an Endress, a Lochman, a Schaeffer, a Ruthrauff, a Shober, a Geissenhainer?

The entire Lutheran population in the world is estimated by accurate authors at from 25 to 30,000,000.

In literary and theological institutions, in learned *theologians*, and in a rich and learned theological literature,[2] the Lutheran church has confessedly surpassed all others. Gratitude for the numerous and signal advantages, reaped by the cause of reformation from the superior learning of her advocates, and the obvious facilities rendered by the revival of letters previously to the reformation, taught the Protestant princes to regard learning as a special gift of God, to deliver them from the bondage of the dark ages. Numerous literary institutions were therefore founded at an early day, and others enlarged. Among the former are the universities of Jena (1558,) and Konigsberg; among the latter Wittenberg and Leipsic. At this day there are in Germany nine universities, wholly Lutheran,[3] one[4] belonging jointly to the Lutherans and Reformed, and four[5] to the Lutherans, Reformed and Catholics in conjunction. In Sweden there are two Lutheran universities, and in Norway one. By the attention of the Protestants to learning and learned institutions, enlightened advocates for the truth were provided, and a pious, learned literature was formed

(1) Now, (in 1851,) this number is 850 ministers, and about 2000 congregations. Of the ministers, nearly one-half are natives of Germany, located principally in the Mississippi Valley.

(2) See Appendix, note C.

(3) Leipsic, Rostock, Greifswalde, Jena, Giessen, Kiel, Halle, Gottingen, and Erlangen universities.

(4) At Berlin.

(5) Heidelberg, Tubingen, Breslau and Bonn.

at an early day, to spread its purifying and enlightening influence over Europe and the civilized world. Had Luther, Melancthon, Calvin and Zwingle not been men of distinguished learning, they could never have drawn from the stores of sacred and patristic literature, the facts which subverted the corrupt pretensions of the papists, and erected a fabric of truth, which remains to this day the admiration of the world. How incalculably would not the Lutheran church in this country have gained in efficiency, in extension, in respectability, in usefulness, had our fathers a century, or even fifty years ago, laid the foundation of some of the institutions which have since then been established? Now the Lutheran church in this country has four theological seminaries in operation, and at least partially endowed, and one college[1] under its particular patronage. In the seminary at Gettysburg alone, upwards of one hundred[2] ministers have been trained in fifteen years, who are now preaching to thousands, the unsearchable riches of Christ, and a large number have proceeded from our other schools of the prophets at Hartwick, at Lexington and at Columbus. Let these institutions therefore share our warmest prayers, and our most zealous efforts; and let no Lutheran rest satisfied, until they are all adequately endowed.

We proceed to contemplate

IV. The progressive development or improvement of the Lutheran church.

Luther had wisely regarded the reformation as unfinished, and exhorted his followers to turn away from his works, and study the bible more attentively.[3] Unfortunately for the cause of truth and peace, the admiration of many of his followers, degenerated into excessive veneration; and death, which translated him to the abode of peace in heaven, made his writings, the source of rancorous contention on earth, imparted a kind of canonical authority to them. Moreover,

---

(1) The number of Theological Seminaries is now increased to six, and that of the colleges to three, by the erection of institutions at Springfield, Ohio, Hillsborough, Illinois, and Columbus, Ohio.

(2) This number has increased to 250.

(3) "I have not kept a list of my publications, nor have I all the works themselves; for I desire much rather that the Bible alone should be studied instead of my works."—*Letter to Ursinus*, 1527; *Thl.* 21, p. 1031.

as the church, established by his instrumentality, was designated by his name, his works gradually were regarded as the standards of orthodoxy, and all attempts to continue the work of reformation so gloriously commenced by him, were denounced as treason to his cause!! "Even, during his lifetime," says the distinguished historian Henke, "there were some who followed him with a slavish servility. A species of canonization of this great man had already taken place; and he was not unfrequently known by the names, megalander, man of God, second Elias, the last prophet, &c.; and when he died, it seemed as if an oracle had been struck dumb."

Had not the church been denominated by the name of this distinguished servant of Christ; had not his works but the bible been regarded as the grand source of religious light, as the grand subject of continued study; and had the Augsburg Confession alone been received as an auxiliary test; the church would have enjoyed much more peace, and the whole field of doctrine, except the few points determined in that confession, would have been open to free continued study and scrutiny in the light of God's word. But instead of finding fault with those theological heroes, who vanquished the hosts of Rome, for not accomplishing every thing; we should be grateful to God that they were enabled to effect so much.

The *first* feature of improvement to which we will advert, is the *entire rejection of the authority of the Fathers in ecclesiastical controversy.* The grand mistake of the earlier reformers was their appeal to this authority. They were, indeed, enabled with these weapons, to overturn the corruptions introduced into the church after the rise of the papal hierarchy; but they also compelled themselves to retain such errors as were of earlier date. The writings of the fathers instead of being good authority for scripture doctrine, are a perfect labyrinth of theological errors, from which it is impossible to escape with safety, and in which we look in vain for that unanimons consent which Rome has so loudly boasted. But it is easy to establish by the authority of Antenicene fathers, the several errors retained by the earlier reformers, and since rejected by the mass of Protestants.

In short it is a principle which the experience of ages has clearly established, that in all controversies about the proper doctrines, or duties, or forms of christianity, *the bible, the whole bible, and nothing but the bible,* must be the armor of the Protestant. To concede to Romanists or others the necessity of an appeal to patristic authority, is a tacit denial of the word of God, as the sufficient and only rule of faith and practice, the only ground on which Protestantism can be permanently and triumphantly sustained.

Another feature of improvement in the Lutheran church consists in her *no longer requiring assent to the doctrine of the real presence of the Saviour in the eucharist.*[1] On this subject her views have not unfrequently been misapprehended and misstated. It is indeed true, that she did entertain opinions on this topic different from the other churches. This difference was however by no means so great as is at present supposed by the less intelligent part of the community. Calvin and the early English reformers, employed language nearly, and in some cases, quite as strong as that found in the Lutheran symbols. The Augsburg Confession affirms, "that the body and blood of Christ are actually present (*vere adsint*), and the German copy adds, under the form or emblems of bread and wine and dispensed to the communicants."[2] Calvin employs language about as strong: he says in the *mystery* of the supper, by the emblems of bread and wine, Christ is really exhibited to us, that is, *his body and blood, in which he yielded full obedience,* in order to work out a righteousness for us; by which, in the first place, we may, as it were, coalesce into one body with him; and, secondly, being made partakers of the *substance* of himself, also be strengthened by the reception of every blessing.[3] In

(1) From this, and the other items of this part of our discourse, the intelligent reader will perceive what gross misrepresentations are circulated, ignorantly we trust, by the publishers of Buck's Theological Dictionary, and by such living authors as Mr. Goodrich, (in his Eccles. Hist.) who represent the Lutheran church of the present day, as resembling the Roman Catholics more nearly than does any other Protestant church! After the repeated publications, made by the Lutherans in this country, it is unworthy of professed historians to transmit to yet another generation these hereditary statements. As to the private ministers, who occasionally inform their hearers, that their Lutheran neighbors believe in consubstantiation, &c.. as we wish not to impute intentional misrepresentation, we must attribute their error to want of information.

(2) Augsburg Confession, Art. x.

(3) Dico igitur in cœnæ *mysterio* per symbola panis et vini Christum vere nobis exhiberi, adeoque corpus et sanguinem ejus, in quibus omnem

the Episcopal church, Cranmer, one of her earliest and ablest reformers, in the reign of Henry VIII., published his translation of the catechism of Justus Jonas, with amendments, in 1548, to which he professed to adhere till his death,[1] and in which he uses this language: "Christ saith of the bread 'this is my body;' and of the cup he saith 'this is my blood.' Wherefore we ought to believe that in the sacrament we receive truly the body and blood of Christ. For God is almighty; he is able, therefore, to do all things what he will."[2] His friend and fellow martyr, Ridley, at his last trial says: "I agree that the sacrament is the very true and natural body and blood of Christ, even that which was born of the Virgin Mary, which ascended into heaven, which sitteth on the right hand of God, the Father, which shall come from thence to judge the quick and the dead, only I differ in the way and manner of being,"[3] &c. It is admitted, these same writers professed to mean a spiritual presence, and so did also the Lutheran reformers, who explicitly declare in the *Formula Concordiæ*,[4] "By that word (spiritually) we exclude those Capernaitish notions concerning a *gross* and *carnal* presence, which have been attributed to our churches by the sacramentarians, in defiance of all our public protestations against them. And when we use this term, (spiritually,) we wish to be understood as signifying that the body and blood are received, and eaten, and drank spiritually in the Lord's supper. For although the participation is effected by the mouth, the manner in which it is done is spiritual." At the present day, it is pretty generally agreed by Protestants, that to talk of the *spiritual* presence of a *material* body, or the *spiritual* eating and drinking of a *material* body and blood, is to employ language that conveys no distinct ideas. We, however, cheerfully concede that the other Protestant denominations relinquished these views of their early reformers, more

---

obedientiam pro comparanda nobis justitia adimplevit: quo scilicet, primum, in unum corpus cum ipso coalescamus; deinde participes substantiæ ejus facit, in bonorum omnium communicatione virtutem quoque sentiamus.—*Institut. Lib.* iv. c. xvii. 11.

(1) See his works, ii. 440; iii. 13, 279, 344; and Hook's Discourse, p. 96.

(2) Hook. p. 96.

(3) Hook's Discourse, p. 99.

(4) Art. vii, No. 21, p. 604.

speedily and with less controversy than did the Lutheran church. It was indeed reported that Luther himself shortly before his death, in a confidential conversation with Melancthon, acknowledged that he had gone too far in regard to the eucharist. But, much as we should be pleased to believe that our great and good reformer had made such an acknowledgment, the evidence appears unsatisfactory; or at most, he may have admitted, that he had exhibited too much warmth in the controversy, or overrated the importance of his peculiar views.[1] At the present day, whilst some shades of difference exist in the Lutheran church, all are permitted to enjoy their opinions in peace, and the most generally received view, if we mistake not, is: "That there is no presence of the glorified *human* nature of the Saviour, either substantial or influential; nor any thing mysterious or supernatural in the eucharist; yet, that whilst the bread and wine are merely symbolic representations of the Saviour's absent body, by which we are reminded of his sufferings, there is also a special *spiritual* blessing bestowed by the divine Saviour on all worthy communicants, by which their faith and Christian graces are confirmed.[2]

The *third* item of improvement is the relinquishment of a much abused custom connected with the preparation for communion. The reformers and their successors had substantially repudiated as unscriptural and corrupting what constituted the essential features of Romish *private confession*, namely: the pretence that the priest is in the place of God; that every individual sin, even the secret thoughts and feelings of the heart must be individually detailed to the priest, as essential to pardon; and that the priest possesses the absolute power to forgive these sins. Yet the reformers deemed it useful, that before communion, each communicant should have a private interview with the pastor, and give him an account of the state of his soul, and his progress in the divine life; in order that the minister might give him instruction and advice, and if the case warranted it, encourage the applicant with the promise of pardon from God. This custom, in order to give as little offense as pos-

(1) It is said, Melancthon communicated the fact to Professor Alesius, of Leipsic, from whom Pfuhlman, one of his students, heard it.

(2) See the Author's Popular Theology, p. 303, 5th ed.

sible, they denominated, though very inappropriately, confession. They had rejected the thing, and therefore it would have been more consistent not to retain the name. Yet, against this custom, it would be difficult to allege any valid objection, except its misapprehension and consequent abuse by the ignorant. Thus explained, confession was approved by Calvin,[1] Peter Martyr,[2] Werenfels,[3] Heidegger,[4] Hornbeck,[5] Jurien,[6] and other distinguished Reformed divines. But even this custom has been almost entirely abandoned, and the preparation for communion consists in a public preparatory discourse, public and united confession of sins, and rehearsal of the promises of divine mercy, similar to the preparatory exercises of other churches. The only difference is, that in the Lutheran and Episcopal churches, which use liturgies, these exercises of confession of sins and exhibition of divine promises of pardon, are conducted according to a settled form, whilst in others they are extemporaneous. Yet in the numerous Lutheran liturgies we have seen, including those of Sweden[7] and Norway, the minister never professes to forgive sins himself, nor even to announce the divine promises of pardon unconditionally to all, but limits them to truly penitent believers; whilst the impenitent and unbelieving are expressly told that God will not pardon their sins, but inflict deserved punishment on them. This formal annunciation of the divine promise of forgiveness, thus conditionally made, is edifying to intelligent minds, especially as the Saviour himself, in the words of the institution, mentions "remission of sins" as the design of that death which we are to commemorate in the eucharist. Yet as it is easily perverted into *certain* pardon by the less informed, who may erroneously conceive themselves penitent, and as the scriptures contain no special promise of pardon at communion, more than in the performance of any other duty; the utmost caution should be observed against misapprehension, and the annunciation itself

(1) Institutions, Christ. Relig; Lib. iii. cap. iv. 12, 13; see Appendix, note E.
(2) Loci Theologici. De Pœnitentia, p. 1023.
(3) Opusc. Theol. Philosph. et Philolog. Tom. ii. p. 320.
(4) Manuduct. in viam concorgiæ Protestantium, Diatr. i. § 20, p. 39.
(5) Koecher's Vertheidigung. p. 529.
(6) Consultat. de pace Protest. Pt. ii. cap. xiii. p. 272.
(7) Shubert's Schwedische Kirchenverfassung, vol. ii. p. 63.

is very properly often thrown into the form of a prayer,[1] as is also done in the Episcopal liturgy.

The *fourth* item of *improvement* is the entire rejection of every remnant of papal superstition in the administration of baptism. The Romanists maintain, that unbaptized persons are possessed by evil spirits, and that the priest possesses the power by adjuration to expel them. This ceremony, termed exorcism, is performed by the priest with a multitude of formalities. Luther, and the other early reformers, rejected both these principles; yet retained some kind of adjuration as a symbolic acknowledgment of the natural depravity of all men. To this they were probably led by their lingering regard for the early fathers. For, something of this kind was practiced even in the third century, when the corrupting influence of the New Platonists was first felt in the church; and it was defended by such men as Cyprian[2] and Augustine.[3] Yet many of our churches were from the beginning unwilling to retain the semblance of this ceremony, even as a declaration of natural depravity, and accordingly it was totally rejected from the liturgy and directory for worship, published at Augsburg seven years after the celebrated diet of that place, namely in 1537; as also in that of Strasburg, published in 1543, of Nuremberg, published in the same year, and in many others.[4] In different kingdoms it was long since wholly rejected, whilst in others, phraseology more or less resembling it was long retained.

The *fifth* item of improvement in the Lutheran church is the more *systematic adjustment of her doctrines*. Luther was so incessantly employed in the great work of reforming the church from the corruptions and superstitions of Rome, that he had little leisure for abstract reflections on the reciprocal relations of the scripture doctrines, and on the

(1) "Almighty God, our Heavenly Father, who of his great mercy hath promised forgiveness of sins to all those who with hearty repentance and true faith turn unto him, have mercy upon you; pardon and deliver you from all your sins; confirm and strengthen you in all goodness; and bring you to everlasting life, through Jesus Christ our Lord. Amen."—*Episcopal Communion Service*, p. 155.

(2) Epist. 69, p. 187; Epist. 75, p. 223.

(3) In Lib. de Fide et operibus, cap. vi. and Lib. 7, cap. 34, contra Pelagium, Lib. ii. cap. 40, and Koecher's Vertheidigung, p. 509.

(4) Siegel's Handbuch, vol. ii. p. 686.

entire and minute consistency of his views with each other. It is certain that in the earlier part of his life, he believed the Augustinian view of predestination. His work, on the Bondage of the Will, published in 1525, must put this question to rest. But he at the same time entertained other views inconsistent with this. Melanchton, who had embraced Luther's unadjusted views of doctrine, led the way in the process of harmonizing their conflicting elements, by the rejection of absolute predestination. Luther himself adopted these modifications, and long before he died, preached and taught what have ever since been the doctrines of the Lutheran standards. The particulars of this interesting process are detailed in Dr. Plank's invaluable History of the Risê, Changes and Formation of the Protestant System of Doctrines.[1] During the reign of infidelity in Europe, when an unbaptized philosophy had desecrated the sanctuary of God, and so far effaced all lineaments and extinguished all attachment to genuine protestant Christianity, that even a Buonaparte could contemplate as a matter of state policy the re-establishment of the Romish religion over all protestant Germany;[2] the doctrines of great reformers were forsaken by many. But thanks be to God, the cause of truth is again prospering, orthodoxy is again preponderant in Germany; and in the Lutheran church in this country the great doctrines of the reformation are taught as universally, as in any other denomination of Christians in our land.

The *sixth* feature of improvement is the adoption of a more regular and rigid system of church government and discipline in this country. The union between church and state has prevented the adoption of an independent and thoroughly scriptural discipline in the Lutheran, as well as in all the other established churches of Europe. Kings and princes are not willing to be disciplined by humble ministers and lay elders. Accordingly, the systems of discipline in different provinces and kingdoms are different, and generally very lax. In this country our General Synod has adopted and recommended a system, which, it is believed, contains all the prescriptions of the Saviour and his apostles,

---

(1) Dr. Plank's Geschichte &c., vol. vi. p. 806—809. See Appendix, No. H.

(2) Butler's Reminiscences, p. 200.

and all that appeared most valuable in the systems of the different other churches. The government and discipline of each individual church, is essentially like that of our Presbyterian brethren. Our Synods, also, in structure and powers, most resemble their Presbyteries, having fewer formalities in their proceedings, and frequently couching their decisions in the form of recommendations. Our General Synod is wholly an advisory body, resembling the consociations of the Congregational churches in New England. In addition to these regular ecclesiastical bodies, constituting our system of government, we having special Conferences, for the purpose of holding stated protracted meetings. These are subdivisions of Synods, containing ordinarily from five to ten ministers each, who are annually to hold several protracted meetings within the bounds of their district. The chief object of these meetings is, to awaken and convert sinners, and to edify believers by close, practical preaching. This feature mainly resembles the quarterly meetings of our Methodist brethren, and presents to pious and zealous ministers, who are thirsting for the salvation of souls, the most direct opportunity they can desire, to glorify God, and advance his spiritual kingdom. Yet all these meetings are to be conducted as the scriptures enjoin, "decently and in order."[1] This system of government is not yet adopted by all our Synods; yet its general features, with perhaps a greater admixture of Congregationalism, substantially pervade those Synods also, which have not yet united with the General Synod.

The *last* item of improvement to which we shall refer, is the practice of the Lutheran church in this country, not to bind her ministers to the minutiæ of any human creed.

(1) The views of Christian order in worship, inculcated by our standards, may be seen from chap. vii. sec. 1, of our Formula. "These meetings (prayer meetings) may be held in the church, school-house, or in private houses; and their object is the spiritual edification of the persons present; but the utmost precaution must ever be observed, that God, who is a Spirit, be worshipped in spirit and in truth; that they be characterized by that solemnity and decorum which ought ever to attend divine worship, and that no disorder be tolerated, or any thing that is calculated to interrupt the devotions of those who are convened, or prevent their giving the fullest attention to him who is engaged in leading the meeting,—in short, that according to the injunction of the apostle, all things be done "decently and in order."

The bible and the belief that the *fundamental doctrines* of the bible are taught in a manner substantially correct in the Augsburg Confession, is all that is required. On the one hand, we regard it as certain, that if we would be faithful to the injunction of our text, "not to receive any who come to us bringing another doctrine," an examination of applicants for admission among us is indispensable. Such an examination is virtually a requisition of their creed, that we may compare it with our own. Now, whether the articles to which we require their assent be few or many, be written or oral, they are a creed, and obviously its reduction to paper, presents some material facilities in the examination. A written creed, therefore, seems necessary to the purity of the church. On the other hand, history informs us, that for several hundred years after the days of the apostles, no other creed was used in the whole church than that called the Apostles' Creed, because admitted by all to contain the principal doctrines taught by the apostles. This creed embodied only the cardinal doctrines of the gospel, which all the so called orthodox denominations of the present day do actually believe; and yet the assent to these few doctrines did for centuries after the apostolic age, secure admission to any and every part of the Catholic, that is, the universal church on earth. By what authority then did the several Protestant denominations after the Reformation adopt creeds ten, and some of them, a hundred times as long as that used in the earlier ages, and require assent to these interminable instruments as a condition of admission to their churches? The bible certainly confers no such authority. But does the experience of three centuries prove their influence to be salutary? Have they not rather been the occasion of endless strife in all the churches adopting them? Have they not proved wedges of dissension to split asunder the body of Christ? It is matter of historical certainty, that the orthodox denominations of the present day coincide as much in doctrinal views, as did the Christians in the golden age of Christianity. If they could walk together in love, and their minor differences created no difficulty then; why should not Christians in the present day unite in the same manner, instead of rending the body of Christ asunder, creating separate and conflicting interests among brethren in Christ, alienation and prosecutions for minor differences, which would not have been noticed in the apostolic, and primitive, and purest age of the church. The duty of all parts of the Christian church seems therefore to be, to return to the use of shorter doctrinal creeds as tests of ecclesiastical, ministerial, and sacramental communion. This noble course the Lutheran church has already virtually taken, by requiring assent only to the fundamental doctrines of the Augsburg Confession, together with an approval of our principles of government and worship. This course cannot fail to promote brotherly love, and fraternal appreciation between different denominations, by giving prominence to their actual unity in doctrine, and restoring a proper unity of spirit among the disciples of Christ. Happy, thrice happy too is the Lutheran church, that she, who was first to cast off the yoke of Roman superstition and oppression, should lead the way in breaking the bonds of Protestant sectarianism; be first in practically teaching the world: that the apostolic injunction to "receive a brother that is weak in the faith, but not for the purpose of doubtful disputation," does not mean to prosecute and expel him. And happy are all in every denomination who raise their voice in behalf of the lacerated body of Christ, and teach Christians to remember the solemn injunction of the Saviour to love one another; and not only to profess but to practise the principle of our blessed Lord, "one is our Master Christ, and ye are all brethren."

Such, my brethren, are the features of the Lutheran church, of that church, to whose service this chaste and beautiful edifice has been dedicated. She may be emphatically styled the church of the Reformation. She holds the grand doctrines of Christianity, with fewer appended peculiarities than most other denominations. With the Calvinist she holds the graciousness of salvation; with the Congregationalist she believes that Christ tasted death for every man; with the Methodist she approves of regularly recurring protracted meetings; with the Episcopalian she occasionally employs a liturgy and forms of prayer; with the German Reformed she agrees in the instruction and confirmation of Catechumens; and with all she unites in ascribing all the glory of our privileges on earth and hopes in heaven, to that Lamb of God, that taketh away the sins of the world. Long may those blessed doctrines be taught within these sacred walls! Long may they be taught throughout our favored land, purifying and elevating our political and social institutions, providing for our citizens, security of person and property, and especially the privilege of worshiping God under our own vine and fig tree, making it the land of refuge to the virtuous oppressed of all nations.

APPENDIX.

Note A. to page 49.

TESTIMONY OF CARDINAL BARONIUS ON PAPAL APOSTOLIC SUCCESSION.

"What was then (in the tenth century) the aspect of the holy Romish church? How extremely filthy was she, (fœdissima!) When the most powerful and obscene prostitutes governed at Rome; and at their pleasure, the occupants of the holy seat were changed, bishops were appointed, and what is unutterably horrible to hear, their paramours were thrust into the chair of St. Peter as false pontiffs, who are introduced into the catalogue of popes only for the purpose of making a record of the times. For who could pronounce those to be legitimate Roman pontiffs, who were thus intruded by these prostitutes, contrary to law? There is not the least mention made of their having been elected by the clergy, or of their election having been afterward sanctioned by them. All the canons were passed over in silence; the decrees of the popes were suppressed; the ancient usages and rules for the election of the popes, as well as the solemn rites and ceremonies were altogether abolished. Annalium ecclesiast. Tom. X. ad An. 912 num. 8 p. 685. apud Kœcher's Vertheidigung, p. 124.

Note G. to page 49.

MINISTERIAL ORDINATION.

The subject of ministerial *ordination* has been involved in some extraneous and unnecessary difficulty, partly by the incidental usage of language, partly by the progress of superstition in the lapse of ages, and partly by the introduction of diocesan episcopacy into the Christian church in the second century. The term ordination (ordinatio) has, in the Christian church, generally acquired a technical character, and is used to designate the specific method or formalities with which it is customary in any particular church to invest a candidate or licentiate with the ministerial office. But in the New Testament, no such a technical word is found. On the contrary, different words are used in the several passages, and all of them are appellative terms, signifying merely to appoint, to induct, or to admit; and they are also applied to other objects. In some cases, the laying on of hands is mentioned, as the method by which the individual was set apart; and it was the superstitious notion of after ages, that some mystic influence was imparted by "the laying on of the hands," which probably led the Romish church to exalt this rite into a sacrament. This error, the Reformers rejected and brought back the ceremony to its original simplicity.

To ordain, according to the New Testament, merely signifies to induct into the sacred office. It implies that some care was exercised, and not every one indiscriminately allowed to perform the duties of the sacred office; but it does not in the least imply that any particular influence or power is transmitted by lineal succession from the apostles.

As to the persons who are to perform this rite, that is, are to induct others into the sacred office, we find that Paul and Barnabas, in traveling through Antioch and other places, "*chose* (ordained) elders for them." *Paul* and *Barnabas* had been set apart for the missionary work by the laying on of the hands, not of a diocesan bishop, but of certain prophets and teachers; namely, Simeon, Lucius, and Manaen. Timothy was inducted (ordained) by the laying on of the hands, not of a bishop of a diocese, "but of the ministry; that is, eldership, or, to retain the Greek word, the presbytery." In several cases, also, individual ministers, such as Timothy and Titus, were directed to induct (ordain) others.

The principal passages involved in the subject of ordination, are the following, from which the reader may learn the scripture aspect of this rite.

Acts xiv. 23. And when they (Paul and Barnabas) had ordained (χειροτονησαντες, had *chosen;* from χειρ, hand, and τεινω, to stretch forth, voting by uplifted hand; De Wette, erwahlet. See 2 Cor. viii. 19, where the same word is rendered "chosen" in our common version) elders for them in every church, and had prayed with fasting, they commended them to the Lord, on whom they believed.

1 Tim. iv. 14. Neglect not the gift that is in thee, which was given thee by prophecy with the laying on of the hands of the presbytery, (πρεσβυτηριυ, the eldership, that is, of the ministers, not of a diocesan bishop.)

1 Tim. v. 22. Lay hands suddenly on no man, (χειρας επιτιθει.)

Acts xiii. 3. And when they (that is, not bishops, but "certain prophets and teachers, as Barnabas, and Simeon, and Lucius, and Manaen, v. 1) had fasted and prayed and laid their hands on them, (επιθεντες τας Χειρας,) they sent them away.

Acts vi. 6. Whom (namely, the seven deacons whom the "multitude of the disciples" had chosen, v. 4, 5) they set before the apostles; and when they had prayed, they laid their hands on them, (επιθηκαν αυτοις τας χειρας.)

The above are all the actual ordinations recorded in the New Testament. The following are the other passages in which the word "ordain" occurs in our English New Testament in reference to the church. We add the Greek to show how various the words are in the original.

Mark iii. 14. Jesus ordained (εποιησε, made, appointed; Stoltz, bestimmte; De Wettė, bestellete) twelve to be with him, &c.

1 Cor. vii. 17. So ordain I (διατασσομαι, direct; Schleusner verordne) in all the churches.

1 Tim. ii. 7. For this purpose (says Paul) I am ordained (τεθην, appointed; Stoltz, gesetzet; De Wette, bestellet) a preacher, (κηρυξ.)

Heb. v. 1. For every high priest is ordained for men, &c., (καθισταται, placed, appointed; Stoltz, eingesetzt; De Wette, bestellet.)

Heb. viii. 3. For every high priest is ordained, (καθισταται, placed, appointed; Stoltz, eingesetzt; De Wette, bestellet.)

Tit. i. 5. For this end left I thee in Crete, (says Paul to Titus,) that thou shouldst ordain elders (καταστησης πρεσβυτεϱϗσ, Stoltz, einsetzest; De Wette, anstelletest,) as I appointed (διεταξαμην σοι, directed; Stoltz, geboten; De Wette, geboten) thee.

From these passages, it is evident, that the scriptures contain not a word about the transmission of any mystic, or sacred influence or power, by *succession* from the apostles. And it is also evident, that in not one of the three examples of ordination or induction, mentioned in the New Testament, was that rite performed by one man, and he a diocesan bishop; but always by several persons, in the one case, by Paul and Barnabas, in another, by "certain prophets and teachers, Barnabas, Simeon, Lucius and Manaen; and in the third, by the eldership, that is, the ministry. Yet, as the apostle Paul directed Timothy and Titus to admit men to this office, we regard the ordination of one minister as valid, whether he be called bishop, or minister, or elder.

Note B. to page 56.

LUTHERAN CHURCH IN SWEDEN, NORWAY AND FINLAND.

A most interesting, satisfactory and authentic work on the state of the Lutheran church in Sweden, was published in 1821–1822, by Dr. Frederick William Von Shubert, professor of Theology in the university at Greifswald. From this work, it appears that Sweden is at present divided into twelve dioceses or districts, as follows;

1. The diocese of *Upsala*, in which the archbishop resides. This diocese contains 166 pastoral districts, and 244 churches.
2. The diocese of *Linkoping*, embracing 147 pastoral districts, and 216 churches.
3. The diocese of *Skara*, includes 113 pastoral districts, and 360 churches.
4. Diocese of *Strengnas*, contains 102 pastoral districts, and 170 churches.
5. Diocese of *Westeras*, has 84 pastoral districts, and 120 churches.
6. Diocese of *Wexio*, includes 98 pastoral districts, and 185 churches.
7. Diocese of *Lunds*, has 223 pastoral districts, and 431 churches.

8. Diocese of *Goetheburg,* includes 102 pastoral districts, and 262 churches.

9. Diocese of *Salmar,* contains 45 pastoral districts, and 58 churches.

10. Diocese of *Carlstad,* embraces 40 pastoral districts, and 129 churches.

11. Diocese of *Hernosand,* includes 63 pastoral districts, and 162 churches.

12. Diocese of *Wisby,* contains 43 pastoral districts, and 92 churches.

FINLAND

Embraces two dioceses, viz: that of *Abo,* containing 127 pastoral districts, and that of *Borgo,* including 83 pastoral districts, including a German one in Wiborg.

NORWAY

Is divided into four districts or dioceses, viz:

1. Diocese of *Christiania* or Oggerthus.
2. Diocese of *Christiansand.*
3. Diocese of *Bergen.*
4. Diocese of *Drontheim.*

NOTE C. TO PAGE 58.

Of the *Theologians and Theological Literature* of the Lutheran church in Europe, our space will not allow us to attempt even an outline. A volume would be requisite for this purpose. A catalogue of the publications by Lutheran divines in this country, may, however, not be uninteresting to many of our readers. All these works, with the exception of a few, are contained in the writer's library. Of that few, the following notices are given from memory.

LIST OF PUBLICATIONS BY LUTHERAN MINISTERS IN THE UNITED STATES.*

The names are arranged chronologically, as far as known to the writer.

HENRY MELCHIOR MUHLENBERG, D. D., principal author of the Hallische Nachrichten, 1 vol. 4to., pp. 1580 Halle, 1747-1763.

---

*For a select list of the principal Lutheran Theologians and theological productions of Europe, see the author's Popular Theology, 5 ed., Appendix. The above list, first prepared by us for this work, in 1840, has been transferred to the Lutheran Almanac for 1851, with some later additions, which, in turn, we also adopt, with other additions.

JOHN FREDERICK HANDSCHUH, next principal author of Hallische Nachrichten, 1747-1763.

JUST. H. HELMUTH, D. D., Pastor in Philadelphia:

Taufe und Heilige Schrift, Germantown, 1793, 8vo., pp. 336.
Unterhaltungen mit Gott, 8vo., pp. 180, (anonymous.)
Geistliche Lieder, 12mo., pp. 200.
Numerous pious works for children.

JOHN C. KUNZE, D. D., member of Am. Philosophical Society, Pastor, N. Y.:

Ein Wort fur den Verstand und das Herz, 8vo., pp. 243, Phila., 1781.
English Hymn Book—much of it tranlasted from the German.
History of the Christian Religion, and History of the Lutheran Church.
Geistliche Gedichte, in 1 vol. 12mo., pp. 200.
New Method of calculating the great Eclipse of June 16th, 1806.

GOTTHILF HEN. MUHLENBERG, D. D., Pastor in Lancaster:

Rede bei der Einweihung des Franklin Collegiums, Lancaster, 1788.
Catalogus Plantarum, &c.
Flora Lancastriensis, 8vo.
English and German Lexicon and Grammar, 2 vols. 8vo.
Grasses of Pennsylvania.

Rev. JACOB GOERING, Pastor in York, Pa.:

Besiegter Wiedertaufer, 1 vol. 8vo., pp. 92, 1783, (anon.)
Answer to a Methodist's Remonstrance, York, (anon.)
Der Verkappte Priester Aaron, (uber die Siebentager,) about 1790.

Rev. F. V. MELSHEIMER, Senior Pastor, Hanover, Pa.:

Wahrheit der Christlichen Religion, mit Beantwortung Deistischer Einwurfe, 1 vol. 8vo.
Gesprache zwischen einem Protestanten and Romischen Priester, Hanover, 1797, 1 vol. 18mo., pp. 122.

FRED. H. QUITMAN, D. D., Pastor at Rheinbeck, N. Y.:

Sermons on the Reformation, Hudson, 1817.
Evangelical Catechism, Hudson, 1814.
Hymn Book of the Synod of New York edit., 1817.
Treatise on Magic.

J. D. KURTZ, D. D., Pastor, Baltimore:

Gemeinschaftliches Gesangbuch, editor, Balt., 1817.

Various articles in the "Evangelische Magazin."

PAULUS HENKLE, Newmarket, Va.:

Sammlung Geistreicher Lieder, Newmarket.
Also, several small works for children.

J. G. SCHMUCKER, D. D., Pastor, York, Pa.:

Prophetic History of the Christian Religion, or Explanation of Revelation of St. John, 2 vols. 8vo., Balt., 1817.
Vornehmste Weissagungen der Heiligen Schrift, Hagerstown, 1807, 1 vol. 12mo.
Wachterstimme an Zion's Kinder, Gettysburg, 1838, 1 vol. 12mo. pp. 233.
Reformations Geschichte zur Jubelfeier der Reformation, York, 1817, pp. 32.
Elegie zum Andenken an Goering.
Schwarmergeist unserer Tage, entlarvt, zur Warnung erweckter Seelen, York, 1827, pp. 52.
Lieder Anhang, zum Evang. Gesangbuch der General Synode, 1833.
Erklarung der offenbarung Johannis, Balt., 1 vol. 8vo., pp. 347.

J. GEORGE LOCHMAN, D. D., Pastor, Harrisburg, Pa.:

History, Doctrine and Discipline of the Lutheran church, 1 vol. 12mo., pp. 165, Harrisburg, 1818.
Evangelical Catechism, Harrisburg, 1822, pp. 56.
Introductory Sermon, Harrisburg.
Valedictory Sermon, Lebanon, 1815.
Hinterlassene Predigten, 1828, 1 vol. 8vo., pp. 334.

Dr. ENDRESS:

Christi Regiment mit weltlicher Monarchie und Aristocratie unvereinbar, 12mo., 1791.
Also, posthumous Sermons, published in Lutheran Preacher and Pulpit.

Rev. FLOHR, Wythe County, Va.:

Sermons, (posthumous.)

Rev. G. SHOBER, Pastor, Salem, N. C.:

History of the Lutheran Reformation and Lutheran Church, Baltimore, 1818, 12mo., pp. 213.
Scenes in the World of Spirits, translated from the German of Stilling; Review, &c., 8vo.

E. L. HAZELIUS, D. D., Prof. in Theol. Seminary, Lexington, S. C.:

Life of Luther, New York, 1813, 12mo., pp. 169.

Life of Stilling, from the German, Gettysburg, 1831, pp. 415.
Augsburg Confession, with Annotations.
Evangelisches Magazin, edit. 1831.
Materials for Catechisation on Passages of Scripture, 1823, pp. 76.
Church History, Balt., vol. 1, 1842, pp. 277.
History of the Lutheran Church in America, Zanesville, Ohio, 1845, 1 vol. 12mo., pp. 300.
Inaugural Address, Lexington, S. Car., 1834.

AUGUSTUS WACKERHAGEN, D. D., Pastor, Clermont, New York:

Inbegriff der Glaubens und Sittenlehre, Philadelphia, 1804, 1 vol. 12mo., pp. 299.

F. D. SCHAEFFER, Sr., D. D., Pastor, Phil'a.:

Antwort auf eine Vertheidigung der Methodisten, Germantown, 1806.

JOHN BACHMAN, D. D., Charleston, S. C.:

The Quadrupeds of North America, 3 vols.
The Doctrine of the Unity of the Human Race examined on the Principles of Science.
The Design and Duties of the Christian Ministry, a Sermon, preached before General Synod, N. Y., 1848, pp. 23.
A Sermon on the Doctrines and Discipline of the Lutheran Church.
Funeral Discourse on the Death of Rev. John G. Swartz.
Address before the Washington Total Abstinence Society of Charleston.
An Inquiry into the Nature and Benefits of an Agricultural Survey.
An Address before the Horticultural Society of Charleston.
Catalogue of Phaenogamous Plants and Ferns growing in the vicinity of Charleston.

F. C. SCHAEFFER, D.D., Pastor, New York:

German Correspondent, 1 vol., 8vo.
Sermon at Centurial Jubilee of Reformation, N. York, 1817, pp. 56.
Parables and Parabolic Sayings, 1 vol. 18mo.

Rev. Dr. ERNST, Lebanon, Pa.:

Sermon on the Death of Washington.

B. KURTZ, D.D., Editor Lutheran Observer:

First Principles of Religion for Children, Hagerstown, 1821.

Sermon on Sabbath Schools.
Faith, Hope, Charity, Hagerstown, 1823.
Pastoral Address during his tour through Europe.
A door opened of the Lord, Introductory Sermon, Chambersburg, Pa., 14th August, 1831.
Ministerial Appeal, a Valedictory Sermon, Hagerstown, Md., 4th Sept., 1831.
Infant Baptism and Affusion, with Essays on related subjects, 1840, 1 vol. 8vo., Balt., pp. 370.
Address on Temperance, 1824.
Why are you a Lutheran? 1843, 1 vol. 12mo., pp. 227.

D. F. SCHAEFFER, D. D., Pastor, Frederick, Maryland:

Lutheran Intelligencer, editor, 4 vols. 8vo., 1826-1830.

J. HERBST, Pastor, Gettysburg:

Evangelisches Magazin, editor, 1830.
Inaugural Address of Dr. Schmucker, translated into German, 1826.

Rev. Dr. MILLER, Prof. Hartwick Seminary.:

On the Fundamental Principle of the Reformation, 1831.
Also, Sermons in the Lutheran Preacher, 1834.
Sermon on Doctrines and Discipline of the Ev. Luth. Church, Nov. 12, 1837.
Sermon on the semi-centennial celebration of N. York Synod, 1845, pp. 25.

G. A. LINTNER, D. D., Pastor, Schoharie, N. York:

Lutheran Magazine, co-editor, 2 vols., 1827-'28.
Liturgy, published by the General Synod, 1832.
Sermon at the Installation of Rev. Lawyer, 1828.
Augsburg Confession, with Notes, 1837.
Sermon on Truth as the Bond of Union, 1841, pp. 19.

C. R. DEMME, D. D., Pastor, Philadelphia:

Die Werke des Flavius Josephus, in berichtigter Ubersetzung, und mit Anmerkungen, Phil'a., 1839, 1 vol. 4to.
"Die Letzte Ehre," eine Leichenrede, beim absterben des Hochw. J. H. C. Helmuth, Phil'a., 1825.
Synodal Predigt, 1839.

C. P. KRAUTH, D. D., Prof. at Theo. Sem., Gettysburg:

Lutheran Intelligencer, co-editor, 1826.
Lutheran Sunday School Hymn Book, editor, Philadelphia.
Oration on the advantages of a knowledge of the German lan-

guage, before the Students of Theological Seminary, Gettysburg, 1832, published by request.
Evangelical Review, editor, 1850.

S. S. SCHMUCKER, D. D., Prof. Theological Seminary, Gettysburg:

Biblical Theology of Storr and Flatt, translated from the German, Andover, 1826, 2 vols.
Elements of Popular Theology, Andover, 1834, 1 vol. 8vo.
Kurtzgefasste Geschichte der Christlichen Kirche, auf der Grundlage des Busch'en Werks, Gettysburg, 1834, 1 vol. 8vo., pp. 352.
Evangelisches Magazin, editor, 1830.
Hymn Book of General Synod, compiler, 1828.
Formula of Gov. and Discipline for Congregations and Synods, published by the General Synod, 1823-1829.
Inaugural Address, Gettysburg, 1826.
Discourse in commemoration of the Reformation, preached before Synod, 1837, pp. 142, 18mo.
Fraternal Appeal to the American Churches on Christian Union, Andover, 1838, 1 vol. 12mo., pp. 149.
Discourse delivered at the request of the Board of Managers of Amer. Sunday School Union, Philadelphia, 1839.
Christian Temple, a Synodical discourse, 1824.
Plea for the Sabbath School System, 1830.
Oration on Anniversary of Washington's Birth day, 1839.
Psychology, or Elements of Mental Philosophy, New York, 1842, 1 vol. 8vo., pp. 329.
Discourse on Capital Punishment, Phil'a., 1845.
Portraiture of Lutheranism, 1840, pp. 89.
Retrospect of Lutheranism, 1840.
Patriarchs of American Lutheranism, 1845.
Christian Pulpit, 1846.
Papal Hierarchy, 1845.
Church Development on apostolic principles, 1850.

Rev. WALTZ, Pastor, Hamburg, Pa.:

Erklarung des Calenders, nebst Unterricht uber die Himmelskorper, Reading, 1830, 1 vol. 8vo., pp. 315.

Rev. H. N. POHLMAN, D. D., Albany, N. Y.:

A Catechism.
Address on Temperance.

Rev. H. W. SCRIBA, Pastor, Strasburg, Pa.:

Anfangsgrunde des Christenthums fur die Jugend, aus dem.

Franzosischen ubersetzt, Chambersburg, 1834, 1 vol. 8vo., pp. 143.

Rev. D. Henkel, Pastor, Lincoln, N. C.:

On Regeneration, Salisbury, 1822, pp. 48.

Rev. Probst:

Wiedervereinigung der Lutheraner und Reformirten, Allentown, 1826, 1 vol. 12mo., pp. 172.

Rev. C. Henkle, Pastor, Somerset, Ohio:

On the Reformation, a Synodical discourse, 1838.
Ueber die Kinderzucht, 1822.

Rev. A. H. Lochman, York, Pa.:

Rosa of Lindenwald—translated.

Prof. L. Eichelberger, A. M., Lexington, S. C.

Lutheran Preacher, editor, 2 vols. 8vo., 1833, Winchester.
Sermons on National Blessings and Obligations, 1830.

Rev. J. G. Morris, D. D., Pastor, Baltimore:

Catechumen's and Communicant's Companion, Baltimore, 1831, 1 vol. 12mo., pp. 250.
Catechetical Exercises on Luther's Catechism, altered from the German, Baltimore, 1832, 18mo., pp. 72.
Henry and Antonio of Dr. Brettschneider, translated from the German, 1824, 1 vol. 8vo., pp. 254.
Lutheran Observer, editor, 2 vols., 1831-1832.
Von Leonard's Lectures on Geology, translated from the German, Baltimore, 1839, 1 vol. 12mo.
Popular Exposition of the Gospels, for families, Bible classes, and Sunday schools, 2 vols., Balt., 1840.
Address on the Study of Natural History, 1841.
Sermon on the Reformation.
Address at the Dedication of Linnæan Hall.
Luther's Catechism Illustrated.
Address at the Dedication of Mt. Olivet Cemetery, Balt.

Rev. J. N. Hoffman, Pastor, Chambersburg:

Arndt's True Christianity, translated from the German, 1 vol. 8vo., Chambersburg, 1834.
Evangelical Hymns, original and selected, for families and private circles, 1 vol. 18mo., 1838.
A collection of Texts, &c. &c., publisher.

Rev. T. Lape:

Theological Sketch Book, 3 vols.

Mourners Comforted, 24mo., pp. 178, N. York.
On Infant Baptism, Balt., 1843, pp. 93, 18mo.

W. M. Reynolds, D. D., Pres. Capital University, Columbus, O.

Monthly Magazine of Religion and Literature, editor, Gettysburg, 1840, 1 vol. 8vo.
Discourse on the Swedish Churches.
Inaugural Address, 1850.
Evangelical Review, editor, 1849.

Rev. H. L. Baugher, D. D., President of Pennsylvania College, Gettysburg:

Sermon on the Providence of God, 1831.
Also, Sermons in the Lutheran Preacher, 1834.

Rev. P. Rizer, Dayton, Ohio,

Sermon in behalf of Foreign Missions, 1850, pp. 19.

H. I. Smith, D. D., Prof. of German Lit., Columbia College, New York:

History of Education, 1 vol. 12mo., 1839.
Inaugural Address, 1848.
Discourse on Sabbath Schools.
Address before the Phrenakosmian Society, Gettysburg, 1843.

Rev. J. C. Hope, S. C.:

On Modern Universalism, Columbia, S. C., 1841, pp. 60.
Sermon on the Missionary Cause, Lexington, S. C., 1844, pp. 24.

Rev. L. Sternberg:

Sermon on the Death of Gen. Jackson.

Rev. R. Weiser, Pastor, Woodsboro', Md.:

On Revivals of Religion, 1840.
Life of Luther, 1 vol. 8vo., pp. 443, Balt., 1849.
Mourners Bench, Bedford, 1844, pp. 32.

Rev. C. A. Smith, Rhinebeck, N. Y.:

Illustrations of Faith, 1850, 1 vol. 12mo., pp. 160.
Sermons on Missions.
Parables translated from the German of Krummacher, New York, 1833.
Catechumen's Guide, 1 vol. 12mo.
Popular Exposition of the Gospels, &c., 2 vols., Balt., 1840.
Lutheran Pulpit, 2 vols., edition, 1838-'39.

Rev. S. W. Harkey, Pastor, Frederick, Md.:

Lutheran Sunday School Question Book, Fredericktown, 1838.
Address before Phrenakosmian Society of Pennsylvania College, Gettysburg, 1837.
The Visitor, editor, Frederick, 1840.
Translation of Starke's Prayer Book, 1 vol. 8vo., 1844.
The Church's Best State, 1 vol. 12mo.
Sermon on the Death of Gen. Harrison.
Sermon on National Thanksgiving, 1842.
Prisons for Women, Frederick, 1847, pp. 32.

Rev. J. H. Bernheim, Pastor, Venango, Pa.:

Ueber das Heilige Abendmahl, 1834, 1 vol. 12mo.

Gottlieb Yeager, Hamburg, Pa.:

Leben des Andreas Jackson aus dem Englishen Uebersetzt.

Rev. Schmidt, Pastor, Pittsburg, Pa.:

Evangelische Kirchenzeitung, editor, 2 vols., 1839-'40.

Rev. Solomon Ritz, Xenia, O.:

Scriptural Dialogue on Protracted Meetings, Revivals, Prayer Meetings, &c., Canton, O., 1844, pp. 35.

Rev. S. Sprecher, D. D., President Wittenberg College, Springfield, Ohio:

Inaugural Address, 1849, pp. 24.

Rev. C. C. Guenther, New Franklin, O.:

Dialogue on Baptism, 1 vol. 12mo., 1848.

C. F. Schaeffer, D. D., Lower Red Hook, N. York:

Discourse on the Reformation of Luther, 1837.

Rev. C. Martin, M. D.:

Lecture on the Deleterious Effect of Tobacco, 1836.

Rev. S. A. Mealy, Pastor, Philadelphia:

On the Death of Rev. Bergman, 1832.
Also, Sermons in Lutheran Preacher, 1834.

Rev. D. Kohler, Kutztown, Pa.:

Biblische 4ti Juli Predigt, 1847.

Rev. E. Keller, D. D.:

Address before the Alumni of the Theological Seminary at Gettysburg, 1844.
Inaugural Address, Springfield, Ohio.

Rev. C. W. Schaeffer, Germantown:

Sermon on History of Church in Harrisburg.

Rev. G. Diehl, Easton, Pa.:

Thanksgiving Sermon, Easton.

Rev. J. F. Smith, A. M.:

Sermon on the Silent Influence of the Bible, 1850, pp. 26.
Hints to Church Members, Winchester, Va., 1845.
Sermon before the Foreign Missionary Society of the Lutheran Church, 1845, pp. 50.
Address on Pulpit Eloquence, 1848, pp. 35.

Rev. D. F. Bittle, A. M., Pastor, Middletown, Md.:

Remarks on New Measures, 1839.

Rev. C. A. Hay, Harrisburg, Pa.:

Essay on Lexicography, 1845.

Rev. C. P. Krauth, A. M., Winchester, Va.:

The Transfiguration, 1850.
"The Pastoral Office, a Farewell Discourse," Balt., 1845.

Rev. W. A. Passavant, Pittsburg:

Address before the Franklin Literary Society of Jefferson College.
Funeral Sermon on the Death of Rev. M. J. Steck, pp. 29, 1848.
Missionary, editor, **3 vols.**, 1848-51.

Rev. S. M. Schmucker, Germantown, Pa.:

Modern Infidelity Refuted, 1 vol. 8vo., pp. 480.

Rev. Jos. A. Seiss, Cumberland, Md.:

Thanksgiving Discourse, 1847.
Lectures on the Epistle to the Hebrews, 1 vol. 8vo., 1846.
Address before the Excelsior and Philosophian Societies of Wittenberg College.
Address on Intemperance, 1845.

Rev. F. Wyneken, St. Louis:

Spruch Buchlein.

Rev. J. Winecoff:

On Modern Dancing.

Rev. C A. Brandt, Manayunk, Pa.:

Rede bei der Grundsteinlegung d. Luth. Kirche, zu Manayunk.

Rev. J. ALBACH :

Translation of Meurer's Life of Luther.

Rev. H. L. DOX :

Sermon on the True Foundation.

The following ministers have contributed sermons to the Lutheran Preacher :

D. F. Schaeffer, D. D., Rev. Dr. Miller, Rev. Dr. Hazelius, Rev. S. A. Mealy, Dr. G. A. Lintner, Dr. Baugher, W. D. Strobel, D. D., Rev. T. Lape, Rev. L. Eichelberger, Rev. F. W. Geissenhainer, Jr., Rev. J. Medtart, Rev. C. Weyl, C. F. Schaeffer, D. D., Rev. J. C. Hope, J. G. Schmucker, D. D.

Contributors to the Lutheran Pulpit :

Rev. C. A. Smith, editor, Rev. D. Eyster, Rev. T. Lape, Rev. Edward Meyer, F. W. Geissenhainer, Jr., H. I. Smith, D. D., Rev. Dr. Miller, Rev. R. Weiser, Rev. W. D. Strobel, Rev. Dr. C. P. Krauth, Rev. Dr. A. Wackerhagen, Rev. J. Berger, Rev. S. A. Mealy, Rev. Dr. G. A. Lintner, Rev. L. Eichelberger, Rev. C. B. Thuemmel.

NOTE E. TO PAGE 64.

CALVIN'S OPINION OF CONFESSION AS FORMERLY PRACTISED BY SOME PROTESTANTS.

Having no copy of the Translation of the Institutes at hand, we render the following extract from the original Latin, (Tholuck's edition, Pt. 1, p. 411, 412,) that our readers may have access to the opinion of this truly great and illustrious divine. "The Scriptures, moreover, (says Calvin,) approve of two kinds of private confession. The one, which is made for our own benefit, is referred to by James, (James v. 16,) in the declaration that we should " confess our sins one to another ; for he supposes that by disclosing our infirmities one to another, we shall be profited by mutual advice and consolation. The other is that, which is to be performed for the sake of our neighbor, for the purpose of appeasing him, and reconciling him to us, if he has in any way been injured by our fault. In the former kind of confession, although St. James, by not specifying any one, into whose bosom we should unburden ourselves, has left us unrestricted choice to make our confession to any one in the whole church, whom we regard as most suitable ; yet, as ministers must be considered much more appropriate than others, we ought especially to select them. I affirm, that they are better adapted to this work than others, because, by their very call to the ministry, they are pointed out to us by God as the persons, by whom we are to be taught how to correct and subdue our sins, that we may derive comfort from the confident expectation of pardon."—"Therefore, every believer should remember, that, if he be so troubled in mind, and distressed by a sense of his sins, that he cannot extricate himself without the aid of others, it is his duty not to neglect the remedy, which the Lord offers to him; but for the purpose of obtaining relief, to avail himself of private confession to his pastor, and in procuring consolation privately to solicit the aid of him, whose office it is both publicly and privately to comfort the people of God with the truths of the gospel." "Moreover, that the flock present themselves to their shepherd, as often as they desire to partake of the Holy Supper, I am so far from objecting to, that I very much desire that this should be done everywhere. For both those who are straightened in conscience may obtain great advantage from it, and those who ought to be admonished, thus afford an opportunity for admonition; but all superstition and coercion must ever be avoided."

Note H. to page 66.

ON LUTHER'S CALVINISM.

As this is a subject on which it is easy to err, and on which men of Christian spirit and learning have entertained different opinions, it may be useful to devote a few moments to its elucidation. It is of no use here to quote passages from Luther's works teaching the doctrine. Luther's former adhesion to the Augustinian view of this subject is admitted. In reply to the passages so often appealed to from Luther's work to Erasmus, which was written in the earlier part of his life, about twenty-one years before his death, when he had not yet laid off many of the Romish and Augustinian opinions which he subsequently rejected, we might present hundreds of passages teaching and implying the contrary opinion. We present a single specimen, carefully translated by us, from Walch's edition (the best) of Luther on the Galatians. We select this that those who have the old English translation of this excellent work, may compare it, and see how uncertain a guide such translations are on disputed points. "And all the prophets foresaw in Spirit, that Christ would be the greatest sinner, whose like never appeared on earth. For as he is made a sacrifice for the sins of the whole world, he is not an innocent person and without sin, is not the Son of God in his glory, but he is a sinner for a season, forsaken of God. Psalm viii. 6. He bears the sin of St. Paul, who was a blasphemer, a persecutor and injurious; of St. Peter, who denied Christ; and of David, who was an adulterer and a murderer, and caused the name of the Lord to be blasphemed among the Gentiles. In short, he is the person who hath taken upon himself, and bears in his own body *all the sins of all men in the whole world, who ever have lived, are now living, or who shall hereafter live;* not as if he had himself committed those sins, but being committed by us, he took them on his own body, in order to make an atonement for them with his own blood"* We might refer the reader to a work entitled "Lutherus Lutheranus," of 700 pages, 8vo, consisting entirely of extracts from his works, showing that on all the distinguishing points between Calvinists and Lutherans, Luther occupied the ground subsequently maintained by his followers. But obviously, even this would not settle the point. The only impartial and decisive course is to examine all his works, and also all his correspondence, according to their date, and trace the gradual change in his opinions. This, according to the unanimous testimony of all Germany, no man has ever done more impartially than the celebrated Dr. Plank, Professor of Theology at Gottingen, in the preparation of his invaluable work, entitled, "*History of the Rise, Changes, and Formation of our Protestant System of Doctrines,* from the commencement of the Reformation till the Introduction of the form of Concord. (1580.) The entire impartiality and great ability of this work, which cost the author twenty years of labor and investigation, are conceded by all parties. The result of his examination may be seen in the following valuable quotation, which, whilst it fully sustains the positions of this dis-

* See Walch's edition of Luther on the Galatians, p. 276. "In summa, er ist die Person die an ihrem Leibe tragt, und auf sich geladen hat alle Sunden aller menschen in der ganzen Welt, die da gewesen noch sind, und seyn werden." See also the common English version, p. 254.

course, also renders it intelligible, how such a diversity of sentiment might naturally exist on this subject. "Nevertheless, the Lutheran divines did not, for a long time, see proper to take any notice of it, (viz: of the prominence and full development given to this doctrine by Calvin, and of its introduction into the Swiss churches;) and even the zealots of Lower Saxony, who had taken occasion from the Geneva 'Consensus,' to renew the contest concerning the Lord's supper, observed a perfect silence on this incalculably more important doctrine, although Calvin appeared to urge them the more explicitly to its adoption. Melanchthon alone declared to him, that although he would not quarrel with him about it, he would never consent to adopt his (Calvin's) views on predestination.* But the silence of the other Lutheran divines on this subject, although it might appear to have been the result of indifference, was owing to a very satisfactory reason, of which the greater part of them were well aware. It cannot be denied, that the Augustinian theory of predestination had already been forsaken by the Lutheran church. Yet her divines could not but feel, that they had *changed* their ground. The fact could not be concealed, that Luther had once embraced this doctrine in its full rigor, and even zealously defended it against Erasmus, and that his early adherents, including even Melancthon himself, had at first done the same. It is indeed true, they could prove that the doctrine was not long retained, and *that Luther himself had abandoned it!* But even this concession would give an advantage to an opponent in this dispute, which they were utterly unwilling to concede to Calvin. They therefore determined, rather not to dispute with him on this subject at all. But there was another reason, which probably aided in causing them to keep silence on this subject. The greater part of Lutheran divines had, like Luther himself, receded from the Augustinian theory of predestination, very probably without themselves being fully aware how this result had been brought about. They found themselves removed from it, before they had wished to be; and it was Melancthon, and no one else, who had produced the change. In the first improved

* Melancthon did not even answer the first letter of Calvin, in which he requested his assent to the doctrine. See Calvin' epist. p. 133, 153.

edition of his *Loci Theologici,* and doubtless still earlier in his oral lectures, he had proposed a theory, which, both in its principles and consequences, was in direct contradiction to the Augustinian view. This contradiction, which Melancthon himself took no pains to bring to light, was however, at first, not generally perceived. Hence several of the principles of his new theory were adopted with the less apprehension, especially as each one of them, considered by itself, appeared to be incontestibly true, both according to reason and Scripture. Thus his cardinal ideas of the divine election of all men in Christ, of the universality of divine grace, of the extension of the atonement and merits of Christ to all men, had been embraced by nearly all the divines of their party, and *by Luther himself,* before they perceived that their views of an absolute decree of God, and the Augustinian doctrine of predestination, were utterly irreconcileable with them. But, when at last they made the discovery, they found their position in several respects an embarrassing one, and were unable immediately to extricate themselves. They felt unwilling, not only so suddenly to abandon a doctrine which they had professed, but even to abandon it at all. They were conscious that Augustin's doctrine of predestination appeared to be inseparably connected with some other parts of his system, such as the total inability of man to do any thing good, which they were firmly determined never to relinquish. On the other hand, they were just as anxious to retain the features of Melancthon's theory, which they had adopted; and were therefore brought into a dilemma, which they could not but feel. The greater part of their divines now adhered to the view of Melancthon, that God desires and strives to bestow salvation on all men in and through Christ, from which it necessarily followed, that his decree concerning the destiny of each individual could not be absolute. But they, at the same time, retained the opinion of Augustine, that depraved man can do nothing at all in the work of his salvation, cannot exert even the feeblest effort of his will; which seemed just as necessarily to imply that the salvation or damnation of each individual, could be decided only by an absolute decree of God. Some of them probably had an impression, that there must be some method of avoiding the last mentioned inference; but their views were indistinct. Hence it happened, that during the Synergistic controversies some of them again embraced the Augustinian theory in full. The greater part of them, however, believed that all they wanted was a more systematic adjustment and connexion of the opinions they entertained, and this conviction was undoubtedly the principal reason for that caution, with which, in direct opposition to the polemic spirit of that age, they evaded a controversy on this subject. It was, therefore, not until 1561, that a formal dispute on this subject occurred between the Lutheran and Calvinistic divines, the occasion of which was the celebrated Zanchius, at that time professor of theology at Strasburg." Here, then, is a correct and impartial statement of the facts in the case, which never has been, and never can be successfully controverted.

III. DISCOURSE.

PATRIARCHS OF AMERICAN LUTHERANISM.

RESPECTED AUDITORS,

WE congratulate you on the formation of the Historical Society of the Evangelical Lutheran Church in our country, as an event of no small significance in itself, and destined by Providence to exert a salutary and enduring influence on our portion of the Redeemer's kingdom. History is the great storehouse of human experience. Without it each individual can profit only by the observations of his own threescore years and ten; but with it he can lift the veil of past generations and draw wisdom from the incidents of thousands of years. All that is valuable in physics, in philosophy, and in religion, is thus made tributary to our improvement. It is therefore not without ground that Dionysius, of Halicarnassus, even as early as the age of Augustus, describes history as philosophy teaching by examples. But when applied to the church of God, and viewed in connexion with the inspired oracles, history assumes a new aspect, and may be styled "*religion, teaching by examples.*" And has Christ, as perpetual Head of the church, promised to abide with her even to the end of the world? Is the tuition of the Comforter, the Holy Ghost, the privilege of God's people in every age? Then may we regard the history of any branch of Christ's church, viewed in the light of God's word, and studied under the guidance of the Holy Spirit, as inculcating the continued and progressive instructions of the Saviour to his followers.

History, impartially and pragmatically studied, is therefore the best test of the influence of different measures, in reference to points not determined in the inspired statute-book. Such points are the proper degree and kind of ministerial training desirable in any age, the most successful method of preaching the gospel, whether with or without notes, and of conducting the several parts of public worship, of prayer with or without liturgies, the effects of different modes of church-government, the practical influence of different systems of doctrine, the best method of conducting revivals and of promoting the spiritual interests of the church, and topics of a similar nature. If, then, church-history be so rich in various instruction, a society designed to preserve and cultivate any portion of that history must be an interesting phenomenon, and may, if rightly conducted, become highly important, especially in our age of radical inquiry, and in our land of constitutional divorce between church and state.

Of the American church, in all her branches, it may emphatically be affirmed, that she is in a *transition state.* Our country itself is yet in its nascent era. With few exceptions, the principal churches of our land have been transplanted from countries where they were connected with the civil government. Such was the case with the Lutheran, the Presbyterian, the German Reformed, the Dutch Reformed, the Episcopal and the Papal. All these, except the last, have thrown off all allegiance to foreign powers. Released from the oppressive embrace of civil rulers, the American church, in all her Protestant branches, is left to breathe freely, and to adopt such rules of selfgovernment as from time to time command her conscientious judgment.

Perhaps an extensive induction of facts would show it to be an established law of God's mediatorial kingdom, that the church untrammelled by the state, is seldom or never entirely stationary. Indeed, even when controlled by the political government, she has been stationary only in her external forms and rites. The life of godliness in her ministers and members has been subject to frequent fluctuations. Of this the history of the Lutheran, the Reformed, the Episcopal and the Presbyterian churches in Europe, afford striking examples. Nor have the different churches in this new world been exempt from similar fluctuations, both internal and external. As the Presbyterian church was originally constituted by two co-ordinate Synods, subsequently united into one General Assembly, and then after the lapse of years again divided into two General Assemblies,—divided also in the days of Whitefield and the Tennants into old and new lights;—and as the Episcopal church was originally organized into separate and independent dioceses without any connection between them, subsequently united into a General Convention, and is now agitated by the Semi-Romish or rather Pene-Romish errors of Puseyism;—so also the Lutheran church at first existed in separate churches, before the Synod of Pennsylvania was formed, and afterwards in separate and independent Synods, until the General Synod was established in 1820, in which the major part of the Synods is already united. So also has she fluctuated in zeal and enterprize, and will, in common with her sister churches, continue to do so. The state of the church in any particular age, is ordinarily in some degree the result of gradual development under the various influences in which she is placed, and in which the gospel is called to act on the minds of her members. Whilst, therefore, the truths of the bible remain unchanged, and the fundamental attributes of piety and prosperity in a church, are the same in every age; variations in collateral circumstances and customs naturally will and must occur. We conclude accordingly, that the efforts of some ultra Lutherans in our Fatherland, to roll back the wheels of time about three hundred years, and to bring the Lutheran church to the standpoint of the 16th century, is no less unphilosophical than anachronistic, and like the similar efforts of a few European brethren in our American church, necessarily must and ought to meet with signal defeat.

The present is an era of improvement in the American church in general, and our branch of it in particular. As one amongst many pleasing evidences, may we not refer to the formation of that association under whose provisions we are now convened? In selecting a subject for this occasion, I had first fixed upon the general history of the earliest, the colonial era of our history in this country. But having received the promise of several valuable documents at a future day, I resolved to change the subject, and have selected as my theme:

THE FATHERS OF THE AMERICO-LUTHERAN CHURCH, THE ENLIGHTENED FRIENDS OF SPIRITUAL RELIGION, AND OF SCRIPTURAL RELIGIOUS REVIVAL.

The grand design of all religion and of all christian church organizations, is to glorify God by promoting the sanctification of the church, and her preparation for heaven. Did not the Saviour give himself for us that he might redeem us from all iniquity and purify unto himself a *peculiar people*, zealous of good works? This peculiar people is his church. The association is represented as embodying in it, "those that are sanctified in Christ Jesus, called to be saints;"[1] "who are children of God by faith in Christ Jesus;"[2] "those whom he designs to sanctify and cleanse, that he might present them to himself a glorious church, not having spot or wrinkle or any such thing."[3] The design of the church is therefore eminently spiritual, and that church, and that state of the church, are most prosperous, in which this design is best accomplished. But the incessant admonitions of the scriptures, "to watch," "to arise," "to return to our first love," "to awake out of slumber," as well as the experience of all ages, show a constant tendency in Christians and Christian churches to relapse. When a church awakes from this state of lethargy, she improves in spirituality, and is in a *state of revival;* and it is in this general sense that we here use the term, as signifying the spiritual prosperity or improvement of the church, including alike individual and simultaneous conversions. This state of revival has been happily styled, "*the church's best state*," by a writer, whose productions the Lutheran church will cheerfully acknowledge as part of her literature. This state should always be aimed at by the church. Then she enjoys the blessedness for which the Psalmist prayed: "Oh! God of our salvation, wilt thou not revive us again that thy people may rejoice in thee;" and which Habakkuk implored: "O Lord, revive thy work in the midst of the years, in the midst of the years make known; in wrath remember mercy." Then do individual Christians rejoice in the enjoyment of that divine manifestation, the temporary loss

(1) 1 Cor. i. 1.
(2) Gal. iii. 26.
(3) Eph. iv. 26.

of which Job deplored in this pathetic language: "O that I were as in months past, as in the days when God preserved me, when his candle shined upon my head, and when in his light I walked through darkness."

In examining the patriarchs of American Lutheranism from the point of observation thus defined, we propose to inquire:

I. WHAT WERE THE VIEWS OF SPIRITUAL RELIGION AND RELIGIOUS REVIVAL, IN WHICH THESE MEN WERE EDUCATED?

II. WHAT WAS THEIR PRACTICE AMID THEIR ALTERED CIRCUMSTANCES IN THIS WESTERN WORLD?

What were the views on the subject of our theme, which these men had imbibed in their youth? Not long before the period under consideration, the church in Germany had experienced a very extensive and remarkable change. That spirit of indomitable adherence to every item of what we regard as truth, and of polemic zeal in its defence, which were necessary to make the reformers equal to the trials of their day, was not easily laid aside after the necessity in which it had originated had passed away. It was transmitted to successive generations, and contributed, in connexion with other causes, to impress a peculiarly polemic character on the German churches throughout their history.

But whilst the fathers of our Lutheran Zion were growing up, the church in their native land, was enjoying a glorious state of revival. The dead formality of the 17th century had been broken up by the influence of Spener and his coadjutors. This effect was chiefly due to their practical and biblical preaching, to Spener's various publications, especially his Pia Desideria, and his Spiritual Priesthood of the Laity; as also to his Collegia pietatis, or private biblical prayer-meetings, in which after a lecture by the pastor on some part of scripture, any male member present was permitted to address the meeting on the same subject, decently and in order.[1] By all these means, soon employed by numerous other pastors, a great and extensive reformation, or revival of spiritual religion, was effected in the

(1) Walch's Streitigkeiten &c. p. 560.

church in Germany. The influence of Franke, and the establishment of the orphan-house and theological school at Halle, gave rapid and general extension to this reform, and supplied a large part of Germany with pious and practical preachers. Listen to the testimony of Franke, the elder, himself, even in his own life-time: "Many thousands of souls have been wakened up to true repentance; yes, many thousands of ministers have been awakened."[1]

In the discussions of the so called Pietistic Controversies, these men exploded the old notion of adiaphoristic actions, or actions, which though not good, were said by their opponents also not to be sinful; such, forsooth, as dancing, attending the theatre, playing cards, &c.;[2] and gave currency to the only view, which can satisfy a spiritually enlightened mind, namely, that every action, word and thought is embraced in the divine law, and is either sinful or holy. They also vindicated the necessity of regeneration and true piety to the minister of the gospel, the necessity of a better observance of the Christian Sabbath, and the spiritual priesthood of all Christians, that is, their duty to labor for the kingdom of Christ. These views, which fall little if any thing short of our ideas of true piety and ministerial fidelity at the present day, were generally received by the evangelical party in Germany in the time of Franke and his successors; and it was from them that these views were imbibed by the fathers of our church at Halle. Indeed, Muhlenberg himself was called to his work by Franke the younger.

Of the deep-rooted and formidable opposition to this great moral regeneration of the church in Germany, the pietistic controversies, and the hundreds of publications concerning them, and even the edicts of civil rulers bear ample testimony. Yet those holy men maintained their ground, and yielded not an iota of what they regarded as the truth of God. With such examples before their eyes, were such men as Muhlenberg, Brunholtz, Handschuh, Schultz, Bager, Krug, Kunze and others educated: and as several of them had labored for a season as teachers in the school at Halle, it was but natural to expect that in pursuing their convic-

(1) Paroenetic. Prelect. VIII, pt. 4, and Guericke's Kirchengeschichte, p. 885.

(2) Guericke's Kirchengeschichte, p. 875.

tions of duty in this western world, their course would be substantially the same.

II. We are thus conducted to the *second* topic of our inquiry:

WHAT WAS THEIR PRACTICE AMID THEIR ALTERED CIRCUMSTANCES IN THIS WESTERN WORLD?

When they arrived in this country, they found the public attention much excited on the subject of religion. *Whitefield* had arrived here four years before Muhlenberg, and was electrifying our different cities and towns by his apostolic eloquence; the pietistic influence had reached England, and Wesley, after having spent two years in our Southern States, had returned to England, and there commenced his indefatigable labors and wonderful enterprises, which excited attention even on this side the Atlantic. Muhlenberg and his coadjutors were animated by a similar spirit, and tasked their utmost powers for the furtherance of the gospel among their German brethren. Whitefield, Tennant, and the fathers of our church, held each other in high and mutual esteem. They cultivated each other's acquaintance, and preached for each other. Of Tennant, Mr. Handschuh thus expresses himself in his diary: "May 17th, 1748. This afternoon, the Rev. Mr. Tennant, a Presbyterian minister, visited us, who is much beloved by us. Our conversations were edifying, agreeable and affectionate. To our great gratification and edification, he tarried with us till late at night."[1] The estimate which Whitefield placed upon their character, is evinced by his personal efforts in taking collections in aid of our brethren in South Carolina, and his preaching for Muhlenberg in Philadelphia; as also by the fact, that, at the death of the pious Handschuh, though unable from sickness to walk in the funeral procession, he had himself conveyed alongside of it in his carriage. Hear from the lips of Muhlenberg himself, an account of that solemn event, which is interesting also as showing the general estimation in which the fathers of our church were held by the public in this great city, at that time however containing a population of only 15,000 souls, with seven churches, viz: a Swedish Lutheran,

(1) Hallische Nachrichten, p. 104.

an Episcopal, a Presbyterian, a Baptist, a Moravian, and a Romish church, together with the meeting-house of the Society of Friends.[1] "It was Thursday, October 11th, 1764. At 1 o'clock, P. M.," says Muhlenberg, "eight bells were rung on the high church, and three on the cupola of our school-house, in memory of the deceased, which produced considerable sensation in the city. At 2 o'clock the teachers and ministers assembled in the conference room, in the school-house. Two Doctors of Divinity, two Professors from the English Academy, three ministers of the Episcopal church, two Presbyterian ministers, one Baptist, one Swedish Lutheran, and two German Reformed ministers, were in attendance, as also Whitefield, with his faithful companion, Mr. Wright, who accompanied him from England. Therewith the Rev. Hartwick, Voigt and myself, constituted the clerical attendants, and all walked before the corpse except Mr. Voigt and myself, who, together with the widow and children, followed the coffin as mourners. Then came the English physician, the church council, after which the citizens of different denominations followed in procession. When we arrived at the church, a great number of persons had entered through the windows, for the doors were yet locked. The church was soon so crowded that we were apprehensive the galleries might break down, and many persons be killed or wounded."[2] It seems evident, therefore, that the framers of the Americo-Lutheran church were in habits of cordial intercourse with Whitefield and Tennant, the two most active revival preachers of that day in our whole country; and no man acquainted with their reports to Halle, made during many years, will doubt that their whole ministry was conducted in the same devotional and fervid spirit.

What was the condition of the Lutheran church at the time of their arrival? Let Muhlenberg himself be our informant. In his diary of 1763, about a year after he reached his field of labor, he says: "It seems as if this were the time in which God will visit us with special gracious influences. And indeed it is high time. If our poor Lutherans had been neglected a few years longer,

(1) Heinsius Kirchengeschichte, p. 685.
(2) Hallische Nachrichten, p. 1166–7.

they would have been scattered altogether, and relapsed into heathenism. There are, moreover, almost numberless sects, opinions and temptations. Nor is there any lack of atheists, deists, naturalists and free-masons. In short, it seems as if there were not a sect in the world, which is not fostered here. There are people assembled here from nearly all parts of the world. What would not be tolerated in Europe, finds full scope here. The most scandalous things against God, and his word, are freely and publicly uttered here. Throughout the whole land there are many thousands, who were baptized and confirmed as Lutherans, but are now scattered abroad and neglect religion. Such is the lamentable condition and religious decline amongst our own poor Lutherans, that tears of blood could not sufficiently deplore it. Parents in many cases suffered their children to grow up unbaptized, without instruction, and to run into heathenism. The great mass of them are yet wild, and it may easily be supposed, that one year will not suffice to root out the disorder and confusion which crept into the people in thirty.[1]" And what was the course by which they hoped to remedy these disorders, to promote spirituality in religion, and to build up the kingdom of the Redeemer, among the lost sheep of the German fold? The amplest investigation will prove, that they pursued the good old gospel plan. They preached the word with great zeal and fidelity, in season and out of season, publicly and from house to house. They administered the sacraments with great solemnity, and in all their pastoral duties throughout the week, they watched for souls as those that must give an account. In short, they belonged to the most zealous and faithful preachers of the pietistic school, of Spener and Franke, in the land of our fathers, and modified their ministrations to suit the altered circumstances of our country. In Germany the pietistic reform was hampered by civil interference. Here in Pennsylvania, the union of church and state was happily abolished, even prior to our independence of Great Britain. For the enlightened and benevolent William Penn at once proclaimed universal tolerance for all religions. Thus did our fathers find themselves free to follow the dictates of their own conscience in

(1) Hallische Nachrichten, p. 17.

the forms of worship, government and discipline. And what was their practice?

1. They proved themselves friends of spiritual religion and religious revival by *their diligence and faithfulness in preaching.* They stood up, not as philosophers to publish the speculations of Plato or Aristotle, of their own far-famed Leibnitz or of Locke, but as ministers of the New Testament, to preach Christ crucified, to the Jews a stumbling block, and foolishness to the Greeks. This duty they performed, not as hirelings, glad when their day's work was over; but like the primitive apostles before them, "daily in the temple and in every house, they ceased not to teach and to preach Jesus Christ." The manner in which they preached, may be aptly learned from a minute of a Pastoral Conference, held at the house of Mr. Muhlenberg, Oct. 20th, 1760, in which the question, "What is the best method of preaching," was fully and freely discussed. There were present, Dr. Muhlenberg, Provost Wrangel, of the Swedish Lutheran church, Rev. Wm. Kurtz, Jr., Rev. Gerock, of Lancaster, Rev. Nicholas Kurtz, of Tulpehocken, Rev. Hansile, of Reading, Rev. Weigand, of New York, and Bryzelius, of the Swedish Lutheran church. Rev. Wrangel, being requested to present his views, said, "it was his habit to take a portion of the New Testament, and to discuss it analytically, exegetically, and by way of application." His sermons are carefully premeditated, and usually of three quarters of an hour's length. Afterwards he questions his hearers in order to learn what they retain of the sermon, "and," says Muhlenberg, "show them the *nervum probandi* of the texts adduced, and how to make a suitable application of them to themselves." Another pastor, says Muhlenberg, in a country station, (probably he meant himself,) pursues nearly the same course, first preaching, and then recapitulating the discourse by question and answer. "In our discourses," said this pastor, "we ought to make no ostentatious display of learning, but study simplicity; we should neither strike into the air, nor employ low and vulgar expressions, not introduce too much matter into a sermon, but discuss the subject fully, and apply it to the heart. Our sermons should not be dry, but practical. Religion should be presented not as a burden but as a pleasure. Avoid personalities. Let personal difficulties be set-

tled in your pastoral visits. The *elenchus* must not be neglected. Present your *thesis* rightly; neglect not the *antithesis*. As our members are resident among all kinds of hostile errorists, controversies cannot be avoided, yet you should not mention names. Carefully inquire into the moral condition of the members of the church, and let it serve as a homiletic rule for you. Let us sow with tears, let us aim at the edification of each individual soul, and give heed to ourselves and our doctrine."[1] Certainly, we seldom find more homiletic wisdom compressed into so small a compass. The custom of examining the congregation on the principal topics of the sermon, also led to the practice, then prevalent, of the hearers taking their bibles into the church, and, during the sermon, referring to the passage quoted by the preacher.[2] Nor ought the moderate length of Dr. Wrangel's sermons be forgotten by those who often lose sight of Luther's maxim, that "one of the cardinal excellences of a preacher is *to know when to leave off*."

Nor did these holy men shun to expose the fashionable vices of the day. They seem to have felt the truth of Paul's maxim: "If ye yet seek to please men, ye are no longer the servants of Christ." So faithfully did Dr. Kunze direct the artillery of the pulpit against the vice of Sabbath breaking, then as now specially prevalent among European Germans, that they became greatly excited, and published some abusive articles against him in the English newspapers, the German editor wisely declining to insert such articles. Like Paul these devoted servants of Christ seem "to have kept back nothing that was profitable," and could say, "we are pure from the blood of all men, for we have not shunned to declare the whole counsel of God."

Muhlenberg availed himself of various suitable expedients, some of which might be called new measures, to arrest the attention of the hearer. "A young man," says he, between twenty and thirty years of age, has frequently visited me and engaged in edifying conversation and prayer. He told me that he had been awakened to seek his salvation in Christ, by impressive evangelical hymns. It is in my custom (he added,) occasionally after sermon to read

(1) Hallische Nachrichten, p. 859, 860.

(2) Hallische Nachrichten, p. 624.

a stirring and edifying hymn adapted to the discourse, to expound several of its phrases, and to recommend these hymns to my hearers. Nor has the practice been unblessed, for the audience more easily understand such representations, and often wonder, that they have sung these hymns a hundred times without having understood their force and beauty.[1]"

The subjects of their discourses were generally of the most practical kind. Of them could not be affirmed what the celebrated author of the Task said of the Episcopal ministers of England:

> How oft when Paul has served us with a text,
> Has Plato, Tully, Epictetus preached ?

Not only their subjects, but the whole character of their preaching was eminently practical and *biblical*, as their diaries abundantly prove. May 24, 1752. "This forenoon," says Muhlenberg, "I preached at Hackinsock on *regeneration*, and this afternoon on the *conversion* of Cornelius, the centurion. The crowd was so great, that not half of it could gain admittance to the church. The others drove their vehicles near the windows of the church, and standing in numbers on them, listened to the sermon." On the 25th, he catechised the young, and on the 26th preached again at the same place. I cannot forbear to call the special attention of this audience to the record of that day's labor. "This morning," says he, "I preached in the Low Dutch, on John vii. 38, and the hearers received the word with great avidity amid many tears. In the afternoon, I preached English, because a number of English families reside here and have no preacher. They offered to unite with our church, if I would remain and preach for them."[2] Happy would it have been not only for the Lutheran church as such, but for the souls of thousands and tens of thousands, descended from the Germans of that day, had the other ministers of our church imitated the example of Muhlenberg, in cultivating an acquaintance with the English language, or had they at least trained young men for this

(1) Hallische Nachrichten, p. 204.
(2) Hallische Nachrichten, p. 488.

work, and thus furnished the rising generation with the ordinances of God's house in a language they could understand. Instead of five or six Lutheran churches in this city, we should doubtless now have at least twenty, and thousands of the young, who, suspended between attachment to the church of their fathers on one hand, and their better acquaintance with the language of the land on the other, never attached themselves to any church, would probably have been saved from entering eternity in that unblessed state, unsheltered by the covenant of God's people. But, excepting Dr's. Muhlenberg and Kunze, we are not aware that any of the others attempted to preach in the English language. Dr. Hellmuth at one time instructed catechumens in English, but subsequently adopted the contrary course. No provision was made to train up an English ministry. Indeed the majority of those fathers appear to have set themselves to work to banish the English language entirely from their churches, to induce as many of the young as possible to learn German, and to hand over those who either would not or could not, to the spiritual care of any English denomination, into whose hands they might fall. In their liturgy, published in 1786, they have introduced a prayer, for which we should be hard pressed to find either scripture, precept or example, and which is not altogether unlike the use made of religion by Buonaparte, on a different occasion. Well knowing the power of early religious education, and feeling that the throne which he had usurped, needed some strong pillars for its support, that remarkable man, alike the blessing and the curse of Europe, summoned before him the dignitaries of the Gallican church in 1806. He commanded them to frame a catechism to be taught to the children of the French nation, and insert into it a series of questions and answers, teaching that God by his special providence had raised up Napoleon as the deliverer of France, that he had endowed him with extraordinary qualifications in times of great difficulty; and that it was the duty of all good Christians, to honor him, pay tax to him, serve in his army, to pray for him as the instrument of God, and yield him a cordial allegiance. Thus our fathers, in their liturgy, taught their churches to pray "that the *Germans* of our land might never disown their ancestry, and that the *German* churches, and *German* schools might be perpetuated here."[1]

In regard to public worship, it is evident that their grand design, to convert sinners and edify saints, led them to some new measures, to some innovations on the customs of Germany. It appears that for about twelve years they used no liturgy at all in ordinary worship. After some time they were induced, in order to preserve uniformity in modes and ceremonies, to compose a liturgy for themselves. In 1754 Muhlenberg, Brunholtz and Handschuh, in their joint report to Halle, say: "We found it necessary for present use, to compose a short directory for worship, (Agende or Kirchenordnung) for the sake of unity (uniformity) in the ceremonies of public worship. We adapted it to the circumstances of our congregations, which had come from different parts of Germany. We took as a basis the directory of the German Lutheran Church at Savoy, in London, *as we had no other at hand*."[2] If they had no other, they had not the Hallish liturgy, to which they had been accustomed in Germany; and it follows, that during the previous twelve years, they probably used none, except on special occasions, when that of Savoy was perhaps employed. Even after this time we rarely find in their detailed descriptions of their preaching, any reference to the liturgy; except on sacramental or ordination occasions. At other times their prayers at public worship appear, during that period, to have been extemporaneous. That they studied simplicity in adopting set forms of the church in Germany, is evident from the directions given by the Synod in 1784, to the committee appointed to prepare and publish a hymnbook for this country, namely, chiefly to follow the hymnbook of Halle; *but to omit the gospels and epistles, for the day of the Apostles, and for all other unusual festivals*, that is, festivals observed by the church in Germany but not in this country. They reduced the festivals to those few which are now observed by us, Christmas, (New Year,) Good Friday, Easter, Ascension day and Whitsunday. Their liturgy, as published in 1786, is, as its preface informs us, longer than the forms

(1) See p. 7 of Kirchen-Agende der Evangelisch-Lutherischen Vereinigten Gemeinden in Nord America, Philadelphia, gedruckt bei Melchior Steiner, in der Reesstrasse. 1786.

(2) Hallische Nachrichten, p. 675.

previously used by them; yet it is not as long as the one published by the Synod of Pennsylvania in 1819; nor more than half as large and copious as the one recently adopted by several Synods, and accepted by the last General Synod. They seem to have thought, and we think justly, that the formal, or stereotyped part of worship, ought to be short, that the time may be chiefly employed in exercises of prayer and preaching. That liturgy leaves it optional with the preacher to read the gospel or epistle of the day, or the portion of Sacred Scripture containing his text, and *it contains no prayers whatever for any festival.* The custom in our church in this country, as also in the Dutch Reformed church, has been from time immemorial, to use the liturgy only on synodical, sacramental, funeral and wedding occasions, excepting in the cities and a few larger towns, where the populace appears to look with a more favorable eye upon forms and ceremonies. To this individual liberty of each minister, we would adhere as a fundamental principle of our American Church, never to be relinquished for any consideration whatever. These chastened views on the subject of forms in worship, go far to explain the reception given by these fathers, to the invitation addressed to their Synod by the late venerable Bishop White of this city, to unite in a body to the Episcopal church. That proposition was treated with due respect, but unhesitatingly declined, although the bishop explicitly offered that their Lutheran ordination should be acknowledged as valid. That bishop was an honor to his church. He had studied his bible and the ancient history of the church of Christ with an enlarged heart and enlightened views, and never dreamt of denying the ministerial character of his brethren in other churches, or of claiming divine authority of diocesan episcopacy. Of similar nature were the views of the most learned and distinguished divines and scholars, even of the Episcopal church itself, such as Archbishop Whitgift, Dr. Willet, Bishops Bilson, Morton, Jewell, Croft, and Burnet, Drs. Whitacker, Stillingfleet, and Hawies, Sir Peter King, and Archbishops Usher and Tillotson. A single quotation may suffice from a pamphlet of Bishop White, written principally to recommend a temporary departure from the line of episcopal succession, on the ground that diocesan bishops could not then (during the American Revolution) be had. "Now, (says he) if even those who held episcopacy to be of divine right, conceive the obligation to it not to be binding when that idea would be destructive of public worship; much more must they think so (referring to himself and others,) who indeed venerate and prefer that form as the most ancient and eligible; but *without any idea of divine right in the case.* This the author (viz. Bishop White,) believes to be the sentiment of the great body of Episcopalians in America, in which respect, they have in their favor unquestionably the sense of the Church of England, and, as he believes, the opinions of her most distinguished prelates for piety, virtue and abilities." With this manly and truthful acknowledgment, how ludicrously does the sentiment of the Puseyites and some other high-churchmen of the present day compare, who virtually unchurch all other denominations of our land, except their own and their twin sister of Rome, and who either have, or seem to have, seriously persuaded themselves, that all other ministers are but laymen, and their ministrations destitute of the divine seal!

If, then, it is asked, was their preaching spiritual, was it revival preaching? We would answer, that, in the true and best sense of the phrase, it was. They evidently aimed with the utmost sincerity and faithfulness to awaken and convert careless sinners, to edify the true believer and to revive, to build up the church of the Redeemer.

Yet it is worthy of note, that nowhere in any of their reports, so far as we know, is there any evidence of their ever having designedly made or allowed any disorder, or unnecessary noise during worship. We say *designedly,* made—for we are convinced, that no minister will long be disturbed by unnecessary noise during worship, who is known to disapprove of it, and who does not either tacitly or expressly, yield it some encouragement. We say *unnecessary* noise: because awakened sinners did sometimes groan or weep audibly, and such unavoidable groans are far less objectionable than lifeless formality. They practised upon the same principle adopted by the General Synod of our church, that God is a God of order; that order and not confusion, is the congenial element for the converting, the regenerating and sanctifying agency of the Holy Spirit.

It is true, they never called out awakened sinners before the congregation, to be made the subjects of special prayer and special instruction, except on confirmation occasions. But they had enjoyed no opportunity to witness the operation of this method, except in connexion with noise and confusion. Whether, if they were now living, they would do it is uncertain. Father Muhlenberg did, what resembles it. He conversed individually with his catechumens during his public meetings on the state of their souls. And the Scriptures seem to justify some method, by which the willing convert decides on the spot, whether he will obey or not. Did the Saviour, or his apostles after preaching, leave the place without ascertaining who were willing to be their followers? Our Saviour, at the close of his sermon, (Matth. xi. 28,) said to the weary and heavy laden, that is to the anxious and inquiring souls, " Come unto me and I will give you rest;" but he did not say, Come to-morrow. And if they came to him, we cannot see how he would give them rest, except by further instruction and advice as to their conduct. We have so long been accustomed to a spiritual application of this invitation of the Saviour, that we forget that its primitive meaning was literal. In many other occasions, Jesus exhorts his hearers to follow him. "Sell that thou hast and follow me"—"if any man will serve me let him follow me." Acts ii. 41. After Peter had preached at Pentecost, and many were pricked to the heart, he exhorted them to be *baptized* for the remission of sins. We are told, "Then immediately those who received the word gladly, were baptized, being about three thousand." Now, how did the apostle know, who among his hearers received the word gladly, unless he gave them an invitation to manifest it, in some way or other? And how could he baptize them unless they came to him? Yet this was done *immediately* and not the *next day*.

2. The *establishment* of *prayer-meetings* by the patriarchs of our American church, is another proof of their friendship to spiritual religion and scriptural religious revivals. The public exercises of the pulpit are such plain and universally conceded duties of a minister, that in Protestant churches all practice them. Manifestations of zeal in the pulpit, may also be found among such as are at heart, either hostile ,or at least indifferent to the cause of true piety. Animal feeling, and the desire of popularity as public speakers, may induce some, practising on the well known rule of

Horace,[1] that feeling in the orator is essential to its production in the hearer, to yield themselves to the impulses of natural feeling and thus without that blamelessness required by Paul, or that moral virtue which both Cicero and Quintilian describe as essential requisites of true eloquence, they may pass for reputable preachers. But when we see the zealous preacher, also zealous in sustaining those less ostentatious modes of worship, and means of doing good, we have additional reason to regard him as one of those who watch for souls, as those that must give an account. The mere formalist is averse to genuine religious excitement, because its regulation and improvement, make demands on his time and exertions. But the faithful servant of Christ rejoices to witness the power of the Holy Spirit moving the hearts of his hearers, and is ready to spend and be spent, in the appropriate labors of his profession. Such was the character of our fathers. They introduced prayer-meetings, not merely in the form of the *Collegia pietatis*, to which they had been accustomed in Germany, but also adopted, what to them were new measures. They adapted them to the necessities of their people, and conducted them according to the customs of England and this country. Their journal, published at Halle, specifically mentions Muhlenberg,[2] Brunnholtz, Krug, Kunze, Helmuth and others, as favoring and holding these meetings, and we have no reason to regard this as a peculiarity in them. They allowed laymen to hold these meetings alone in the absence of the pastor.

Like Luther, and Knox, and Spener, and Franke, and Wesley, they appear to have been eminently men of prayer. We would look in vain, even amongst the most zealous ministers of any denomination at the present day, for a parallel to some of their specimens of abounding prayer. At the consecration of St. Michael's church in this city, in the year 1748, after the name of Michael's had been given it, the ministers all kneeled around the altar, and there were not less than six prayers offered up, viz: two in Swedish by Provost Sandin and Rev. Nusmann, and four in German by Rev. Brunnholtz, Hartwick, Handschuh and Kurtz.[3] And

(1) Si vis me flere, &c.
(2) Hallische Nachrichten, p. 915 917.
(3) Hallische Nachrichten, p. 569.

at the consecration of the church in Germantown in 1752, the pious Handschuh remarks, "After the act of consecration was performed by the Rev. Acrelius, of the Swedish Lutheran church, we ministers all fell upon our knees around the altar, and each offered up a prayer according to the circumstances, in the following order, Muhlenberg, Kurtz, Schaum, Weygand, Heinzelman, Schultz, Schrenk, Raus, and myself."[1]

A prayer-meeting was commenced in Philadelphia, by Muhlenberg himself, who had held them daily on board the ship crossing the Atlantic,[2] and continued until the time of Dr. Helmuth. Another was sustained in Lancaster, conducted by the lay-members alone, of which the pastor, Dr. Helmuth, gives the following interesting account: "Those who had learned to know the truth, meet on two or three evenings of the week, at different places for the purpose of singing, praying, reading a chapter of the Bible, and also of Arndt's True Christianity. The number attending was often inconveniently large, amounting to from thirty to forty. These meetings were several times disturbed by wicked men, both young and old, by standing around the windows listening, and sometimes by casting stones against the doors for the purpose of exciting those within to resistance. They reviled them publicly on the streets, stigmatizing them as pietists, hypocrites, &c.

My conduct, adds Dr. Helmuth, has also given much offense, in as much as I would not, and could not discourage such meetings. On the contrary, I loved them, and praised them both publicly and privately, with suitable caution against their abuse."[3]

It is evident, therefore, that those among us, who are most zealously engaged in promoting prayer-meetings, conducted in christian order, are the genuine old school Lutherans, and if necessary we can plead the example of the fathers of our church in our defense.

3. Their *private pastoral* labors prove them to have been friends of spiritual religion and of religious revival. They seem to have not only aimed at the conversion of sinners, in

---

(1) Page 285.
(2) Page 49.
(3) Hallische Nachrichten, p. 1352.

their sermons and prayer-meetings, but they also faithfully followed up those labors by more private efforts with individual souls. Their journal abounds in detailed narratives of individual cases of experience, evincing their deep solicitude for souls, and showing that, like the apostles, "they preached privately to those of reputation, lest they should have run and labored in vain."[1] Listen to an extract from Dr. Muhlenberg's diary, taken from multitudes almost at random. May 27th, 1752: "I visited Mr. ——, the senior officer of the government, whom I mentioned before. He professed to have been greatly encouraged by the four sermons I had preached here. We had an edifying, confidential conversation, and mutually encouraged each other. Afterwards I visited a young deacon, who also appeared to be revived, and determined to give his whole heart to God. Finally I visited the sick woman before referred to. She thanked me heartily that I had spoken to her concerning death. She had subdued all fear of her approaching end, and had a deep sense of her depravity, and a godly sorrow on account of it. She felt and acknowledged herself the very chief of sinners, as destitute of even the least power to help herself. But although her heart seemed thus bruised and humbled, she could not yet console herself by the merits of the Saviour. At her request, I prayed for her, and spread her wants before the Lord, and instructed her from the word of God."[2]

Touching a visit paid by him to the congregation in Tulpehocken, he bears this pleasing testimony of the fidelity and success of his fellow-laborer, Rev. N. Kurtz. "After the preaching was over," says he, "I was informed by various individuals, that they had been awakened from the sleep of sin, by the preaching of the Rev. Mr. Kurtz, and brought to repentance, and a hungering and thirsting after righteousness."[3]

One other case I cannot omit. It is from the journal of that venerable father in Christ, with whom in early life, I had yet the pleasure of personal acquaintance during several years, though the heat and burden of many years had im-

(1) Gal. ii 2.
(2) Hallische Nachrichten, p. 489.
(3) Hallische Nachrichten, p. 229.

paired his intellectual as well as his bodily energies. "To day," says he, "I visited several sick persons, among whom was a naturalist, (deist.) He had travelled much in the world, and had been a captain in the Danish army. He urged the principal, customary objections to the divinity of Christ, and other truths of the gospel. Grace was given me to reply to him in a becoming, affectionate and convincing manner. How great was my joy, when, in the midst of my conversation with him, he seized my hand, and with tears in his eyes exclaimed, you have convinced me, dearest friend, you have reclaimed a wandering sheep to the Great Shepherd! He then uttered a heartfelt prayer, and with many tears besought the Saviour as the true God-man, and Redeemer of the world, to pardon his sins. I reminded him of the Saviour's declaration: Whosoever heareth my sayings, &c. I told him, he must persevere in prayer, through every difficulty, until he obtained lasting peace of mind."[1] This convert not long after died in the hopes of the gospel, and Dr. Helmuth took occasion to add interest to his funeral discourse by a narration of his conversion, a practice, which, if judiciously followed, we would recommend to our younger brethren occasionally to pursue.

Nor were their self-denying labors at all confined to the rich, or those in middling circumstances. They freely "condescended to those of low estate." The poor, yea those who might be emphatically styled *God's poor*, for they are despised by many for the skin which He gave them, we mean the neglected colored population, shared in their faithful labors. Under date of February 15th, 1745, he states: "I visited a female of the Reformed church, who seems to be truly pious, and a colored woman, a slave, (for then, alas! even Pennsylvania had slaves!) entered the room, who appeared to be a friend of true religion, and to possess an experimental acquaintance with it. I conversed with her in the English language, in order to encourage her mind."[2] On another occasion, during his residence in the city of New York, he says: (July 26th, 1752.) "This forenoon I preached in Low-dutch on the *unjust steward*, and this afternoon, in German, on the words, "I am crucified to the

(1) Hallische Nachrichten. p. 1473.
(2) Hallische Nachrichten, p. 49.

world," &c. A widow of the congregation had a mulatto slave, who was in the habit of attending our English and Low-dutch meetings, and by her consistent walk put many nominal christians to shame. She brought me my dinner from her mistress. I offered her a piece of money as a token of my gratitude, but she absolutely refused to take it, and began to weep bitterly, because she had heard that I was about to leave them. She said, she had experienced the power of the preached word in her heart, and had never before obtained so much consolation for her soul, and now I was about to leave them. I must confess my heart was ready to break. I admonished her to adhere closely to the Lord Jesus, who shed his blood for her too. After the afternoon sermon, three inquiring sinners visited me in my house, and desired a word of instruction. At night, I preached in the English language on the condition of the church at Laodicea,[1] Rev. 3. In the journal of the Rev. Handschuh, also, we find six or eight entries detailing his faithful labors in instructing a colored man[2] of genuine piety, and admitting him into the church. Noble example! How few among us have done likewise! Have not some of us been ashamed of the poor negro? Or at least, have we not neglected him? How few of us have remembered them that are in bonds as bound with them?

They discouraged vice in every form, as hostile to the interests of the soul. Has the cause of temperance enlisted all the wise and good of our age? Here we find temperance men before the age of temperance; men who discouraged all use of ardent spirits a century ago. Muhlenberg describing the custom which even at this day disgraces some enlightened neighborhoods, of giving intoxicating liquors as a supposed refreshment, at funerals in the country, dilates on its soul-destroying effects, and praises those who gave bread, and some innocent beverages in its stead. His description of rum, then a novelty, is worthy of note. He says: "There is a species of spirit of wine in this country, which is distilled from the West India sugar-cane. It possesses a concealed, exciting, deceptive, and corrupting tendency, and can gradually enslave and ruin the strongest

(1) Hallische Nachrichten, p. 502.
(2) Page 564—570.

constitution. If a person take a spoonful to-day, to-morrow his nature demands two, and next day three, and thus on until he acquires such a thirst for strong drinks, that he can pour in the strongest brandy like water, and still cannot slake his thirst. It may well be compared to the pestilence that walketh in darkness, and the destruction that rageth at noon-day, by which a thousand are slain on our side, and ten thousand on the other.[1]" Yet impartiality, one of the cardinal virtues of the historian, requires us to add, that though a temperance man in the literal sense, and in regard to rum a total abstinence man, the grand idea of the present age of moral reform, total abstinence from all that intoxicates, whether vinous or distilled liquors, had not yet dawned on his mind. But who can doubt that if he had lived in our day, he would be found in the foremost ranks of thorough reformers?

That they were the ardent friends of genuine religious revival, is doubly evinced by the manner in which they speak of the *special blessing, sometimes attendant on their labors.* Says Dr. Helmuth, in 1772: "As to the spiritual condition of our church, there is at present an unusually blessed state of revival. Aged, dead sinners have been brought to life, and cried out weeping for mercy. Sinners whose case I had often regarded as hopeless, are powerfully affected, and many of them truly converted to Christ. How greatly has my despondent mind been cheered, and my sluggish heart been roused, especially during the past weeks! I published a sacramental season, and in order that I might have opportunity to probe the hearts of my dear people, I gave them an invitation to call on me from eight to twelve o'clock, A. M., every day for two weeks. I thus had an opportunity to converse with each one separately, and to learn the extent and depth of this revival in many souls, by which the labors of these fourteen days were greatly sweetened. Through occasional neglect of my meals, and through excess of speaking and concern of mind, I was very much debilitated at the end of this time."[2] This same father, speaking of some

---

(1) Hallische Nachrichten, p. 986. See, also, p. 477, and on p. 1196, the case of an intemperate female! and p. 1479, a case of delirium tremens, the subject of which was truly converted and remained faithful at least to the date of the report in 1784.

(2) Hallische Nachrichten, p. 1344.

catechumens, who were deeply impressed during his address to them, says: "Their hearts were so deeply moved, that they could not contain themselves, nor refrain from disturbing me during the services by their audible weeping."

Dr. Kunze, one of the most learned and enlightened of that noble band, thus expresses himself in 1782: "Especially," says he, "among the young in this place, a fire has been kindled, which to the mutual joy of my colleague, Dr. Helmuth, and myself, has been burning upwards of a year."[1] Speaking of New York[2] in 1785, to which city he had removed, he says: "By the grace of God my labors are not in vain. The number of souls who have been gained by the word, is not yet large. Several have, however, come to me with tears, and expressed a desire to converse with me about the concerns of their souls. Of more extended fruit, I have as yet heard only faint indications; but that the preaching of the word has somewhat affected the souls of my hearers in general, I infer from evident proofs in the whole congregation."

4. Their conscientious and faithful labors to train the rising generation in the nurture and admonition of the Lord, proves them the friends of genuine religion, and of religious revivals. One of the cardinal characteristics of the Lutheran church, has always been her systematic provision for the thorough religious education of the young. In no other church on earth are the children more fully indoctrinated in the way in which they should go. Yet the value of this provision depends much upon the manner in which it is executed, and this depends upon the piety of the minister. It is therefore not the mere fact that catechetical instruction was given, and given extensively; but the manner in which it was done, to which we appeal in proof of our theme. These fathers gave all due prominence to the practical aspects of instruction. They labored to make that instruction the means of conversion to those on whom it was bestowed. So that at the great day they might be able to say, "Here Lord am I, and the children thou hast given me." It was customary for them to preach in the country stations but once a day, and immediately after the public

(1) Hallische Nachrichten, p. 1423.
(2) Page 1509.

service, to devote an hour to the catechetical instruction of the young. But their diary pays the special tribute to the Rev. Van Buskirk, of Macunschy, that he possessed particular excellence in this department. Sometimes they catechised the congregation on the gospel of the day.[1] The common book of instruction, however, was ordinarily Luther's German Catechism. Of this valuable little manual, an English translation of it was made at a very early period, for we find that version of Dr. Wrangel, in 1761, is called a *new* one. Another version into the Indian language had been executed before by Campanius, Lutheran pastor of the Swedes. It is worthy of remark, that even at that early day, the opposition of several sects to this important method of instruction was very strong; and it is recorded that some of their enemies termed the catechism "the devil's book."[2] No well grounded objection, however, can be made against the fact of catechetical instruction, though it justly may against the practice of some negligent pastors, who conduct their instruction in a careless manner, and admit their catechumens to sacramental communion without the requisite attainments in religious experience. Rightly conducted, the course of instruction preparatory to sacramental communion, ought not to consist mainly in reciting or explaining the catechism, which should be done in earlier years; but principally in a course of lectures on practical piety, based on the catechism, explaining the rise, progress, nature, evidences of true conversion, and the duties of professed disciples of Christ. Thus conducted, it furnishes to the pious pastor, a series of practical meetings, giving him free access to the hearts of his catechumens, and enabling him to accomplish all that spiritual good, aimed at and doubtless often attained by others, under the name of class meetings or conference meetings, &c. After many years of experience and observation, we regard this peculiarity of the Lutheran church as one of her moral glories; and we trust no Lutheran minister will be found disparaging it. But we will let these fathers speak for themselves. Says Mr. Brunholtz, of Philadelphia, in 1752: "I find, that my catechetical instructions of the young, which I have from the beginning conducted

(1) Hallische Nachrichten, p. 927.

(2) Hallische Nachrichten, p. 289.

in the church, (to which I have added another exclusively for children, on Friday, at my residence,) has excited a greater interest, not only in the youth, but also amongst others, than could be done by preaching alone; because the people are better able to understand instruction in question and answer, than a didactic discourse. These Sunday afternoon exercises are almost as numerously attended as the discourses of the morning."[1]

Of the faithful manner in which Muhlenberg himself conducted the course of instruction preparatory to confirmation, let us hear his own testimony. "In the month of November, I confirmed and admitted to the Lord's supper, the young people whom I had instructed in New Hanover. They were twenty-six in number, chiefly adults, one of whom was a married man. They had committed to memory the questions on the plan of salvation with considerable accuracy. I labored earnestly to impress them with the proper import of what they had learned, and without ceasing admonished them to frequent prayer, and to reduce to practice the instructions they had received. They cannot, therefore, plead as an excuse before God, that they have not been sufficiently impressed and urged. The major part of them have also assured me in the individual communications I had with them, that they have often been upon their knees in private prayer at home, and have experienced in their souls the operative influence of the Spirit of God, through his word. At their confirmation, they renewed their baptismal vows, amid many tears, upon their knees, before God and the congregation."[2] Such was their instruction, and thus conducted it can never fail to eventuate in blessing.

5. That they were ardent friends of spiritual religion and religious revival might be proved by the various efforts they made to improve the state of *discipline* in their churches. This is indeed an all-important feature of a well conducted church. Even the heathen Seneca has said, *bonis nocet, qui malis parcit,* and a greater than Seneca has said, "Them that sin, rebuke before all, that others may fear." Our Saviour enjoins that after having admonished

(1) Hallische Nachrichten, p. 305.

(2) Hallische Nachrichten. p. 340.

an offending brother in private, the admonition should be repeated under the associate influence of two or three others. If he will not hear them, tell it to the church, and should he still refuse to hear, then esteem him as a heathen or publican, i. e. exclude him from Christian privileges. It was for this purpose that Christ gave his disciples the keys of the kingdom of heaven, the control of ingress and egress from the church, and told them that whatsoever they bound on earth, should be bound in heaven, and whatsoever they loosed on earth, should be loosed in heaven. Without this provision for eclecticism and self-purification, the people of God would not be "a peculiar people," nor would they long continue "zealous of good works." In Germany, as is well known, the unhappy union of church and state has entirely defeated all efforts of discipline. But Muhlenberg and his coadjutors saw the error, and determined to reform. They, in fact, on this, as on some other points, introduced a *new measure*.

In 1762, a system of church discipline was introduced by the Philadelphia church, highly respectable in the standard of Christian propriety assumed.[1] One based upon similar principles was adopted by the church in Lancaster; but Dr. Helmuth, at that time pastor, complains in 1772, of great difficulty in enforcing it.[2]

In 1784, it was resolved at a synodical meeting, that all communicants who had been guilty of licentiousness, should be required to make public confession of their sin, or be excluded from church privileges.[3]

But these fathers unhappily failed to adopt any uniform, general system, based upon scriptural principles. Nor did they print the resolutions actually adopted, for general circulation among the people. Thus they lost the influence which education and public sanction would have given to the discipline they actually adopted, and as their members had never been accustomed to any discipline in Germany, and were, therefore, peculiarly difficult to control, the discipline was soon partially relaxed, and in course of time almost totally neglected.

---

(1) Hallische Nachrichten, p. 963.
(2) Page 1345.
(3) Page 1458.

6. *Finally*, their *synodical meetings* and *special conferences* were conducted in such a manner, as to prove them the ardent friends of spiritual religion, and of religious revival. The light in which they viewed these meetings, is indicated by the minute made of one of them in 1760, after the discussion of the question, whether it is useful and necessary that the annual meetings of the ministers and elders should be continued. "It is necessary (say they,) in order that the servants of one master and laborers in one vineyard, may become acquainted with each other, may become more closely united in love, and in mutual consultation concerning the best interests of the church (ecclesiae plantandae,) and the propagation of the Christian religion. They are useful, in order that each individual may communicate the grace and gift he has received, for the common good,—that they may encourage, admonish, and comfort each other, and decide cases of conscience,—that they may make known to each other in love, simplicity, meekness, and humility, their personal faults of which they themselves might not be aware,—and remove all contention and jealousy; because a house divided against itself cannot stand, and harmony among ministers of the same denomination, (and we would add, of all fundamentally orthodox churches,) "makes a great impression upon friends and foes."[1]

The zeal and brotherly love actually abounding among them, was such, that, during the meeting above referred to, whilst they regularly dismissed the congregation at a seasonable hour and retired to the residence of Dr. Muhlenberg, there to spend some time in private conference on experimental religion and the duties and difficulties of the pastoral office, they thrice continued these private consultations and devotional exercises till long after midnight, viz.: on the 18th, 19th and 20th of October, 1760.[2]

As early as 1772, the practice of holding *special conferences*, in the interim of the synodical meetings, was commenced, and their design is thus described by Dr. Helmuth: "A conference is to be held once every three months, to be attended only by those ministers who reside nearest together, and they differ from the General Conference (the

(1) Hallische Nachrichten, p. 857.
(2) Pages 854, 855—862.

Synod,) in this, that their object is not to attend so much to the external affairs of the congregation, but chiefly to aim at edification and at improvement in brotherly love. The contiguous brethren in the upper part of Pennsylvania, (Lancaster,) are Messrs. Kurtz, Sen'r., Kurtz, Jr., Krug, Wildbahn, Enderlein, Fred. Muhlenberg and myself (Helmuth.) We held our first meeting in a village, called New Holland, and spent our time in a truly brotherly manner. Each brother proposed something, which tended to edification or instruction, and which was made the subject of prayer."[1]

How pleasing to find one of the most important measures for promoting religion, which is but now beginning to gain currency amongst us, we mean *special conferences,* sanctioned by something so much like them, in the practice of the illustrious pioneers and fathers of our church! Would that the provisions of our Formula on this subject were more generally reduced to practice. Then should we witness more frequent revivals of religion amongst us, and see spiritual religion more extensively prevail.

In conclusion, we see that the spirit of our Fathers was a spirit of *Eclecticism.* They called no man master, they acknowledged no head but Christ; no absolute authority but the Bible. They bound themselves to no set of forms derived from the old country, but retaining the grand landmarks of Lutheranism, doctrinal, practical, and liturgical, they adapted them to their altered circumstances in this country. Thus with the Bible in their hands, and their eyes fixed on the leadings of God's providence, they passed forward, and felt at liberty to adopt any improvement which was developed in the progress of society, and of the church, and which commended itself to reason and to scripture.

Thus O may it ever be with our Zion! Far be the time, nay, may it never come, when the Lutheran church shall be robbed of her liberty for free and unshackled investigation, or shall again be enslaved to voluminous creeds and detailed confessions. But with the Bible, and the brief doctrinal articles of the Augsburg confession, may that church, which is emphatically styled *the church of the Reformation,* continue to deserve the name, and as she owes

(1) Hallische Nachrichten, p. 1339.

her existence to the Reformation, never be the enemy of Reformation. For the sake of substantial uniformity, let her have a brief liturgy, but never, never, bind the conscience of her ministers as to the frequency of its use. Let her be cautious in rejecting the old, but not prejudiced against all that is new. Let her try every doctrine and every measure by the touchstone of God's word, and whatever the oracles of Jehovah sanction, and the providence of God blesses, let her not be ashamed to practice and profess.

Then, my beloved brethren, may we hope to find our church ever the friend of spiritual religion and religious revival; then may we hope to train up Christians and Christian ministers of enlarged views, of liberal, charitable feelings, of expanded enterprises, of millenial schemes. Thus may we hope she will co-operate most harmoniously, and most efficiently with the other churches of our land, and of all lands, in advancing the mediatorial reign of our blessed Master, and preparing the way for the second glorious coming of the Lord.

IV. DISCOURSE.

THE NATURE OF THE SAVIOUR'S PRESENCE IN THE EUCHARIST.

When the Divine Author of our holy religion, gave us an inspired, written record of its sacred principles, precepts and institutions, through the men whom he had personally instructed, he also taught us to regard this record as a sufficient rule of faith and practice, as able to make us, individually, "wise unto salvation." Through these same honored instruments he informs us, "that all scripture was given by inspiration," for the express purpose, "that the man of God may be perfect, thoroughly furnished unto every good work." To the close of the whole canon, that is, to the last (as we believe) of the inspired books, the Revelation of St. John, the Saviour appended this solemn warning, speaking in his own person: "I Jesus have sent mine angel to testify unto you these things in the churches. If any man shall add unto these things, God will add unto him the plagues that are written in this book; and if any man shall take away from the words of the book of this prophecy, God shall take away his part out of the *tree* (var. lect. for Βιβλιω book) of life, and out of the holy city, and from the things which are written in this book." Rev. xxii. 18, 19.

From these solemn declarations it is evident, that God will hold every man to strict responsibility for the conformity of his religious opinions to the teachings of the inspired word; and, therefore, in forming our doctrinal views, we ought to study the utmost possible objectivity, ought to labor to divest ourselves of all preconceived opinions, either for one or other interpretation of a disputed point, and let the Scripture, as much as possible, be made to interpret itself. These remarks are peculiarly applicable to the doctrine which is at present to claim our attention. It has been a bone of contention in the Protestant church, with but little intermission, ever since its origin, until about fifty years ago, when the Lutheran church almost universally abandoned the views, which Luther and his co-laborers, with few exceptions, entertained. We, therefore, feel the deepest obligation, in endeavoring to investigate this subject, to be governed entirely by the word of God, interpreted according to the correct principles of common sense, which is the only true system of Historical Exegesis.

Let us *first* briefly recall to mind those principles of Hermeneutics, which particularly come into question in these passages of Scripture on this subject.

§ 1. General Principles of Interpretation.

1. The general nature of language implies, that the words of a speaker be regarded as definite signs of his ideas, and that the signification of these signs is *conventional:* that is, the signs or sounds called words, derive their meaning, not from their intrinsic structure, but from the current practice or usage of the people at the time they are employed. Thus, Σῶμα signifies body, σάρξ flesh, and αἷμα blood, ἄρτος bread, and οἶνος wine, simply in consequence of conventional usage. The few words in different languages, which express sounds not unlike that of the words themselves, such as roar, crash, &c., are, like some of the admired lines of Virgil or Homer, in which the sounds of the whole sentence bears some analogy to the idea expressed, but exceptions which confirm the general rule.

2. The language of Scripture and of inspiration, does not differ from other language in its general principles. That this would be the case, might *a priori* be expected: for if it were otherwise, such language would not be intelligible. As words in any language convey to the hearer, not whatever ideas the speaker may choose, but those of which conventional usage has made them the authorized exponents; the inspired writers could be intelligible on no other supposition.

Accordingly, it is admitted by all enlightened exegetical writers, that the language of Scripture must be investigated on precisely the same principles which are applied to uninspired language.

The actual examination of the Scriptures *a posteriori*, proves the above expectation, or supposition to be correct. The diversity of style, of literary excellence, and of psychological peculiarity, belonging to the different books, incontestably establishes the homogeneity of the language of the Bible, with that of uninspired writers. Generally, the Scriptures have been interpreted on this supposition, by the great mass of christians in all ages, and found to be intelligible.

3. The rules of Sacred Hermeneutics must therefore, also, like those of Hermeneutics in general, be based on the nature and general principles of language, and arise out of them.

Thus we must study the historical import of the individual words employed: the context and scope of the passage must be investigated, the circumstances and design of the writer are to be examined, and in short all the light of archæology is to be employed, to ascertain what ideas the passage in question would have conveyed to the persons of the age and country, to whom they were first addressed. The sense thus acquired is to be regarded as the true one, and is termed the historical sense. Luther himself, in most instances, practiced on this system, and termed the signification thus acquired the *literal* sense.

4. Experience, however, proves, that in fact, general usage has, in all languages, given different significations to many words. The causes of this fact, we will not here stop to discuss; its reality is undisputed, and familiar to all.

That signification of a word, in which it is most commonly employed, is usually termed its natural or *literal* import. The others are called *figurative*.

The *figurative* meanings of words are of various kinds, metaphysical, typical, allegorical, &c., &c.

5. Yet the great mass of men ordinarily employ words, in their natural, most obvious, and literal sense.

Therefore, a sound rule of interpretation is, that *the literal sense must be adhered to in the interpretation of all authors, sacred or profane, until reasons occur to justify us in deviating from it.*

6. Such reasons, however, often do occur both in sacred and profane authors, and then a deviation from the literal sense becomes necessary.

These reasons are 1.) When the passage literally interpreted *contradicts natural reason, common sense,* or the testimony of our senses.

Thus, for example, in Psalm xviii. 2, and elsewhere, God is termed "a *rock*, a *fortress*, a *buckler*, a high *tower:*" when the Saviour says, (John xv. 1,) "I am the true *vine*, ye are the *branches*,"—or "I am the *door*," x. 9: or when Paul says, 1 Cor. x. 4, "That *rock* was Christ," or "Christ our *passover*," was slain for us, &c.; or Matth. xiii. 38, 39, "The *field* is the world—the *seed* is the *word*, &c., the enemy is the devil." See also Matth. viii. 22; or in Gethsemane when Jesus says, "Father, if it be possible let this *cup*," this trial of affliction, pass away. This rule is based on the universally conceded proposition, that the testimony of our senses fairly and fully ascertained, is stronger than any other evidence, which might seem to overturn it; and that the obvious and conceded teachings of common sense and reason are also true.

2) We must depart from the literal sense, when the passage literally interpreted, *contradicts the well known opinions of the author*, or in regard to the Bible, contradicts some other portions of Scripture, and the passage naturally, in accordance with the laws of language, admits another meaning, that does not labor under these difficulties. Thus, the command of the Saviour: "If thy hand, or foot, or eye offend thee, cut it off, or pluck it out," &c., Matth. xviii. 9, 10, literally interpreted contradicts the command in the decalogue, "thou shalt not kill," and, therefore, the literal sense cannot be retained.

3) The deviation from the literal sense is the more natural and allowable, when the composition is *poetic*, in which figurative language naturally abounds, in all languages and among all nations.

4) Also, in popular discourses and even narrative compositions, when the speaker is in the habit of employing figurative style.

Thus, after we know from the discourses of the Saviour in general, that often, very often, he speaks in parables, and employs various kinds of figurative expressions; it is the more probable, that his meaning in a disputed passage is figurative also; and it is the more obligatory on us to adopt a tropical interpretation, when a literal one labors under difficulties. We need not enumerate the parables of the Saviour. It is well known that his discourses are more frequently parabolical or figurative, in some form or other, than literal.

This is also very frequently the case in regular historical and didactic composition in all languages, although the figures occurring are of a more modest nature, are metaphorical rather than allegorical. The tropes are rarely kept up through a whole narrative.

Such a figurative mode of speaking, is more usual among the orientals in general, than among the other civilized nations.

Having thus sketched out the general principles of hermeneutics, so far as they have an immediate bearing on the portions of Holy Writ, relating to the Supper of our Lord; we proceed, in the *second* place, to their application. We shall inquire what is the literal import of the words of the institution; whether sufficient difficulties oppress the literal sense to justify its rejection; what are the several tropical or figurative significations, of which the words in question admit; and which of these commends itself most strongly to our judgment and conscience, as most accordant with the legitimate principles of interpretation.

§ 2. The literal sense of the words of the institution.

What is the literal sense of the Gospel narrative of the institution of the Lord's Supper? Matth. xxvi. 26. (Mark xiv. 22. Luke xxii. 19. 1 Cor. xi. 23, 24.)

Εσθιόντων δε αὐτων, λαβὼν ὁ Ιησȣς τον ἄρτον, και εὐλογήσας, (or according to a various reading, ἐυχαριστήσας) ἔκλασε, και ἐδίδȣ τοις μαθηταῖς, και εἶπε· Λάβετε, Φάγετε· τȣτό ἐςι ςῶμά μȣ. Literally, this means, "But whilst they were eating, Jesus took the bread, (or loaf,) and having offered prayer, or pronounced a blessing, (but not blessed *it*, the bread, "it" not being found in the Greek,) he break and gave to his disciples, and said, Take eat, this (bread) is my body (that is, is no longer bread, but is my body, and having been bread when I took it up, and being now my body, it must have been changed from one substance into another, that is, it must have been transubstantiated.") We, therefore, see that the Romish doctrine is really the literal, and only literal one. And it cannot be consistently denied, that if we are to disregard the testimony of the senses, and to suppose a miracle in the case, the doctrine of papal transubstantiation is the legitimate sense of this passage.

The same remarks and inferences are equally appropriate to the language of the Saviour touching the wine, as given by Matthew xxvi. 27–29. Πίετε ἐξ αὐτου πάντες· τȣτο γάρ ἐστι τὸ αἷμα μου, &c. That is, literally, *Drink ye all of it,* (*out of this cup,*) *for this* (*bowl or cup*) *is* (no longer a cup, but) *is my blood.* Hence, as it was a bowl or cup when he took it into his hands, and was thereafter no longer a cup, but was his blood, it must have been changed from one substance into another: and here again we have the papal transubstantiation as the legitimate and only result of the literal interpretation. Yet, after all, even the Papists do not adhere faithfully to the literal import here, as they suppose the "cup" (ποτήριον) to be used *figuratively* for the wine contained in it.

This Romish interpretation is wisely rejected by the whole Protestant world, for the following satisfactory reasons:

a) It is contradicted by the clear and indisputable testimony of our senses, which demonstrate that no change has taken place in the nature and properties of the bread and wine. We have this testimony, not of our senses only, but of sight, taste, smell and touch. Nor the four senses of one individual only, but of all men, of every generation and country, where the rite has been celebrated. But no testimony is so strong as that of the senses; because, on it rests our belief even of the Scriptures.

b) It contradicts the universal observation of mankind, that all bodies (material substances) must occupy definite portions of space, and cannot be at more than one place at one time: for according to this interpretation, every portion of consecrated bread is really the whole material body of the Saviour; hence the whole body is locally present in many different places at the same time, which is absurd.

c) The Apostle still calls the symbols bread and wine, *after* their consecration; which he would not have done, if they had been transmuted into the body and blood of the Saviour. 1 Cor. x. 16; xi. 26.

d) Because the bread and wine are subject to the same law of decomposition and corruption as if they were not consecrated.

e) Because it was a comparatively recent doctrine, unknown in the Christian church generally, until about a thousand years after this ordinance was instituted.[1]

§ 3. THE FIRST FIGURATIVE INTERPRETATION (BY LUTHER.)

What is the first *figurative* interpretation of the words of the Institution?

It is that of Luther, and his coadjutors in the sixteenth century, retained by the great mass of the Lutheran church till half a century ago, from some apparent scriptural authority aided by respect for Luther, and the penalties which followed the rejection of a material feature of the state religion. It amounts to this: The words of the Saviour, "Take, eat, τȣτο ἐϛι το σωμα μȣ," (take, eat, this is my body,) mean, "*Take, eat this bread, which is not my body, and remains bread, but which is the outward element, in, with or under which my true body is truly and substantially present, and is distributed with the bread, and received by the mouth, by all communicants.*"[2]

---

(1) See the writer's Popular Theology, 5th edit. p. 296, &c.

(2) That there may be no doubt in the minds of those unacquainted with the symbolical books, as to the accuracy of our representation of the views taught in them on the subject of the real presence, we annex several proof passages:

1) The Augsburg Confession says (Art. X.): "The *true* (*wahre*,) or *real* body and blood of Christ are *verily* (assuredly, truly, "*wahrhaftiglich*) present, and distributed and received by the communicants. &c."

2) The Apology to the Confession, Art. X. states: "The tenth Article (of the Augsb. Conf.) is not objected to by our opponents, (the Romanists) in which we confess that the body and blood of the Lord are *truly* and *substantially* (vere et substantialiter) present, and tendered, and received, *as the* (*Romish*) *church has hitherto believed* (wie man bis anher in der Kirchen gehalten hat".) That is, the Augsburg Confession was intended by Melancthon, who wrote it, and was understood by those who received it to teach the actual presence of the real body and blood of Christ, in the sense in which it had been taught by the Romish church generally, and also by the Greeks, who are named in the context, and also believed in transubstantiation.

3) The Form of Concord, Pars. I. § VII. De Cæna Domini, employs the following language, affirming that the body and blood of Christ are

The language of Jesus relative to the wine, "Drink ye all out of it," (the cup,) τȣτο γάρ ἐστι τὸ αἷμα μȣ, &c. (for this is my blood,) is to be thus interpreted: "*Drink ye all of this wine, which is not my blood, and remains wine, but which is the outward element, in, with, or under which my true blood is truly and substantially present, and is distributed with the wine, and is received by the mouth by all communicants.*"

The objections to this interpretation, are very similar to those which oppress the Romish doctrine of transubstantiation, though not quite as strong.

a) It contradicts the clear and indisputable testimony of our senses. This theory requires us to believe, not as the Papists do, that the bread ceases to be bread, and has been transmuted into the body and blood of the Saviour; but, still, that the true body of Christ is actually and *substantially*, or as the German copy says, *essentially* present, and yet it cannot be perceived by our senses. The body of Christ, whilst on earth, was always perceptible by the senses, like other bodies: and even after his resurrection and glorification, whenever he was present at any place,

---

truly and *substantially* (or, as the German copy states, *essentially*) present: "Quæritur an in sacra Cœna, verum corpus et verus sanguis Domini nostri Jesu Christi vere et *substantialiter* sint presentia, atque cum pane et vino distribuantur et ore sumantur ab omnibus illis qui hoc sacramentum utuntur—Cingliani negant—nos vero asseveramus." "Ob in dem Heiligen Abendmahl, der wahrhaftige Leib und Blut unseres Herrn Jesu Christi *wahrhaftig* und *wesentlich* gegenwartig sei, mit Brodt und Wein ausgetheilt und *mit dem Munde* empfangen werde, von allen so sich dieses Sacraments gebrauchen. Die Sacramentirer sagen nein, *wir sagen ja*."

We are aware, that the Form of Concord rejects the idea of a gross *Capernaitish* eating and drinking in the eucharist, according to which the flesh of the Redeemer is manducated by the teeth, and digested like other food. Muller Symb. Books, p. 543. It would therefore be the height of injustice to charge the adherents of the symbols with believing these consequences. Yet, if they properly flow from their doctrines, they may justly be alleged as objections to the doctrine itself, by all who regard them as its legitimate consequences.

They further pronounce the mode of eating and drinking to be a "*spiritual*" one, to which in its natural import, we ourselves believe; but they also add, "we believe that the body and blood of Christ are received *not only spiritually* by faith, but also *by the mouth*," and those are condemned who affirm that this reception is "*only* spiritual by faith," and not *oral*. The symbolical books also claim for the glorified body of Christ, by virtue especially of the hypostatic union, the possession of properties different from those of other matter, and even of other glorified bodies. Yet, as

his *glorified body also* was perceptible, even the nail prints in his hands and the wounds in his side. This glorified body, like that of believers in general, will still be a body, however elevated and refined in its properties; and being a body, it remains matter, and like all human bodies, visible and tangible.

It cannot indeed be denied, that God, by *a miracle,* might so interpose as to make the body of the Saviour invisible on sacramental occasions; but where is the intimation in any part of the narrative, that there should be a miracle wrought? Or is there the least shadow of evidence, that the apostles thought any thing miraculous had occurred? Do they manifest any surprise? Certainly not, and we have, therefore, no authority to suppose the existence of a miracle.

b) It also contradicts the observation of all ages and nations, that every body, or that material substance must occupy a definite portion of space; and cannot be at more than one place at the same time. According to this view, the body of Christ must be able to occupy different portions of space at the same time. It must be here, in Gettysburg, and in New York and Boston, and London and in Africa,

---

this assumption is considered gratuitous by those who reject this doctrine, they, of course, do not admit its force. And it deserves to be ever remembered, that only fourteen years after the Form of Concord was published, when Duke Frederick William, during the minority of Christian II. published the VISITATION ARTICLES OF SAXONY in 1594 in order to suppress the Melancthonian tendencies to reject this and other peculiarities of the symbols, the article on this subject framed by men confessedly adhering to the old symbols, and designing to re-enunciate their true import, and enforced upon the whole church in Saxony as symbolic, give the most objectionable view of this doctrine, viz.: I. "The pure doctrine of our Church is that the words, "*Take and eat, this is my body: drink, this is my blood,* are to be understood *simply and according to the letter.*" II. That the body (which is received and eaten) is the *proper* and *natural body* (der rechte naturliche Leib) of Christ, *which hung upon the cross;* and the blood (which is drunk) is the *proper* and *natural blood* (das rechte naturliche Blut) *which flowed from the side of Christ.*" Muller's Symb. Books p 847. Now we cannot persuade ourselves, that this is the view of a single minister of the General Synod, or of many out of it; and yet these are the views they are obligated to receive if they avow implicit allegiance to the former symbolical books of our Church in Europe. If they adopt the modification received by many of our distinguished divines, such as Mosheim, Reinhardt and others, they do not faithfully embrace the symbolical doctrine, and should not profess to do so.

and in Asia, at the same time, if Christians are simultaneously celebrating the holy supper; and yet his body was a human body like our own, whilst on earth, and even after its glorification, was confined to one place at a time, as it had been before. When the glorified Redeemer appeared to Mary Magdalene at the tomb, he was not also with his disciples in Jerusalem. When he appeared to Cleopas and another disciple on the way to Emmaus, he was not simultaneously among the apostles in Jerusalem. When he appeared to the assembled apostles in the absence of Thomas, Thomas did not see him elsewhere at the same time. When he was on the mount in Galilee, or at the sea of Tiberias, or finally at Bethany, whence he ascended, he was seen no where else. In short, his body seems to have been as much confined to one locality at a time, after his resurrection, as before his death. Since, therefore, we have no intimation in the Scriptures, that glorified bodies, in general, can occupy different portions of space at the same time, and since the body of Christ after his resurrection did in every instance appear under this restriction to one locality, and there is no intimation of a miracle in the Eucharist; the evidence all seems to be against the doctrine of the real presence of the body of Christ at the eucharist, in different places, at the same time.

Nor can the assumption of the Form of Concord (Muller, p. 667–8,) that the *body* of Christ possesses two other modes of presence, beside the local presence, be sustained, either by reason or the word of God. The alleged "*spiritual*" presence of the Saviour's *body*, is, literally interpreted, a contradiction in terms. And the other, the "*divine* or *heavenly*" presence, which is attributed to his body in common with the Deity, is wholly unscriptural, as well as opposed to the essential, unchangeable difference between the creature and the Creator, the finite and the Infinite.

c) This interpretation cannot be correct, because the glorified body, which is said to be received with the elements, had actually not yet any existence, and therefore could not have been given by the Saviour to his disciples at the Holy Supper. The idea, that it is impossible for the same thing to be and not to be at the same time, is not only an immutable law of all created things; so far as the human mind can perceive, it is applicable to the Deity himself, and it is usually admitted, that things contradictory in their nature, are not embraced in the range of the divine omnipotence. Hence, if Christ had intended his supper for this purpose, he would have told his disciples, "Ye cannot indeed now receive this supper in its proper import, nor receive my body in it, as I am yet alive and amongst you;" or rather, if it had been the intention of Christ to give us his real glorified body in the eucharist, he would have deferred the institution of the ordinance till after his resurrection, or have left it to his apostles to institute it, after he had wholly left this world, and ascended to his heavenly glory.

d) The eucharist could not have conferred the *broken* body to the disciples at its institution; because it was not yet broken, crucified, dead: nor to the followers of Christ after his resurrection, because it no longer exists in a broken, dead state, but in a risen, re-animated, glorified condition. Therefore, the words τȣτο ἐϛι, "this is," must, of necessity, have been figuratively understood by the disciples at the time of their delivery, in the institution of the supper.

e) The old Lutheran theory cannot be correct, according to the language of Christ, because he says, Luke xxii, 19, "Do this in *remembrance* of me," ἐις τήν ἐμήν ἀνάμνησιν, i. e. in mei recordationem, (Schleusner,) in commemoration of me; but we perform an act in remembrance of any person or event, only when it is *past* and *absent*. We deliver a sermon in commemoration or memory of the Reformation, or of General Washington, only because they are past and absent. Even when we commemorate the deeds of living men, those deeds must be past, which are to constitute the burden of our eulogy.

f) That the doctrine of the *real presence* cannot be true, is proved by those passages of scripture which represent Christ as having left this world, as having returned to the Father, and as being seated at his right hand in heaven; John xvi. 28, "I came forth from the Father, and am come into the world;" again, "I leave the world, and go to the Father." Matth. xxvi. 11. "For ye have the poor always with you; but me ye have not always." John xvi. 7. "It is expedient for you that I go away, for if I go not away, the Comforter will not come unto you; but if I depart, I will send him unto you." We are told by the Saviour himself, not to yield credence to such as say, "Lo, here is Christ or there." Matth. xxiv. 23.

When he took his final leave of his disciples, Luke tells us, "he was carried up into *heaven*." And although the Saviour left on record the delightful promise, that he would be always with his disciples till the end of the world; it was in his *divine* nature, which is omnipresent; and his next *visible* appearance, the angels informed the men of Galilee at his ascension, would again be from heaven in like manner, as they had seen him ascend. Acts i. 11.

In Acts iii. 21, Peter declares, that "The *heavens must receive him until* the times of the restitution (ἀποκαταστασις, fulfillment or accomplishment,) of all the things which God had spoken by the mouth of all his holy prophets, since the world began." We are told by Paul, "That the Lord will descend *from heaven* as with the voice of an archangel," 1 Thess. iv. 16; and again, the same inspired writer exhorts the Colossians, "Seek those things which are above, where Christ *sitteth* on the *right hand of God*." iii. 1. Now whilst all these passages and many others, teach us that Christ has left this world, and is now seated in heaven, we know of not a single passage which intimates that he is present at any sacramental celebration. But if it were true, that his body, which was last seen ascending to heaven, is all the while present on earth, at one or other place where the supper is commemorated, and often at thousands of places at the same moment; is it unreasonable to suppose, that such a remarkable fact, such an almost incessant miracle in the church of all ages, would at least be alluded to in a single instance in the New Testament?

g) Again, whilst the idea, that Christ is figuratively represented as the *spiritual food* of the believer, is a delightful, consoling and becoming one; the supposition that the believer is to eat the actual flesh of his best friend, and drink his real blood, is a gross, repulsive and unnatural idea, which nothing but the clearest evidence would authorize us to adopt. The eating of flesh and *blood* even of beasts was forbidden by the Jewish law, Gen. ix. 4.; with how much more horror would the disciples of the Saviour have been filled, had they understood him as enjoining on them habitually to eat and drink his body and blood? Yet they exhibit no indication of such horror or surprise, and, therefore, did not understand the Saviour as requiring such a repulsive act. Yea, the council of apostles and elders, at Jerusalem, after the Saviour's death, prohibit the eating of blood. Acts xv. 28. Hence, it is not surprising that, amid the long catalogue of Protestant creeds, of every denomination, there is not a single one, which adopts this doctrine of the real presence of the body and blood of Christ in the eucharist, except the Augsburg Confession and the other former symbolical books of our church. Several Protestant symbols do indeed employ language seemingly implying this doctrine, but they explain it away in other passages, so that this doctrine is not understood to belong to any other church. We know the Form of Concord rejects the idea of gross Capernaitish eating; but it at the same time denies that it is mere figurative eating, eating by faith alone, and between literal and figurative eating of a real body of flesh and blood, there is no third or intermediate mode of eating conceivable. The term "*spiritual*" is used by the Form of Concord; but applied to eating and drinking material flesh and blood, it must signify figurative eating, or it signifies nothing intelligible at all.

But are there no arguments in favor of the doctrine of the real presence?

There are several expressions, in the portion of Scripture discussing this subject, which have been supposed to favor Luther's interpretation. At first view, and especially in our vulgar version, they may seem to possess the appearance of force; yet, on close examination, this will disappear, especially before the mass of contrary evidence, pervading the whole passage.

1. 1 Cor. xi. 27. "Wherefore whosoever shall eat this bread and drink this cup (wine) of the Lord, unworthily, shall be guilty of the body and blood of the Lord," ἔνοχος ἔσται τȣ σώματος και τοῦ ἀιματος του Κυριȣ: "shall be guilty of the body and blood of the Lord;" that is, "shall commit sin in regard to the body and blood of the Lord," viz., by treating the solemnly appointed commemoration of them with levity or irreverence. It has been said, "How could we be guilty of the body of Christ, if it were not present?" We answer: To be guilty of the body, means in the original, to be guilty or commit sin in reference to the body; that is, to make the body of Christ the occasion of commit-

ting sin. And must not all admit, that we can and often do commit sin in regard to absent persons and things? May we not sin, or be guilty in regard to an absent friend, by slandering or even thinking ill of him, just as well as when he is present? Do we not insult the majesty of an absent king, when we treat with indignity a monument or other memorial which has been established in honor of him? And the unworthy communicant is specifically said to have been guilty in reference to the *body* of Christ, because it was his body, which was specially represented by the symbols which he treats irreverently in the Lord's Supper. He is guilty of treating with irreverence, that sacred institution which the Saviour appointed under the most affecting circumstance, to commemorate the breaking of his body and shedding of his blood upon the cross, and thus commits sin in regard to the body and blood of the Lord. Thus, James ii. 10, the phrase, "*guilty of,*" ἐνοχος, is used in the same general acceptation: Whosoever shall keep the whole law, and yet shall offend in one point, is guilty of all (γεγονε παντων (νομων) ἐνοχος), commits sin in regard to all other points of the law.

The reason of their guilt is further described by Paul thus, "*not discerning the Lord's body,*" that is, not distinguishing between ordinary bread and these consecrated symbols of the Lord's body and blood. *Ernesti* justly remarks,[1] that this use of the term employed by the Apostle, "discerning," (διακρινων,) originated from the Jewish habit of distinguishing clean from unclean meats, according to the law of Moses. Those were said not to discern or distinguish the meats, who ate indiscriminately both clean and unclean or forbidden meats. See Ezek. xliv. 23. This remark is the more important, as the Apostle Paul had, in the previous context (x. 18 and 27) spoken of things offered in sacrifice both by the Jews and Gentiles.

2. The other passage, is 1 Cor. x. 16. The cup of blessing which we bless, is it not the communion of the blood of Christ? The bread which we break, is it not the communion of the body of Christ? "ουχι (το ποτήριον) κοινωνία τȣ ἄιματος τȣ Χριςȣ ἐστι;—("τον αρτον) ουχι κοινωνία τȣ σώματος τȣ Χριςȣ εστιν;"

(1) Opusc. theol. p. 136.

Κοινωνια. The term κοινωνια, *communion*, has several significations in the N. T. 1, communication or bestowment of a benefit, beneficence. See Rom. xv. 26. 2 Cor. ix. 13.

2, conjunction, society, spiritual communion. Acts ii. 42. And they continued steadfastly in the Apostles' doctrine and *fellowship*, (κοινωνια.) 1 Cor. i. 9. God is faithful by whom ye were called to the *fellowship*, (κοινωνια,) of his Son Jesus Christ our Lord.

2 Cor. vi. 14. What *communion*, (κοινωνια,) community of interest, or adaptation for close union, hath light, the children of light, christians, with darkness, the children of darkness, "unbelievers."

2 Cor. xiii. 13. The grace of the Lord Jesus Christ and the love of God, and the *communion*, (κοινωνια,) *of the Holy Ghost*, be with you all.

Gal. ii. 9. And when James, Cephas and John, who seemed to be pillars, perceived the grace that was given me, they gave to me and Barnabas the right hand of *fellowship*, (κοινωνια.)

Ephes. iii. 9. And to make all men see what is the fellowship (κοινωνια) which hath been hid in God.

Philipp. i. 5. I thank my God—for your fellowship (κοινωνια) in the Gospel from the first day until now.

——ii. 1. If there be—any fellowship (κοινωνια) of the Spirit,—fulfil ye my joy, &c.

——iii. 10. That I may know the power of his resurrection and the fellowship (κοινωνια) of his sufferings.

Phil. v. 6. That the communication (κοινωνια) of thy faith may become effectual..

1 John i. 3, 6, 7. That ye also may have *fellowship* (κοινωνια) with us, &c.

As to the Lutheran and Romish interpretation, which supposes this passage to teach the actual presence of the body and blood of Christ, it is liable to all the objections above enumerated in regard to that doctrine. But a moral signification, as is evident from the passages just quoted, is far more agreeable to the usus loquendi, and is perfectly easy and natural. The cup of the blessing—is it not the communion, does it not bring us *spiritually* into communion with the body of Christ, &c. In the same sense it is said of the Jews in v. 18: "are not they who eat of the sacrifices, partakers of the altar? ουχι—κοινωνοι του θυσιαστηριυ ειϛι, in communion with the altar? here we find the very same word, κοινωνοι, employed, and yet, who would infer, that the Jews ate the God whom they worshipped, or the altar on which they sacrificed, or any thing more than the outward offerings? In like manner, in the next verse, 20, "The things which the Gentiles sacrifice, they sacrifice to devils or demons,—and I would not that ye should have fellowship, communion, κοινωνους των δαιμονιων γινεϛθαι, with devils. Who would suppose, that the Gentiles, in their sacrifices, had communion with the bodies of the dead heroes and demigods whom they worshipped? Yet if the word, κοινωνια (and κοινωνȣϛ,) in the one case, means the actual participation of the flesh and blood of the being commemorated, what reason can be assigned for its having so different a signification in the other? The language in both cases is substantially the same, yea, the identical word, only in one case used substantively, and with the other adjectively. If, then, the words mean, that the sacramental communicant receives the flesh and blood of Christ, in addition to the outward elements, they also teach, that the partakers at heathen altars, likewise eat the flesh and drink the blood of those heroes and demigods to whom they offer sacrifice.

In addition to the scriptural passages in favor of the presence of the body of the Saviour in the Lord's Supper, there is a theological argument or theory, which, though in part rejected by Luther himself, was adopted by some of his followers, and about a quarter of a century after his death, was introduced in its full development into the Form of Concord, which became the standard of Lutheran orthodoxy in some parts of Germany. Luther's view of the personal union of the two natures in Christ he thus judiciously expresses: If it should be objected on the ground of reason, "That the Godhead cannot suffer nor die; you must answer: That is true; nevertheless, as the divinity and humanity in Christ constitute one person, therefore the Scriptures, on account of this personal unity, also attribute every thing to the Deity, which occurred to the humanity, and vice versa. This is, moreover, accordant with truth; for you must affirm that the person (Christ,) suffers and dies. Now the person is the true God, therefore it is proper to say, the Son of God suffers. For although one part (if I may so speak) namely, the Godhead does not suffer; still the person which is God, suffers in its other part, that is in its humanity (denn obwohl das eine Stueck (dasz ich so rede) als die Gottheit nicht leidet; so leidet dennoch die Person, welche Gott ist, am andern Stuecke, als an der Menschheit.) Thus we say, The king's son has a sore, and yet it is only his leg that is affected: Solomon is wise, and yet it is only his soul which possesses wisdom: Absalom is beautiful, and yet it was only his body that is referred to: Peter is gray, and yet it is only his head of which this is affirmed. For as soul and body constitute but one person, every thing which happens either to the body or the soul, yea even to the smallest member of the body, is justly and properly attributed to the whole person. This mode of expression is not peculiar to the Scriptures, but prevails throughout the world, and is also correct. Thus the Son of God was in truth crucified for us, that is, the person which is God; for this person, I say, was crucified according to its humanity." (Luth. Works, Jena edit. vol. 3, p. 457.) Yet Luther, also, sometimes employed language inconsistent with the statements which he here makes. The theory above referred to, was claimed by its advocates as a legitimate sequence of the hypostatic union of the two natures of Christ, and is known as the *Communicatio Idiomatum,* or supposed reciprocal communication of attributes between the two natures of the Saviour, one result of which is to be, that his body now possesses *ubiquity;* and, therefore, can not only be present simultaneously wherever the Holy Supper is administered, but actually is present every where else in the universe. In support of this opinion several Scripture passages are alleged:

Coloss. ii. 9. For in him dwelleth the fullness of the Godhead, *bodily,*" σωματικῶς. This passage, we think, naturally signifies, in Christ the real, not imaginary, the full divinity and not an inferior deity dwells; that is, with his human nature the truly divine nature is really, not figuratively, or typically, but actually united σωματικῶς personally, that is, into one person. This signification of the term σῶμα, as signifying person, is found both in the N. T. and in classic Greek. James iii. 6. So is the tongue among our members that it defileth the whole body, i. e. person (ὅλον τὸ σῶμα,) for certainly the fact, that "the tongue is a world of iniquity," does not consist in its polluting the literal body, but the person, the character of the individual. Thus also Xenophon uses σώματα ἐλεύθερα, for freemen, free persons. Lycurgus, and Aeschynes employ σῶμα in the same sense, to signify a person. The same usage meets us in the Latin language: Longeque *ante* omnia *corpora* Nisus emicat. Æneid v. l. 318, where the reference is to the person in general. And even in our own tongue, the term body has the same meaning, in such phrases as "some body," "no body," &c., for some person, no person, &c.

John iii. 34. "For God giveth not the Spirit by measure unto him," (but ἀμέτρως). This may signify, that the inspiration of the Holy Spirit did not rest on the Saviour, only at particular times and in a limited degree, as it did on the prophets of the Old Testament; but at all times and in an unlimited degree. Or the idea may be, that the actual or entire divinity dwelt in him, i. e. was personally united with him. But there is certainly no intimation in it of the transfer of the divine attributes to the humanity of Christ.

Matth. xxviii. 18. "All power (πᾶσα ἐξουσία all *authority*, not πᾶσα δύναμις) is given unto me in heaven and on earth." This certainly does not signify power, omnipotence; but all or full *authority* to command and direct all things on earth to the accomplishment of the purposes of his mediatorial reign.

In this sense the word (ἐξουσία), translated *power* in the passage under consideration, is often employed in the New Testament. Thus, Matth. xxi. 23, the chief priests and elders, came to him, when he was teaching, and said: "By what *authority* (ἐξουσία) doest thou these things?" And (vii. 29,) the people were astonished at his doctrine, "For he taught them as one having *authority* (ἐξουσία), and not as the scribes." In the same general sense, as signifying authority, liberty, &c., having no reference to omnipotence or physical power, this word is employed in many other passages, so that the declaration of the Saviour: "All power or authority is given to me," has no necessary reference to physical power or omnipotence. See Matth. ix. 6. Mark ii. 10. Luke v. 24. 1 Cor. ix. 4, 18. 2 Thess. iii. 9. In perfect accordance with this import, is the classic usage of the word ἐξουσία, as signifying "licentia, potestas, auctoritas, jus sive facultas *moralis;* at δύναμις vis activa, seu facultas *naturalis,*" licence, power, authority, a moral right;

whilst δυναμις signifies a physical or natural faculty or power.

To this doctrine of the ubiquity of the body of Christ, numerous and formidable objections present themselves.

1. The idea that the properties of one substance can become the properties of a different substance, is a philosophical absurdity.

2. It is impossible, in the nature of things, that the infinite properties of God, the uncreated one, should be communicated to any creature. The difference between the creature and the Creator is an infinite and unchangeable one. Yet, if the human nature of Christ acquired possession of divine attributes, it must itself be divine.

3. Wherever any one divine attribute is found, there the others must also be, and that is God. If then the body of Christ, or his humanity in general, possesses one divine attribute, it must possess them all and must be God. Yes the finite has become infinite, the creature has become the Creator, and a feeble mortal like unto us in all things, sin only excepted, has become the immortal God.

A distinction has been made between mediate and immediate communication, and it has been affirmed the attributes of Deity have been communicated to the man Jesus only mediately. But mediate communication in reference to this subject is no communication at all, and can only signify, that the divine nature of Christ is at all times ready to exert his divine attributes for the accomplishment of the purposes of the associated humanity, and this no one denies, but this cannot with propriety of language be styled communication of attributes.

4. If the hypostatic union in Christ implies a communication of attributes, it must be reciprocal; and whilst the humanity of Christ is clothed in the attributes of divinity, his divinity must also have assumed the attributes of humanity: have become human; which the opponents are unwilling to admit.

5. If this hypostatic union is attended by a transfer of attributes, it necessarily involves a confusion of natures, which error was condemned by the ancient church in the Eutychians. And if it was such as to preserve the attributes of each nature distinct, then there can be no real transfer of attributes.

6. The doctrine of the ubiquity of Christ's body instead of conferring more importance on the Eucharist, actually robs it of all special interest, and gives no more to the sacrament than to every other object and place. We may upon this theory, as well say that Christ's body is in, with or under, every apple and pear, peach and cake, as in the consecrated bread.

7. Nay this doctrine is not entirely exempt from liability to the charge of favoring *pantheism*. If Christ's *body* is omnipresent, we are in him and he in us, whether believers or unbelievers we are one: especially as all bodies must have extension, and occupy space, and exclude other bodies. The idea also that Christ's *body* nourishes our *souls* has a similar tendency, by leading to the supposition that soul and body are ultimately identical, or of the same substance.

8. If the glorified body of Christ is really in, with, or under the bread, it will be very proper to direct our worship towards the bread, and thus adore the present God-man who is somehow connected with it. For we know that his divine nature is there, as it is omnipresent: and therefore we would have as much reason to worship towards the bread as if he were personally and visibly to appear in connexion with it.

9. It will be admitted that the union of the two natures in Christ, was just as real and intimate during his life on earth as it ever will be; (for it is decided by the Form of Concord, to have commenced at the moment of his conception by the Virgin Mary.) Now as this union produced not even the shadow of a *communicatio idiomatum* (transfer or communication of attributes) on earth, it is not probable that it will hereafter. It certainly proves, that such communication is not the natural result of the hypostatic union in Christ, and therefore it cannot be true, unless the Scriptures expressly teach that this union will produce very different results in eternity from those which attend it in this world, which is not contended.

Finally, the discourse of our Lord to his disciples at Capernaum, recorded in John vi. 25–55, has sometimes, though contrary to the example of Luther and the other principal reformers, been supposed to refer to the holy supper, and to teach the literal manducation of the Saviour's body and the drinking of his blood. It is true our Saviour here employs the language, "I am the bread of life," as he elsewhere does the expression, "I am the vine," and "I am the light of the world," &c. John viii. 12. Again, the Saviour also says, "Except ye eat the flesh of the Son of man, and drink his blood, ye have no life in you," &c. v. 54. That these and similar expressions in this discourse, can have no reference to the Lord's supper, is evident from the fact, that no such ordinance as the eucharist then existed, or had been heard of. This discourse, according to the most probable chronological arrangement of the evangelical narrative, was delivered about a year before the Saviour instituted it, and before his disciples could possibly have had the least idea of such intended memorial. Of course they could not understand these words, as referring to an ordinance of which they had never heard, and to the future institution of which there was not a single allusion in the discourse itself.

Again, that the Saviour in this entire discourse had reference to his being the food of believers, is abundantly evident from the phraseology employed. 1) In v. 35, to the words, "I am the bread of life," he immediately adds by way of explanation, "he that *cometh* to me, shall never hunger, he that *believeth* on me shall never thirst," showing that it is by *faith*, that he becomes the bread of life to us. 2) v. 40. "He that *believeth* on the Son, hath everlasting life," showing the necessity of *faith* to the enjoyment of this spiritual food. Also, 3) v. 47. "Verily, verily, I say unto you, he that *believeth* on me hath everlasting life—I am that *bread* of life." 4) v. 51. The bread which I will give is my flesh, which I will give for the life of the world," i. e. which flesh I will give, not *to* believers to be eaten; but *for* them on the cross; and not for *believers only*, who receive the holy supper, but for the "*world*," many who reject my atonement and never celebrate the supper, which I shall institute in commemoration of my death. If sacramental eating were intended, it must have been limited to his professed followers, who celebrate the ordinance; and could not have been extended to the world at large who neglect it. 5) v. 56. "He that eateth my flesh and drinketh my blood, dwelleth in me and I in him." If this passage teaches a *physical* eating and indwelling of the Saviour's body in the communicant, it also affirms that the communicant's body dwells in the body of the Saviour, which is absurd. 6) v. 63. "It is the Spirit that quickeneth, the flesh profiteth nothing: the words that I speak unto you they are spirit and they are life." Here the Saviour seems, in the closing words of this discourse, expressly to teach that the *literal* eating of his flesh would profit them nothing; that it is the Spirit that quickeneth, and that his words are spirit, are to be *spiritually* and not literally understood. This interpretation is moreover confirmed by the succeeding remark of Christ: 7) v. 64. "But there are some of you that *believe* not," some who have no faith, and therefore cannot thus spiritually feed on my flesh and blood. From all these considerations, we cannot but coincide with the judgment of Luther and the most distinguished divines of ancient and modern days, as expressed by the learned Lutheran theologian Gerhard: "*The passage, John* vi. 53, *does not treat of sacramental but of spiritual eating the body and drinking the blood of Christ, which is essential to salvation for all.*" [1]

§ 4. THE SECOND TROPICAL INTERPRETATION (BY CALVIN.)

The *third* interpretation of these words is that of *Calvin*, which though generally abandoned by his followers in Europe and America, is deserving of a passing notice. That distinguished Reformer, animated by a noble desire to prevent a schism in the Protestant church of Europe, though he could not adopt the view of Luther on this subject, laboured hard to come as near it as possible, without making himselt liable to the grosser objections which lie against the Lutheran dogma. He supposed the words of the institution to teach, not that the body and blood of Christ are present at the celebration of the eucharist; but that they remain in heaven, and from there a supernatural influence emanates from the glorified body of Christ, by which the soul of the believer is animated and strengthened in a mysterious manner.

This interpretation is indeed free from the charge of conflicting with the testimony of the senses; but it seems so entirely different from either the literal or the figurative

(1) Dictum John vi. 53, non de sacramentali sed spirituali corporis et sanguinis Christi manducatione et bibitione tractat, quæ omnibus ad salutem necessaria est. Loci Theol. de Sacra Cœna.

import of the Saviour's words, as to bear evident marks of having grown out of extraneous theological considerations.

Calvin's own language on this subject is: "I therefore maintain, that in the *mystery* of the supper, by the emblems of bread and wine, Christ is *really exhibited* to us; that is, his body and blood, in which he yielded full obedience, in order to work out a righteousness for us; by which, in the first place, we may, as it were, become united with him into one body; and secondly, being made partakers of the *substance* of himself, also be strengthened by the reception of every blessing."[1] The entire opinion of Calvin is thus stated by Dr. Bretschneider, a very distinguished late writer of Germany: "Calvin's spiritual reception of the body and blood of Christ, is indeed a real, but not an oral one, and consists in this: that in the moment in which we partake of the bread and wine, if our hearts are by faith elevated to him, a *supernatural* influence emanates from the substance of the glorified body of Christ, (which is in heaven and remains there,) by which the soul of the believer is animated and strengthened in a *mysterious* manner. But the unbeliever receives nothing more than bread and wine."[2]

It may, perhaps, be regarded as a striking coincidence, that the views of the two most illustrious reformers on this subject, have been almost universally abandoned by their followers; even whilst they adhere to nearly all the other features of their doctrinal system. Yea, the view of Calvin, though the subject of much less controversy, has been more universally rejected by those who bear his name, than has that of Luther by his followers.

§ 5. The true, Historical and Pauline interpretation of the words of the Institution.

We come now, in the last place, to attempt an unbiassed, impartial examination of the words of the institution, ac-

---

(1) Dico igitur in coenæ *mysterio* per symbola panis et vini Christum *vere nobis exhiberi*, adeoque corpus et sanguinem ejus, in quibus omnem obedientiam pro comparanda nobis justitia adimplevit; quo scilicet primum in unum corpus cum ipso coalescamus; deinde participes *substantiæ* ejus facti in bonorum omnium communicatione virtutem quoque sentiamus. Institut. Lib. IV. Cap. XVII. II.

(2) Dr. Bretschneider's Systematische Entwickelung aller in der Dogmatik vorkommender Begriffe. p. 721, ed. 3, 1826.

cording to the fair principles of historical interpretation, as laid down in our introductory observations.

Was there any thing peculiar in the occasion and the circumstances, attending the utterance of these words, calculated to illustrate their meaning?

The Saviour and his disciples had just celebrated the Passover, an institution appointed of God to commemorate an important event of the Old Testament history, at which it was not unusual to use language similar to that of our Saviour. At its institution, though it was expressly appointed to *commemorate* the passing of the angel of the Lord over the Israelites in Egypt, whilst he destroyed the first born of the Egyptians; yet, Moses uses language similar to that of the Saviour: "Ye shall eat it in haste, for it *is* the Lord's passing over," i. e. it *signifies* the angel of the Lord's passing over the house of the Israelites, &c. Exod. xii. 26, 27. No one imagines these words to mean: "The lamb that was slain at the passover, was the passing over of the Lord's angel." All admit that "*is*" here is equivalent to *signifies*.

This ordinance, whilst it commemorated the divine favor to the Israelites in Egypt, also, as Paul tells us, was typical of the Saviour himself.

Now, it was at the close of this mnemonic or commemorative and symbolic paschal supper, where symbolic ideas prevailed, and figurative language is usual among the Jews,[1] even to this day, that the Saviour uttered the words under consideration.

1. After the paschal supper, "Jesus took *bread*." It was *natural* bread, not miraculously furnished. He took the bread, which happened to be prepared for the passover, and which, according to Jewish law, must be unleavened bread. Yet, it is equally certain, from the New Testament, as the primitive christians received the Lord's supper every week, and often more frequently, that on some occasions, they used leavened bread, as no other was at hand.

2. Jesus "offered a prayer." Mark, and perhaps Matthew, use the term ἐυλογήσας, which signifies "to bless," or pronounce a *blessing*. But neither of them says, that he

(1) See Levi's Forms of Prayer for Passover and Pentecost, among the Spanish and Portuguese Jews, p. 20.

blessed "*it*," (τȣτο,) as our English version has it. Very good manuscripts read εὐχαριστήσας "having given thanks," in Matthew. Luke and Paul both say, "he gave thanks," ευχαριστησας. There is not a syllable about his effecting any *change* in the bread, as Romanists pretend, nor of his making those elements the conductors or means of imparting his body to us. In short, according to the original, he did not specifically bless the bread or wine, nor do anything at all to them. He offered thanks, as it was also customary to do at the beginning of the paschal supper, and as is in itself always appropriate, and invoked the blessing of his heavenly Father upon the whole ceremony, of course, also including the elements employed.

3. No change had been effected in the bread. It was still natural bread, as the Saviour broke it; which he would not have done, if his prayer had transubstantiated it into his own body, or in any way made it the vehicle of his material body. It was still natural bread, because the disciples exhibited no evidence of having the least idea, that they received any thing but bread.

4. "He gave it to them and said, *Take, eat, this is my body*," λάβετε φάγετε τοῦτο ἐστι τὸ σῶμα μȣ.

That the literal interpretation of these words by the Romanists, as well as several others, which, though professedly literal, are really figurative, and inconsistent with the context, cannot be sustained, we have endeavored to show in a former part of this discussion. What, then, is their true interpretation? Let us, if possible, derive our guide for the true meaning of these words, from the declarations of the Saviour himself, and of his apostles.

1. Let us inquire, Does the *breaking* of the bread throw any light upon our investigation?

It must have been done by the Saviour, so far as we can judge, from one of two reasons: either because the cake, or loaf of bread, was too large to be conveniently handed around, or because the Lord intended it to possess some significance, either symbolic or other, connected with the design of the whole institution. It seems not to have been the former, because the bread was then, as is still customary among the Arabians, baked in cakes of moderate thickness, easily baked through, and convenient for breaking. See 'Leidensgeschichte Jesu,' p. 45. Stuttgard, 1809. But that he had another and important design in breaking the bread or cake, is evident from the fact, that the Saviour expressly states, that this *broken* bread is, or represents his "*body broken,*" that is, represents the *breaking* of his body, his crucifixion, or death upon the cross. Here then we have the infallible declaration of the Lord himself, that the *broken* bread in the eucharist, represents the breaking or crucifixion of his body. To represent this fact, the breaking of the bread was very appropriate; but to designate the future *presence* of his glorified body, it would have no significance or appropriateness at all, The *broken* bread must be a representative of the *dead*, the *crucified* body, and cannot in any way, be designed to indicate the presence of the living body, either glorified or not. The accuracy of this interpretation is confirmed by the fact of the Saviour's also mentioning that the wine signified not only his blood, which would have been sufficient, if the mere presence of the Lord was to be indicated; but his blood "*shed,*" the *shedding* of his blood on the cross. Should it be said, if the breaking of the bread was significant, then also something should have been done to the wine, to indicate its being shed; we reply: This was not necessary. The fact that his body was broken, already indicates that his blood was shed. Besides, the representation of the blood, as separated from the body, also implies the same fact.

2. This is, or represents *my body* "*given,*" says Luke, and "*broken,*" says Paul, "for you." That by these terms, "given" and "broken" the crucifixion of the Lord is indicated, cannot be denied, and we believe is not. But if the Lord himself teaches us, that to represent his death upon the cross, is *the* object of the Holy Supper; then we are certain of being correct in supposing and teaching this truth; and if others suppose this ordinance was instituted for a *double* purpose, it devolves on them to exhibit proof of the *other*, in the same way as this is established, by declarations of Christ or his apostles. Here the *onus probandi* most justly lies on them, and if they fail to prove a *second* object, then this remains the only one, namely, to represent, in all coming time, that all-important, amazing fact, which "angels desire to look into," the death of the Son of God upon the cross, an event which happened about eighteen hundred years ago. As the Holy Supper was certainly instituted to

commemorate this eternally important occurrence, an event sufficiently momentous to justify the institution of a standing rite for its commemoration, it is not probable *a priori*, that another very different object (the presence of the living, glorified Lord) would be joined to it; and as we find no clear indication of the fact in Scripture, we are compelled to doubt it.

If the Saviour's object had been to represent the *presence* of his body in the eucharist, the bread entire would have been more suitable; and if, in that event, he had even broken the paschal cake or bread merely incidentally, there would have been no object in his stating the fact. But he himself informs us, it signifies his body "*broken*," the breaking of his body, his crucifixion, his death upon the cross. The same remarks are equally applicable to the language of the Saviour in reference to the wine. "Take and drink, this is my blood," and as Paul and Luke says, "this cup is the New Covenant in my blood, '*which is shed*' for you—for many, for the remission of sins." The wine, therefore, most undoubtedly commemorates the *shedding* of the Saviour's blood on the cross.

3. "*Do* this *in remembrance of me*," says the Saviour, according to Luke and Paul. Luke has τȣτο ποιεῖτε εις τὴν ἐμὴν ἀνάμνησιν, do this in *remembrance* or in commemoration of me; Paul has the same words, only adding, οσάκις ἂν πίνητε, *Do this, as often as ye drink it,* in *remembrance* or commemoration of me. Now, the very fact that we are called on to do any thing in remembrance of any person or event, implies two things. *First,* it presupposes the priority or antecedence of the event; it implies that the event is *past.* Even when we commemorate any actions of a living person, those actions must be past. The very import of the word remember, necessarily implies that the thing to be remembered, is a something past. *Again,* the term "remembrance" implies the *absence* of the person or thing to be remembered. When our friend is with us, we do not need any rite or ceremony to remind us of the fact. Nor can we, in propriety of language, be said to "*remember*" a *present* object or friend. The very necessity of such a rite, if our friend were with us, would convey a reflection on our attachment to him. It is, when about to separate, that friends bestow on each other mementoes; or agree on the stated

performance of some act to keep alive the remembrance of each other during their separation. Now, both these implications of the Saviour's words, "Do this in remembrance of me," accord perfectly with the object of the eucharist as explained by himself. At the celebration of this standing rite of the church, in commemoration of the breaking or crucifixion of his body, the fact would be past, and his body would be absent. The glorious fact of his atoning death on the cross, would, from century to century, be receding farther and farther into the past, and as objects are in danger of being forgotten in proportion as they recede farther from us, nothing could be more appropriate than the institution of an ordinance, to keep alive in the forgetful memory of his disciples, that fundamental fact in the history of redemption, which is the ground of every believer's hope, and on which the salvation of a world is suspended.

But, if the design of the eucharist is a two-fold one; if, in addition to the commemoration of the crucifixion of the Son of God, that ordinance was, as some suppose, also appointed for the purpose of commemorating the Saviour's presence with us, and the communication of his body to the communicant, the language, "*in remembrance of me,*" appears not only strange, but inappropriate. It would have been more natural for him to say: "As often as ye eat this bread, and drink of this cup, ye do celebrate my *return* to your midst."

The Pauline Interpretation of the Saviour's Words.

Such are the intimations concerning the design of this solemn ordinance, furnished by the words of the Saviour himself. If we had no other, they would incontestibly establish the fact, that it is a *mnemonic* rite, instituted to *commemorate* the death of Christ on the cross. But we have still another inspired narrative of this institution, from the distinguished Apostle of the Gentiles, twenty-four years after the establishment of this ordinance, and the ascension of the Saviour to heaven. 1 Cor. xi. 23–30. And what did Paul regard as the design of this holy feast of love?

1) He also declares the bread to stand related to the *broken* body, to signify the *breaking* of Christ's body, as

above intimated. "The Lord Jesus, the same night in which he was betrayed, took bread, and when he had given thanks, he *brake* it and said, Take, eat, this is my body which is (or is to be) *broken for you.*"

2) He expressly pronounces the design of this rite to be *mnemonic*, "this do in *remembrance* of me," the force of which words we have above illustrated, as equivalent to "Do this in order to keep alive the recollection of a *past* event and of an *absent* person."

3) But he adds two other importaut indications, which are not contained in the gospels. "For as often as ye eat this bread and drink this cup (the wine in it,) τὸν θάνατον του κυρίȣ καταγγέλλετε "ye do show forth, or publish, *the death* of the Lord." Here then we have the plain, literal declaration of the inspired Paul, as clear as language can make it, that the result of the Holy Supper is to commemorate, not the Lord's presence, nor his bestowing his body and blood on the communicants, but to *show forth the Lord's death,* that amazing display of divine love on the cross, which is the foundation fact, the central doctrine of Christianity, and the recollection and full appreciation of which, is essential to the Christian character. This declaration of the Apostle is of incalculable value. The greater portion of the language of Christ is or may be figurative, and, therefore, admits of a diversity of interpretations, and it may remain questionable which is their true sense. But this language of Paul is literal, nothing figurative about it, and, therefore, in its import all agree. All admit that he designs to say, as often as ye celebrate this Holy Supper, ye commemorate, perpetuate the memory of, revive your recollection of the death of Jesus on the cross.

It is certain, then, that this was the object of the Saviour in this sacred institution. It is certain, also, that, in the view of Paul, this was its great and principal design, if not its only one. And it is probable, that he regarded it as the only one, since he mentions no other. The expressions from which some would deduce another design, "are not the bread and wine *the communion* of the body and blood of Christ," have been explained above, we think, satisfactorily. They teach that the bread and wine bring us into solemn, spiritual, mental communion, or recollection of, and reflection on the

Saviour's body and blood, broken and shed for us on the cross.

4) But this illustrious apostle adds another expression calculated to reflect light on this subject. He adds, "Ye do show forth the Lord's death," ἄχρις οὗ ἔλθῃ, "*until he come.*" This solemn declaration clearly teaches three facts; *first*, that the Lord is himself absent at the celebration of the supper, as well as generally after his ascension; and *secondly*, that he will continue absent personally, as long as the supper is to be commemorated; and *thirdly*, when he comes, his personal presence will supercede the necessity of any further observance of a commemorative ordinance.

About twenty-four years had elapsed since Jesus had ascended to heaven. In the mean time he had been seen by no one of all his friends or enemies on earth. Whether he had appeared unto Paul, fourteen years before this time, when wrapped in holy vision, he was elevated to the third heavens, Paul does not state: yet it is highly probable. Once, he had certainly seen him, during his journey to Damascus. But then he appeared to him in the clouds of heaven, evidently from another world. At other times he received special communications from him, but it is not certain that he again appeared to him personally. All the experience of the Apostle therefore, had connected the present residence or local existence and manifestation of the Saviour with another world, and taught him that Christ was absent.

These words of Paul also imply, that so long as it is obligatory on Christians to celebrate this holy feast, the Saviour will continue absent; for they are commanded to repeat its celebration often, *until* he comes; which involves the consequence, that when he does come, this celebration shall cease. And finally, as this celebration, or commemoration of the Saviour's death, is to cease on his personal return to earth, it seems a natural supposition, that it was appointed to preserve in constant memory something, which in his absence we would be prone to forget; and Paul tells us, this was the grand and cardinal fact in his mediatorial career, his vicarious death upon the cross for the sins of the world.

Since it is certain that the commemoration of the Lord's death is the object of the sacramental institution, the question arises, whether there is any reason to suppose, that the Lord had a double object in view. The only arguments in support of such a supposition are found in the supposed necessity of a literal interpretation of the phrase τουτο ἐστι το σωμα μου, "this is my body," and the phrase of Paul, 1 Cor. x. 16; ουχί (το ποτηριον) κοινωνία τȣ σωματος τȣ Χριστου ἐστι; "is it not (the cup) the communion of the blood of Christ?" &c., και τον ἄρτον, ὀυχι κοινωνια του σώματος τοῦ Χριστου ἐστι; and "the bread, is it not the communion of the body of Christ?" But as we have already proved, that the literal interpretation of the Romanists is utterly untenable; and that the doctrine of the real presence of the body and blood of Christ "*in, with, or under*" the elements, is not a literal one, but figurative and unnatural, and at the same time, liable to many of the objections, on account of which all Protestants repudiate the Romish literal interpretation, we need not repeat them. And having already presented our view of the import of the term κοινωνια "communion," in the Epistle to the Corinthians, the only thing which remains, in order to vindicate the Pauline interpretation, which we adopt as our own, namely, the *mnemonic* import of the rite, its appointment to perpetuate the memory of the Lord's death or crucifixion, is to show that this figurative or tropical interpretation of the phrase τουτο ἐστι το σωμα μου, "this is my body," is perfectly sustained by the *usus loquendi* of the New Testament.

a) Even those who receive the doctrine of the real presence, concede that these words do admit of the figurative meaning for which we contend. The learned and pious Dr. Storr remarks: "The words of our Lord, 'This is my body,' &c., may indeed be explained figuratively without violence to the *usus loquendi* of the New Testament. The figure assumed would not be an uncommon one. Nor can it be said that the nature of the case altogether forbids the supposition of the language being figurative. For it cannot be denied that some of the language used in the institution of the Holy Supper is figurative, (tropical.")[1] Nor is this admission made without cause. The reasons sustaining this opinion are numerous and most satisfactory.

b) The Hebrew language does not contain a word to express the idea, *signify*, and therefore the Hebrews

---

(1) Storr's Biblical Theology, § 114, Ill. 6; p. 537 of 2d ed. of the translation.

always conveyed that idea by other terms, usually by the substantive verb, הָיָה, to be. Or perhaps, more frequently the phrase is elliptical, and the verb entirely wanting, and to be supplied from the context. But the inspired evangelists have given us the verb ἔστι, "is"; and it is the *usus loquendi* of the New Testament, in regard to this term, that we are to investigate.

c) That this method of using the term "*is*" for "signifies," is a very common one among different nations, is well known, and the idiom of the Old and New Testament is, in this respect, the same. Thus, it was customary for the Jews, when interrogated by their children concerning the import of the Passover, to reply: "This *is* the body of the Lamb which our fathers ate in Egypt," that is, it *signifies* the lamb, &c. The Psalmist says, (Ps. xviii. 2:) The Lord *is* my rock and my fortress—*is* my buckler—*is* the horn of my salvation—*is* my high tower. Ps. xxiii. 1. The Lord *is* my shepherd, &c. &c.

But the Scriptures abound in cases of the very same figure, which we are now considering. Gen. xl. 12. Joseph says, "the three branches *are* three days, i. e. *signify* three days. xli. 26. The seven good kine *are* seven years. Danl. vii. 24. "The ten horns out of this kingdom *are* ten kings that shall rise." v. 17. "These great beasts which are four, *are* four kings." viii. 21. "And the rough goat *is* the king of Greece." In all the above cases, though the language is elliptical, the substantive verb is understood, which is expressed in our English Bible. Paul says, (1 Cor. x. 4,) "That rock (that followed the Israelites in the wilderness) *was* (ἦν) Christ." Gal. iv. 24. "For these (Sarah and Hagar) *are* (εἰσιν) the two covenants," i. e. signify them. Luke xii. 1. "Beware of the leaven of the Pharisees ἥτις ἐστιν which *is* (signifies) hypocrisy." Heb. vii. 2. "King of Salem, ὅ ἐστι, that *is* (signifies) king of peace." Mark iv. 15. And these *are* they by the wayside—and on stony ground,—among thorns, &c., that is, these *represent* or signify them. 2 Peter ii. 17. These (the false prophets) *are,* that is, *signify,* wells without water.

But, did the Saviour himself employ such figurative language, in reference to himself, on any other occasion than at the sacramental supper? *He doubtless did on various occasions.* John v. 11, 14. I am the good *shepherd.* vi. 35, 41, 48, 51. I *am* the *bread* of life, ἐγώ εἰμι ὁ ἄρτος. viii. 12. I *am* the *light* of the world, ἐγώ εἰμι το φῶς του κοσμου. x. 7, 9. I am (ἐγω εἰμι) the *door* of the sheep—"I am the door." xiv. 6. I am the *way,* the truth and the life. xv. 1, 2. I am the vine, ye are the branches. I am the resurrection and the life—I am the Alpha and Omega, the beginning and the end. Here, then, we perceive that the Saviour was in the habit of speaking of himself in this tropical manner, calling himself bread, a shepherd, a door. That he should also compare his body to bread and his blood to wine, is, therefore, perfectly accordant with his habits; and the figurative use of the phrase "this is," τουτο ἐστι, is perfectly accordant with the usus loquendi, and therefore we are at perfect liberty, according to the sound principles of interpretation, to give to these words, "*this is my body,*" *this is my blood,*" the meaning, *signifies* my body, *signifies* my blood, as required by the design of the ordinance, as taught by Paul and by the Saviour himself, namely, to show forth *the Lord's death until he come.*

In view of all these facts, it seems evident that the words of the sacramental institution as uttered by the Saviour, recorded by the evangelists, and explained by Paul, are to be understood, so far as the mode of the Saviour's presence is concerned, as follows:

"And as they were eating, (the paschal supper,) Jesus took bread, (the unleavened bread or cake which had been prepared for the passover,) and having given thanks and pronounced a blessing, he gave the pieces of bread to his disciples, and said, Take, eat, this (bread, which is and remains bread and) signifies my (natural, not glorified) body, which is (to be) broken for you, (on the cross, crucified,) do this in (order to cherish the) remembrance of me. Likewise, he took the cup, after (the paschal) supper (was ended,) and when he had given thanks, he gave it to them saying, Drink ye all of it, (of the wine, which was ordinary wine, that had been prepared for the Passover;) This cup (the wine in it) is (signifies or represents) the new testament in my blood, (represents the new covenant ratified by my blood,) which is (to be) shed (on the cross) for you, and for many for the remission of sins. This do ye as often as ye drink it, in (order to cherish the) remembrance of me. For as often as ye (reverently and devoutly) eat this bread and drink the wine in this cup (consecrated by prayer for the sacramental celebration) ye do show forth (perpetuate the memory of) the Lord's death, (upon the cross,) until he returns, (at the latter day, at the close of the present dispensation.) Whoever shall eat this bread and drink this wine unworthily, (irreverently and without faith and a due regard for the solemn design for which they were appointed,) is guilty of (in respect to) the body and blood of the Lord, (guilty of treating irreverently or profanely the emblems or memorials of the Saviour's broken body and shed blood, and thus guilty of casting reproach on the Lord himself.) Let a man, therefore, examine himself (as to his knowledge of the design of the institution and his moral qualifications to receive it;) for he that eateth or drinketh unworthily (in an irreverent manner and without faith in Christ,) eateth and drinketh (judgment, κριμα, not) damnation to himself, not discerning the Lord's body, (not distinguishing between ordinary bread and these elements, instituted and consecrated as emblems of the Saviour's crucified body and blood.)

According to this view of the sacramental narrative, it follows, that in the Holy Supper of our Lord, there is,

1. A *real* presence of the Saviour as to his *divine* nature.

2. A *spiritual*, that is symbolic presence as to his *human* nature, and,

3. An *influential* presence of the God-man, the Theanthropos (θεανθρωπος) as to the blessings flowing from his death and mediatorial work in general.

Hence, the view of the Lord's Supper, which is most scriptural, and also most generally received by the great majority of the Lutheran ministry and churches in this country, is summarily the following:

That there is no real or actual presence of the glorified human nature of the Saviour either substantial or influential, nor any thing mysterious or supernatural in the eucharist; yet, that whilst the bread and wine are merely symbolical representations of the Saviour's absent body, by which we are reminded of his sufferings, there is also a PECULIAR *and special* SPIRITUAL *blessing bestowed by the divine Saviour on all worthy communicants, by which their faith and Christian graces are confirmed.*[1] The further development of the nature and evidences of the various blessings resulting from this ordinance, does not fall within the design of the present discussion. We will in few words merely add, on this interesting and highly practical subject, that whilst the nature of this ordinance, so far as the Saviour's person and its presence are concerned, is merely commemorative or mnemonic, its influence and general relations are by no means exhausted by this term.

Having thus presented the view of the Saviour's presence in the Holy Supper, which we find clearly taught in the records of inspiration, we close with the remark, that whilst we vindicate to ourselves the right to believe and profess what we regard as the scriptural view of this subject, we consider the Protestant diversities in reference to it as of minor moment, and can cordially fraternize with the Zwinglian and all others on the one hand, who attribute to this ordinance no *peculiar* spiritual blessing, beyond that of the other means of grace, and with the rigid adherent of Luther's views on the other, who believes in the real presence, the eating and drinking of the body and blood of the Redeemer in this Holy Feast of Love.

---

(1) Popular Theology, 5th ed., p. 303.

(2) The Holy Supper is indeed a mnemonic ordinance, but it is also much more. In addition to its character as

1. A *mnemonic* or commemorative ordinance; the Scriptures authorize us to regard it also.

2. As a *federal* ordinance. It has a federal or covenant character. "This cup, said the Saviour, is, or signifies the New Covenant (Testament) in my blood." This ordinance represents the covenant of grace, the plan of salvation ratified by my blood, and fully set forth in the books of the New Testament.

3. It is a *professing* ordinance. In it we publicly profess not only our belief in the vicarious atonement through the Saviour's blood, "broken," "shed for many;" but also profess anew our having accepted the offers of mercy, based on this doctrine.

4. It is a *sacramental* ordinance, in the original sense of the term sacrament an oath. By it Christians renew their oath, or vow of fidelity to their Saviour made at their reception into the church, adding new strength to the obligation by their voluntary act.

5. It is a *collative* ordinance. It professes not only what theologians term a *vim significativam*, a symbolic influence; but also a *vim collativam*, a collative influence. That is, it not only possesses a significative import, it is also the means through which the Divine Saviour actually bestows a *special spiritual blessing* on all worthy communicants.

6. It is a *eucharistic* ordinance, because it is a feast of gratitude to the Redeemer for the rich blessings purchased by his death, and secured to worthy partakers of this ordinance. The name is derived from *εὐχαριυτία*, giving of thanks. Matthew 26 : 27. Luke 22 : 19. 1 Cor. 11 : 24.

7. It is a *communing* ordinance. It brings us into communion, not only spiritually with the crucified body of Christ; but also with all true believers, who unite with us in the ordinance; and even spiritually with Christians elsewhere, who partake of the same ordinance. It is the means of *congregational* and of *catholic communion.* "For," says Paul, 1 Corinthians, 11 : 17. "we being many are one bread and one body; for we are all partakers of that one bread."

V. DISCOURSE.

THE DOCTRINAL BASIS AND ECCLESIASTICAL POSITION OF THE AMERICAN LUTHERAN CHURCH.

CHAPTER I.

INTRODUCTORY REMARKS. PROPOSITIONS DEFINING THE DOCTRINAL BASIS. THE NAME LUTHERAN—IT IS GIVEN TO MANY WHO REJECT THE MAJORITY OF THE "SYMBOLICAL BOOKS."

ONE of the characteristic features of the Christian church, by which the wisdom and benevolence of its Divine Author are illustriously displayed, is found in the fact, that, whilst he himself projected the fundamental lineaments of its external, visible organization, he left the great mass of minor features, to be filled up by the discretion of his disciples in the successive ages of the world. It was thus, that the divine truths of his holy religion found, comparatively, easy access to the human heart, under all forms of civil organization. For whilst it taught kings and emperors to rule in righteousness, "to be a terror to evil-doers, and a praise to those that do well," it simultaneously enjoined on those "under authority," to be "subject to the powers that be," as "to the ministers of God, who hold not the sword in vain;" because civil government is an institution "appointed of God." Under the sanction of this discretionary principle, we find not only different denominations of Christians, characterized by diversity of external polity, but even Christians of the same denomination, in different countries, admit of these variations. Thus, the adherents of the Augsburg Confession, the XVth article of which sanctions this principle of diversity in external arrangements, designed to "*promote peace and good order in the church,*" though all designated by the general name of *Lutheran*, or Evangelical, are characterized by strongly marked diversities of organization and polity. For example, whilst all Lutherans of every land, acknowledge the primitive parity of ministers, in Denmark our church has diocesan bishops, and in Sweden also an archbishop; whilst in Germany she has superintendents, and in republican America, adheres to entire parity of ministerial rank in practice, as well as in theory. In like manner, whilst in Luther's lifetime, no symbolical books at all, except the Bible, were imposed on either pastors or churches; after his death, several important documents of historical importance, all (except the Form of Concord,) written for other purposes, were prescribed by the civil authorities, as binding on both pastors and churches. After this system of symbolic servitude had been commenced, more books were invested with such authority in Saxony, than in some other sections of Germany. In Sweden, none of these modern documents were regarded as strictly symbolical, except the Augsburg Confession; and in Denmark, none but that Confession, and the Smaller Catechism of Luther. The Lutheran Church in America, though pursuing some diversity in practice, never entered on a formal settlement of this point, until the General Synod virtually accomplished this end, in her Synodical Constitution, by the requisition of *fundamental assent to the Augsburg Confession*, from all candidates for licensure and ordination. That Lutherans in this country would not be insensible, either to their inalienable rights or obligations, that they would avail themselves of our happy liberty from all entangling alliances with the civil government, and organize their church more closely, according to the Apostolic model, than could be done in Germany, was natural and right. Accordingly, like their brethren of other denominations, our fathers did introduce various improvements on the ecclesiastical institutions of Lutheran Europe, and adopt a system, which, *whilst* it is *Lutheran, is also American,* and more nearly conformed to the

Apostolic model, than has been attained by the Lutheran church in any other country.

To portray the practice of our Fathers, the principles on which they acted, and the organization which has gradually grown out of them, is the design of this essay; as well as to vindicate them against the objections, which may arise in the minds of our friends or foes. As the subject is possessed of a high, enduring interest, these discussions, which first appeared in the Lutheran Observer, are now presented in this permanent and condensed form, entirely divested of the peculiarities in which they originated; and they are circulated, not to provoke controversy, but to present calm, rational and scriptural argument, for the conscientious consideration of those concerned, with the supplication and the hope that a gracious Providence may employ them to cherish peace and harmony within our borders, to promote a Scriptural organization of the Church on earth, and to hasten her triumph over the kingdoms of this world.

We shall devote the present chapter to a statement of the propositions to be discussed, and to several general and preliminary topics.

The doctrinal basis and ecclessiastical position of the American Lutheran Church, may be briefly comprehended in the following propositions:

1. The patriarchs of our church did at first practically profess the former symbolical books of our church in Germany, by avowing them or in most instances the Augsburg Confession at the erection of their houses of worship, and in various cases at the induction of men into the ministerial office.

2. They soon relaxed from the rigor of symbolic requisition, and referred only to the Augsburg Confession, generally omitting all reference to the other former symbolic books, except the use of the Smaller Catechism of Luther in the instruction of the rising generation.

3. Neither they nor their immediate successors ever formally adopted these symbolical books as binding on our church in this country, as tests of admission or discipline.

4. About the beginning of this century they ceased, in fact, to require assent even to the Augsburg Confession at licensure and ordination, and demanded only faith in the word of God, thus practically rejecting (as they had a right

to do) all the symbolical books as tests; though still respecting and occasionally referring to the Augsburg confession as a substantial expose of the doctrines which they taught.

5. The actual doctrinal position of our church in this country at the formation of the General Synod, was that of adherence to the fundamental doctrines of Scripture as substantially taught in the Augsburg Confession, with acknowledged dissent on minor points. Ecclessiastical obligations are voluntary and personal, not hereditary. God deals with every man as an individual moral agent, possessing certain unalienable rights, and owing certain unalienable duties. Hence the ministry and laity, that is, the church of every age have as good a right and are as much under obligations to oppose, and, if possible, change what they believe wrong in the religious practices of their predecessors, and to conform it to the word of God, as were Luther and the other christians of the sixteenth century.

6. Whatever moral obligation their practical requisition of assent to the Augsburg Confession, may have imposed on themselves and those thus admitted by them, it was annulled when, by common consent, they revoked that practice. And as none, so far as we have ever heard, protested or seceded, they thus all practically rejected all those books as binding symbols.

7. Our General Synod found the Lutheran Church in America without any human symbols as tests of admission or discipline, although the Augsburg Confession was still occasionally referred to as a substantial exhibition of the doctrines held by them; and the General Synod ratified the state of doctrine existing among its members, namely, fundamental assent to the Augsburg Confession, with acknowledged deviation in minor or non-fundamental points, and subsequently passed a formal adoption of the Augsburg Confession, in this fundamental way, as a test of admission and discipline.

The American Lutheran Church is characterized by certain definite *features*, and as such is worthy of the highest respect and confidence of her membership, and of the Christian public at large.

In regard to our *first position*, namely, *that our earliest preachers often referred to the symbolical books, and especially to the Augsburg Confession as an expose of their doctrinal views,* no doubt can exist, and therefore an induction of proofs is superfluous. And yet it seems evident that in thus referring, they did not design to profess an absolute conformity; because they had certainly rejected several of the tenets of those books, which are also at present generally rejected, such as auricular confession, which is taught in the Augsburg Confession, Article xi: "*Concerning Confession we teach that* PRIVATE ABSOLUTION *must be retained in the churches and must not be abandoned,*" and also *Exorcism,* which is enjoined in the Directory for Baptism, (Taufbuechlein,) appended by Luther himself to his Smaller Catechism, where we find on the subject of Baptism, the following directions: Let the officiating minister say: *Depart* (or come out, 'fahre aus') *thou unclean spirit, and give room to the Holy Spirit,*" and after a prayer the minister says: "*I adjure thee, thou unclean spirit, by* (bei) *the name of the Father, and of the Son, and of the Holy Spirit, that thou come out and depart from this servant of Jesus Christ, N. N.* (naming the child) *Amen.*" All these things are omitted from the liturgies and catechisms published by our earlier ministers, that we have seen. We know, too, that some of them, such as Dr. Kunze, *rejected the imputation of Adam's sin, or rather of the depraved nature which we derived from him, to his posterity as personal guilt;* and from the general tenor of Muhlenberg's theological views, we doubt not he and others of them participated in this rejection. Now these are the principal points, with the addition of the *bodily* presence of Christ in the Eucharist, which the friends of the "General Synod's basis," or of the "American Lutheran church," object to in the Augsburg Confession, (and exorcism is not even taught in that book); and we are greatly mistaken if one in five hundred of our American Lutherans will ever adopt the views of Luther on these subjects. But if the early fathers of our church in this country had formally adopted the whole mass of the books as symbolical and binding on all future generations, (which they did not,) the writer's views of his own position in the Lutheran church, and of his duty in regard to her, as well as that of his brethren of the General Synod, would not be changed in the least. His reasons are these:

Religious and ecclesiastical obligations are not hereditary. In matters not prescribed by the word of God, I am bound by no other obligations than those which I personally assumed. I was not even requested to pledge myself to any one of the symbolical books on entering the ministry, but to the inspired and infallible word of God. If subscription to the symbolical books is essential to the character of a Lutheran, *then Luther himself was not a member of the church that bore his name;* and a large part of all who were called Lutherans during the first half century of her existence, were in the same condition, as well as all those entire Lutheran countries, which always rejected the ill-fated Form of Concord. The friends of the General Synod's basis believed themselves acting honestly, and honorably in joining the church, then as now called Lutheran; because they believed and still believe and teach all the great and cardinal doctrines which Luther taught, and carry out more fully than he did, the principles of church government and discipline, which he believed to be taught in Scripture.

Again, if the founders of the American Lutheran church even had formally adopted the symbolical books of Germany, it was equally competent for their successors to rescind such adoption; and certainly could not affect our duty and position. It is enough for us, and for the present generation of our ministers and members, that when we entered the holy office, no such obligation was customary or even thought of; no pledge to the symbolical books, or any one of them, was asked of us, or given by us. We selected the Lutheran church as the church of our choice, *as she then was*, not as she had been two or three centuries ago. And, as honest and honorable men, we are answerable for our fidelity only to the promises which we ourselves made, so long as we do not publicly renonunce them, and avow a change of opinion as to our duty; as Luther did when he repudiated the obligation of his monastic vows. It is certain our American fathers did not formally adopt these books, but in several instances practically required assent to them at licensure or ordination, and probably for some years longer, as we have recently been informed by one of the oldest fathers of the church, required candidate's assent to the Augsburg Confession alone, practically rejecting the other books; and they did recommend the smaller catechism of Luther as a book for catechetical instruction; but their successors gradually disapproving of this pledge, practically rejected it, as well as any pledge to the other symbolic books, about half a century ago, *which they had a perfect moral right to do.*

All the while, those venerable brethren, among whom were Drs. Kunze, Helmuth, Schmidt, Streit, Schaeffer of Philadelphia, Muhlenberg of Lancaster, Daniel Kurtz of Baltimore, Krug, Endress, Goering, Schmucker of York, and Lochman, Sen'r., though they no longer required the licentiate to pledge himself to the Augsburg Confession, yet still adhering to the grand doctrines held by Luther, considered it honorable to retain the name of Lutheran, as their successors still do. Dr. Helmuth is known to have been prominent in rejecting the requisition of a pledge to the Augsburg Confession. Whether all the others, above named agreed with him, we know not; yet the majority must have done so, or the practice could not have been changed.

"During the first thirty years of this century, the great body of the American Lutheran church had, therefore, no human creed at all binding upon them, though they always did refer (as we still do,) to the Augsburg Confession, as a substantial expose of their doctrines.

As freemen, and servants only of Christ, they felt that they had the right, and rested under the obligation to worship God, and to conduct the affairs of his church according to the dictates of their own conscience, guided by the Scriptures; and we have yet to see any evidence that they were under any obligation of honor or honesty, to pursue a different course.

Their real doctrinal position, at the formation of the General Synod, was that of fundamental agreement with the Augsburg Confession, and acknowledged dissent from it on some minor or non-fundamental points. This state of doctrine alone could the clause of the General Synod's constitution be designed to perpetuate, which denies to that body "the right to introduce such alterations in matters appertaining to the faith, &c., as might, in any way, tend to burden the consciences of the brethren in Christ". The alterations prohibited, must have been alterations from the state of things and doctrines actually existing. How the "consciences of the brethren could be oppressed" by the General Synod's altering or rejecting any doctrine which they did not believe, we cannot divine; and to maintain that the framers of that article designed by it to perpetuate or shield from alteration any doctrine which they themselves rejected, would evince more zeal than sound judgment.

This doctrinal position of substantial agreement with the Augsburg Confession, with acknowledged privilege of difference on non-fundamental or minor points, was subsequently made symbolic or binding by the General Synod, in her Constitution for Synods, and *this is the official creed of the General Synod.* This doctrinal position had been introduced in the same way and with exactly equivalent restrictions, into the Constitution of the Theological Seminary of the General Synod. This obligation, written by ourselves, we have also taken, and to it we expect to adhere so long as strength is granted us to labor in the vineyard of our blessed Lord. It has sometimes been said, as Lutherans we ought to adhere to the standards of the Lutheran church. This is perfectly true and just, if the standards of the Lutheran church *in America* be intended; for these are none other than the "Word of God and the fundamentals of that Word as taught substantially in the Augsburg Confession." But as to the former symbolical books of the Lutheran church in Germany, we are under no such obligation. Our churches, for near a century, have not acknowledged any one of them except the Augsburg Confession, and *for fifty* years past have received as binding, none at all, until the General Synod formally adopted the Augsburg Confession, and that only as to fundamentals; and probably not a dozen of all our American ministers have ever read all these books. If we ask the question, how could any one suppose us bound by the symbols of our church in Germany? we can perceive no other solution, than the supposition that such person has adopted some phase of the Unlutheran and unscriptural notion, which is beginning to pervade the theology of some other denominations, and regards the church as consisting of an ideal, abstract membership, together with the human Constitution, Creeds, Liturgies, &c., framed and professed by Christians in any particular age, and which fictitiously confers on this ideal church a corporate personality, apart from the individual members who compose it. In this unscriptural sense, a church, that is, her constitution, creeds, liturgy, &c., may be orthodox, and her actual members be infidel. But, we ask, will these creeds, constitutions, or abstract ideal membership appear before the bar of God, to answer for the deeds done in the body; or the professing Christians of every age, who adopted or rejected them? When the apostle of the Gentiles addressed his epistle "to the church at Corinth," did he mean an abstract or ideal membership, or the creeds or regulations of the Christians in that place, or the houses in which they worshipped? Let his own words decide the point for us. "Paul, called to be an apostle of Jesus Christ, &c., unto *the church* of God which is at Corinth, to *them that are sanctified* in Christ Jesus, called to *be saints*, and to all that in every place *call upon the name of Jesus Christ, our Lord.*" Here, real persons, certainly, and not things, are regarded as *the church*. In full accordance with this, the Augsburg Confession teaches, That *the Christian church is nothing else than the congregation of true believers.* Art. VIII. Human creeds are a publication of the doctrinal belief only of those who framed and published them, and of those who subsequently avow their assent to them, either in whole or in part; and they cannot, possibly, be binding on any others, who have not, by personal avowal, adopted them, either as an exponent of their belief, or as a rule of discipline. This view of the subject is clearly taught in the preface to the Form of Concord, where we are told, "Symbols cannot possess the authority of a judge in controversies, which dignity belongs only to the Scriptures,—but they show, how, *at particular times*, the scriptures were understood on controverted points by the teachers in the church of God, who THEN LIVED, (quo modo *singulis temporibus* sacræ literæ in articulis controversis in ecclesiæ Dei a doctoribus *qui tum vixerunt*, intelectæ et explicatæ fuerint.) But, as this subject will be more fully considered hereafter, we here pass it by, and devote the remnant of this chapter to the inquiry:

How much agreement with Luther, and the symbols adopted at different times, during half a century after the organization of the Lutheran church, is requisite in order honestly to retain the name of Lutheran?

In the judgment of some it is necessary to believe not only the Augsburg Confession and Apology to it, and the Catechisms and Smalcald Articles of Luther, which he never designed as binding symbols, and which were not generally received as such during his lifetime; but also the Form of

Concord, which was not in existence till thirty-six years after his death. But if we listen to the judgment of every respectable historian of the last three centuries, who has treated of our church, and of the millions of acknowledged Lutherans, who have rejected one or more of these books; we find the award of the public to be very different.

It was doubtless unfortunate and Anti-protestant, as well as contrary to Luther's solemn protest, for those who agreed with him in sentiment, to adopt the nickname given them by the Papists, and to call the church of the son of God, after any mere man. If an inspired apostle would not suffer the disciples to be called after the name of Paul, or Apollos, or Peter, much less should the name of any uninspired leader be abused to this purpose, and thus practically, though unconsciously, be thrust in between the believer and his Lord. Yet, as this has been done, it becomes a question, whether those who find the church of their choice designated by this name, and who prefer that church on the whole, to all others, shall on account of that name, (a name in itself dear to their hearts) refuse to enter that church, or being in it, shall renounce their private judgment in studying the word of God, or form a new sect. The latter part of this alternative we regard as not only utterly unsustained by scripture, and based on a confused and pernicious over-estimate of the framework of sectarianism; but also radically inconsistent with the scriptural views of the church of Christ. All history has decided against it.

I. The Form of Concord, published 1580, was rejected by the following Lutheran nations, principalities, dukedoms, &c., and yet no one ever attempted to deny their right to the name *Lutheran*.

1. *The kingdom of Denmark.* "The king, though invited to adopt it, refused to do so, by advice of his clergy, who disapproved of it, because peace and unity of doctrine prevailed in his dominions, and he feared its introduction would create strife and divisions. And so bitterly was he opposed to it himself, that he *took the copy (decorated with gold and pearls) sent him from Germany, cast it into the fire, and made it a capital offence* to introduce and publish it in the kingdom. Kœllner's Symbolik, Vol. I, p. 575, 576. And though at a subsequent period it acquired some popularity, and was practically used; it was never publicly acknowl-

edged as a symbol. See Baumgarten's Erlæuterungen zum Concordienbuch, p. 184, 185. Mosheim's Eccles. Hist., Vol. III. p. 155, Murdock's edition.

We add the testimony of Shubert's celebrated work on the Ecclesiastical and Educational Institutions of Sweden, as summarily given by Kœllner. After repeating in full the oath of ordination, which mentions in addition to the three ancient creeds, only the Augsburg Confession, and refers to the Liber Concordiæ as illustration of it, Kollner adds this remark: "Upon the whole, the case of Sweden is like that of Denmark and of Holstein. It was from the beginning customary to bind oneself to the symbolical books, which were not adopted until after the time of the Reformation, *only in as far as they were believed to agree with the holy Scriptures.*" In later times, it is customary in public documents, instead of the phrase, "the *Lutheran doctrine,*" to use the more appropriate expression, "the pure *evangelical doctrine.*" Kœllner's Symbolik, I. p. 122.

2. *The kingdom of Sweden* did not receive it during the first thirteen years after its publication. Hear the testimony of that ultra-Lutheran historian Guericke, (Symbolik, 2d edition, p. 112, 113.) "And if Denmark and *Sweden,* stopping at a still more youthful age in regard to Confessions, did not concede proper symbolical authority to the Apology to the Augsburg Confession, or to the Smalcald Articles, or the Larger Catechism of Luther, (and in Sweden not even the Smaller Catechism,) they would naturally be still less willing formally to acknowledge the Form of Concord." Guericke, Symb., p. 112, 113. Still at a later period, in 1593, the Form of Concord received a *tolerably* formal acknowledgment, (ziemlich formliche Anerkennung.)

3. *Hessia* rejected it.

4. *Pomerania* rejected it.

5. *Holstein* rejected it for more than half a century.

6. *Anhalt;* and the cities of *Strasburg, Frankfort, a. M., Speier, Worms, Nurenburg, Magdeburg, Bremen, Dantzic,* &c., &c. Kœllner, p. 577.

II. The Smalcald Articles, published in 1537, were rejected by *Sweden* and *Denmark.* In Sweden, the symbolic books generally are now regarded as an authorized explanation of the Lutheran faith; yet the "Symbolical Books of the *Danish* church, lately published, like those of the *Swedish* church in 1644, (entitled Confession of the *Swedish* faith, approved by the council at Upsal in 1593,) contains only the three ecumenical confessions; namely, the so-called Apostles' Creed, the Nicene and the Athanasian Creeds, and the Augsburg Confession, to which the Danish collection adds the Smaller Catechism of Luther. Both these collections, however, exclude the *Smalcald Articles.* Guericke's Symb. p. 67. and his History, p. 807, 1st editon.

III. The Apology to the Augsburg Confession, was denied official symbolic authority by Sweden and Denmark. Guericke sup. cit.

IV. The Larger Catechism of Luther was denied formal symbolic authority in Sweden and Denmark. Guericke, sup. cit.

V. Even the Smaller Catechism of Luther was not received as symbolic in Sweden; yet in both these kingdoms they are highly respected, and the Smaller Catechism, if we mistake not, is used for the instruction of youth. Guericke, p. 113.

Here then we have the historical facts, the greater part of them well known indeed to those who are familiar with the history of our church in Europe; but, for the benefit of others, proved by the authority of the accurate Kœllner, and of that bigoted Old-Lutheran, Prof. Guericke.

What now appears to be the result of these facts? Did all these kingdoms and principalities, which are known in history as *Lutheran,* and to whom no writer, not *even Guericke,* denies the name of *Lutheran,* receive all the symbolical books as such? Far,. very far from it? We see, on the contrary, that whole kingdoms, especially Sweden, which has sometimes been held up as the *beau ideal* of Lutheranism, never received as symbolical one-half of them; though they respected and used them as theological productions; just as our church does in this country. In short we find, that the declaration of Dr. Hase, is literally true, when he says the *Augsburg Confession is the only symbolic book, which has been acknowledged by the whole Lutheran church.* Hutterus Redivivus, p. 116, § 50. And it is certain that much more frequent and important deviations from the Augsburg Confession would have been avowed, if the peace of Augsburg, in 1555, had not guaranteed toleration to the Protestant princes *only so long as they and their theologians dhered to the Augsburg Confession;* and if the Papists and especially the *Jesuits had not watched* even every verbal deviation, and used it to excite the Romish Emperor to withdraw his protection, and to put down Protestantism by fire and sword, which efforts actually eventuated in the thirty years' war. It is well known, that even during Luther's lifetime, Melancthon, Cruciger and others, disapproved of a part of the Augsburg Confession, and yet Luther would not suffer them to leave Wittenberg, or the communion of the Lutheran church, when they on one occasion expressed a willingness to do so, if they could not deviate from Luther's views without denunciation from several of his followers. In all ages of the Lutheran church, there have been among her ablest divines some who dissented, at least privately, from Luther's opinion, *that the real or true body and blood of Christ are present in the eucharist, and are received by the communicant,* as taught in the Augsburg Confession. And Guericke himself admits, what is indeed matter of general notoriety, not merely that the neologians, but that *the whole Lutheran church in Germany had rejected this doctrine before* 1817, when the union of the Lutheran and Reformed churches was effected in some parts of that country. *Even to this day, there is not a single Lutheran kingdom or principality, which receives any one of the former symbolical books as binding, except the Augsburg Confession, and this,* as we were informed on the spot, *only as to its substance.* Now if all the world, with the exception of a few bigoted ultra-Lutherans, freely concede the name Lutheran to these millions who bear it; it is rather too late in the day for a few individuals in this country to set up the doctrine, that no Lutheran is entitled to the name, who does not believe and profess the whole catalogue of the former symbolic books, or at least *so* receive the Augsburg Confession, as not to contradict the teachings of any one of the other books! *Our own impression of the equity of the case is this, that so long as the Lutheran church, in this or any other country, adheres to the fundamental principle of Lutheranism, that the Bible is the only infallible rule of faith and practice, and believes the great, the cardinal doctrines of Luther's system, together with so many of his peculiarities, as to agree more fully with them as a whole, than with the peculiarities of any other denomination, she may justly retain the Lutheran name;* and all the world, a few ultraists excepted, will cordially proclaim the equity of the designation. Thus also, will the Protestant churches make some approximation to the precept of the Saviour, who taught us: *one only is your Master, Christ, and ye are all brethren.*

CHAPTER II.

Early abandonment of the strict, symbolic standpoint, by the founders of the American Lutheran Church.

We now come to the second *position* in this discussion. But that our real position on the subject in general may not be misapprehended, it seems proper to premise a few observations. Let it not be supposed that we are hostile to creeds of every description. It is indeed true, that the Word of God neither enjoins, nor expressly sanctions any human creeds. It is itself, professedly, a creed, and an inspired one. In it God himself has taught us what we are to believe, and what we are to do, that is, has given us a rule of faith and practice. It is reasonable to suppose, that such a divine rule would be sufficient for all purposes, and that rule itself professes to be a sufficient one, "able to make us wise unto salvation, through faith which is in Christ Jesus." This is represented as the test by which the opinions of men are to be tried. "To the law and the testimony; if they speak not according to this word, it is because there is no light in them." And Paul declares that, if an angel from heaven should preach "any other doctrine than that which he taught," and which is recorded in his epistle, "let him be accursed." These facts should make us reflect carefully, before we erect any other standard of doctrine, in a manner, which, even indirectly, or by human infirmity, might, in any degree, take the place of this inspired rule. Still, the Saviour and his apostles have prescribed certain requisitions to be demanded by those whom they received into the church, of all others who might subsequently apply for admission. For example, applicants had to express their belief, that Jesus was the Christ, that is, the Messiah, &c. This brief acknowledgment, by frequent repetition, acquired a settled form, which, when it first meets us in the literature of the church, had grown into what was called the *Apostles' Creed,* constituting less than a duodecimo page; and this is all the creed used in the Christian church in the whole world, so far as is known, for several hundred years, during the golden age of Christianity. We fully coincide with the judgment of the early church, thus expressed, that for the purity of the church, and harmony of its operations, a creed of fundamentals is necessary, or at least useful, if properly employed. Yet it is evident, from many considerations, that it should include only fundamentals, only such doctrines as we believe necessary to the Christian character, together with as many points of government and discipline, as are requisite for harmony in action. Otherwise, we destroy the unity of Christ's body, we violate the charity inculcated in the gospel, and wage a war of "doubtful disputations" with the brother, whom we consider "weak in the faith." We, therefore, after much and prayerful study of this subject, in the light of scripture and history, approve of the use of the so called Apostles' Creed, the Nicene Creed, and the fundamentals of the Augsburg Confession, as an expression of the prominent truths we believe the bible to teach, and as tests of admission and discipline in the church. This is the ground which our fathers in this country *practically* adopted, half a century ago; this is the ground which our General Synod has *formally* adopted, and the ground on which we stand. These several positions might be established by numerous, irrefragable arguments, but the present discussion does not properly cover this ground.

We return, then, to our next position, that *the fathers of our American church soon relaxed from their rigid views of obligation to the symbolical books.*

There are numerous reasons to authorize the belief, that Dr. Muhlenberg himself, the principal founder of our American church, was a man of much more liberality and enlarged views of Christian apostolic liberty, than he has sometimes received credit for. As evidence of this fact, we will cite his liberality towards some "Separatists," as they are styled in Germany, before he came to America;

for which he is censured by the historian Heinsius, who was a churchman of the strictest class. Speaking of our church in Philadelphia, he says:[1] "The Ev. Lutheran congregation in that place, has recently obtained a preacher, concerning whom we rather wish than can confidently expect, that he will preserve those churches *in order and in purity of doctrine, without divisions*. This minister is Mr. Muhlenberg, who some time since studied at Goettingen, afterwards officiated as deacon inspector in the baronial Gersdorf-Orphanhouse at Grooshennersdorf, in Lusatia, and *who secretly advocated the course of the Separatists in a publication against Dr. Mentzer*." We do not know what points Dr. Muhlenberg vindicated in this work, but it is well known that those Separatists were generally pious persons, who saw, or thought they saw, defects in the established (Lutheran) church, and wished to worship God in what they considered a purer and a more scriptural manner. This fact, however, proves that Dr. M. was a man who thought for himself, and disapproved of some things in the Lutheran church in Germany, which were approved by Heinsius himself, a rigid Lutheran and a pious man. That Dr. M. did not regard liturgies as very important, is evident from the fact, that twelve years after he had been laboring in organizing and building up churches in this country, where he thought it desirable for the sake of the unity in public worship to compose a liturgy, he had not a copy of a liturgy used in Germany, nor could one be found; so that when he and his fellow laborers, Brunnholtz and Handschuh, undertook to form one, they had to take as its basis, the liturgy of the Savoy Lutheran church in London; for, says he, "we had no other one at hand."[2] "That he did not like a long liturgy, is evident, because they prepared *a short one*," even shorter than "the enlarged" reprint of it in 1786, which is not more than half as large as that now in use. Nor was he a stickler for the *peculiarities of any* part of Germany, for he says; "we adapted it to the circumstances of our congregations, *which had come from different parts* of Germany.

---

(1) Vol. iii. page 389, of his Unpartheiische Kirchen Historie. Jena, 1754.

(2) Hall. Nachrichten, p. 676.

That he and his associates were not ardently devoted to the whole mass of symbolical books, is probable, as they are not named in their Synodical constitution (ministerial ordnung,) so far as appears from our oldest copy, nor in their liturgy, except the catechism, for the instruction of youth. It is worthy of note, also, that the charter for the "congregations in and near Philadelphia," which was probably as usual in the case of such documents, written by some lawyer, under the direction of Muhlenberg and his associates, mentions not one of the symbolical books, though dated as early as 1765, and very extended and minute in its specifications, covering four and a half quarto pages. That they were unwilling to receive as binding any of the symbolical books except the Augsburg Confession, is evident, because in the prominent documents in which they mention that symbol, they say nothing about the others. Thus, in *the (Kirchenordnung) discipline of the church at Philadelphia,* written by Muhlenberg himself, in 1762, the ministers are bound in the very first clause to teach according to the *unaltered Augsburg Confession, but nothing is said about the other symbolical books.* The catechism is subsequently prescribed for the instruction of the young. The same discipline was introduced into the church at Lancaster, *unaltered.* The same is the case in the inscription on Muhlenberg's church at the Trappe, dated 1743, the very next year after his arrival in this country, "this church sacred to the society devoted to the *Augsburg Confession,*" and nothing more. Twenty years afterwards, he remained firm in this distinction, and generally the other symbolical books; for in his address to his congregation, he again speaks of that church as being founded "on the apostles and prophets and the *unaltered Augsburg Confession,*" without even a reference to the other symbols. Can any impartial mind fail to perceive that Muhlenberg desired no other book to be regarded as symbolical, except the Augsburg Confession, when he designedly omits them on these solemn, official occasions? Again, we find another proof in an interesting diary of a voyage made by father Muhlenberg near the close of his life, to Charleston, South Carolina, found in the Ev. Review. In a letter which Dr. Muhlenberg addressed to Europe, requesting the mission of a minister to supply the church in that city, he solicits one "who is able and willing to propagate the gospel according to the foundation of the holy apostles and prophets, whereof Jesus Christ is the corner stone, and to administer the holy sacraments agreeably to the articles of our unaltered *Augsburg Confession.*" Here, too, it cannot fail to be seen, that this indefatigable servant of Christ, again says not a word of the other symbolic books, and certainly if he wished or expected, that the minister who might be sent over, would here be required to bind himself to the other symbolical books also, he must necessarily have mentioned them, as he so distinctly specifies one of them, the Augsburg Confession. But it is evident, that if the expected minister differed from the specifications of all the other symbolical books *on all the various points not determined in the Augsburg Confession,* he would still be such a minister as Dr. M. requested, and as he would not hesitate to ordain. Nay, further, although we do not know this to have been the design of Dr. M., and therefore do not assert it, for our cause needs no doubtful interpretations; yet, he says the gospel is to be preached according to the *foundation of the holy apostles and prophets,* and only of the sacraments does he say they shall be administered according to the Augsburg Confession.

Now, when we recollect he did not feel bound to believe all the minor points even in the Augsburg Confession, that he rejected Auricular Confession, and in all probability, as far as we can judge from his writings, also the imputation of Adam's sin to his posterity; that he did not use the liturgy of Germany, but for twelve years, as it would seem, none at all, and then made a very "*short*" one; we may justly claim him as in principle, the *father of American Lutheranism* "so called." For American Lutheranism, as represented in the General Synod, cannot with truth be represented as a *creedless* system; on the contrary, it adheres to the fundamentals of the gospel as taught in the Augsburg Confession, whilst it refuses to acknowledge as binding, the other books, however much they may be valued by many amongst us, as theological productions.

This is, in fact, also the doctrinal standpoint of the greater part of Evangelical Lutherans in Germany at the present time. With the exception of about one hundred ministers, (the so called Old Lutherans,) out of seven thousand in Germany, none are bound to any thing more than the Augsburg Confession, and that not to every minor doctrine in it. In traveling through Wurtemberg, we made particular inquiry of Dr. Schmidt, the principal professor in the Theological Seminary in Tuebingen, himself an orthodox man, and were informed that the clergy of Wurtemberg are obliged only to teach "according to the principles of the Augsburg Confession," (nach den Principien der Aug. Conf.) or as another eminent minister informed us, (nach dem Geist und Sinn,) according to the spirit and import of the Augsburg Confession. These are *the exact* words as recorded in our diary at the time.

The views of Dr. Muhlenberg as above given, are in perfect consonance with the statements made to us a few days since, by one of the most aged ministers of our church, our venerable father, who was admitted into Penn'a Synod 1792, and has successively held the highest offices of that body. He asserts, that at the time of his admission, the propriety of requiring a pledge was a matter of doubt and debate; that in some instances it was exacted and in others not; but some years later it was wholly omitted; and that Dr. Helmuth, confessedly, one of the most pious members of that body, who was any thing else than a rationalist, and commenced his labors in our church as early as 1769, was prominent in opposing the requisition of any other creed than the Bible. Muhlenberg himself had already been translated to a better world. Another highly respectable and learned minister of our church, who also entered the ministry about the close of the last century, or beginning of this, in a letter now before me, says: "That the exaction of a promise to conform to the symbolic books *was ever habitual*" with the Synod of Pennsylvania "I do not believe." It is, moreover, certain that the Synod of New York, one of the oldest in our church, when framing her constitution, introduced a clause *forbidding* the use of any other doctrinal test than the Bible. If then, our fathers, who in Europe were pledged to the whole mass of the symbolic books, (namely, to the three ancient creeds, the Apostles', the Nicene and the Athanasian, the Augsburg Confession, the Apology to the Confession, the Smalkald Articles, the smaller and larger Catechisms of Luther, and the Form of Concord,) did on their arrival in this country, or soon after, make a distinction between them, and in their Liturgies, church disciplines, and other important official documents, if they refer to any of the symbolic books, mention only the Augsburg Confession, and omit the other confessions altogether; if they, as early as 1792, were divided on the propriety of exacting any other test than the Bible and some years later entirely omitted the requisition of a pledge to any of the symbolical books; if all these things are true, as is certain, then it must be admitted, that our fathers, even the oldest of them, soon relaxed from their rigid views of obligation to the symbolical books, which at that time prevailed in Germany, and with which they probably came to this country.

It has already been stated, that the founders of our American church rejected several of the doctrines of the symbolic books, such as auricular confession, exorcism, the imputation of Adam's sin (or rather of the depraved nature inherited from him,) to his posterity as personal guilt, and we may add, at least in regard to some of them, the lax notions of the Augsburg Confession on the Christian Sabbath. It may not be amiss to show these deviations more fully, and also in later days to exhibit somewhat more in detail the actual, prevailing state of doctrine, at the time of the organization of the General Synod.

Dr. Kunze, probably the most learned of our older ministers, and no less distinguished for his piety,[1] than learning, in his history of the Christian Religion, thus expresses his views on the imputation of Adam's sin: "To derive original sin from the first man's being the federal head or representative of the human race, seems not satisfactory to a mind inclined to derive or expect only good and perfect things from the good and perfect Creator. By one man's disobedience, it is true, many were made sinners, but not on account of an imputation of this man's sin, but because by him, sin entered the world."[2] And on the subject of the Christian Sabbath the Doctor took such high and decided grounds as to excite hostility and even persecution from some of his hearers.

Dr. Lochman himself, speaking of the Article in the Augsburg Confession on Natural depravity, uses this language:

---

(1) See his work, "Ein Wort fuer den Verstand und das Herz passim," and especially p. 208–211.

(2) Lochman's Luther, p. 88.

The last clause in the above article, namely, the clause "condemneth all who are not born again of water and of the spirit," is thus explained by some: "If we suffer our depraved nature to have the rule over us, it will certainly lead us to ruin and condemnation."[1] This we know, from personal interviews with him, to have been the Doctor's own opinion.

The *Rev. Schober*, of North Carolina, though a warm friend of piety and active advocate of fundamental orthodoxy, did not receive the Augsburg Confession implicitly himself; and though he desired to introduce an acknowledgment of it into the constitution of the General Synod, did not design, had his efforts been successful, to require the belief of all its minor doctrines as a term of admission. Had such been his purpose, he would have excluded himself. In the edition of the Augsburg Confession published by himself, he appended notes to several articles, indicating his dissent from them. Hear his own language on the subject of Confession and Absolution, (Art. xi. of Conf.)

"This article was inserted at the time of the delivery of this Confession, chiefly to show a conciliatory spirit to the other party; but the practice of private confession and absolution is entirely discontinued in our Lutheran churches," p. 107. And of course the doctrine on which it is based, is also rejected.

On the doctrine of the Lord's Supper, he follows the Latin copy of Art. x. of the Confession, which omits the word *true* from before "body," in the German, adds the word "*external*" to emblems, which is not found in the Latin or German copy, and in addition to all appends the following note: "As Christ has promised unto his disciples and true followers, that he will be with them to the end of the world, and as he has been pleased to give us the gracious assurance, to be present with us whenever we assemble in his name; how firmly may we not rely on his promises, especially when we celebrate the Lord's Supper according to his holy institution, in solemn commemoration of his sufferings and death, and appropriate his merits to our own hearts." But he says nothing about receiving the body and blood of Christ in the ordinance.

But to place this matter beyond all doubt, both in regard

(1) P. 86—88 articles.

to Rev. Schober, and the ministers of the North Carolina Synod, generally, even as early as the year 1820, we add a document, adopted by that Synod at the very meeting at which delegates were elected, to attend the Convention at Hagerstown, in October of the same year, for the purpose of forming a Constitution for the General Synod. At that meeting a letter was addressed to the North Carolina Synod by a minister of a sister church, to which the following answer, prepared by a committee of Synod, was adopted; and the Rev. Schober requested to forward it to the memorialists, accompanied by "a polite and brotherly address" in the name of the Synod:

"To the Rev. James Hill:

Rev. and Dear Sir,—In answer to your question, whether water baptism effects regeneration? we say we do not fully know what you mean by the word "effects," as it may have many definitions. But we say, that baptism is beneficial, and ought to be attended to as a command of God; but we do not believe *that all who are baptized with water, are regenerated and born again unto God,* so as to be saved without the operation of the Holy Ghost; or, in other words, without faith in Christ. And as to the second question, we do not believe nor teach, that the *body and blood of our Lord Jesus Christ, are corporeally received along with the bread and wine in the Lord's Supper;* but that the true *believer* does *spiritually* receive and partake of the same, *through faith* in Jesus Christ, and all the saving benefits of his death and passion."[1]

Here, then, we cannot fail to see, that this whole Synod, (for they seem all to have been of one mind,) had abandoned the ground of the Augsburg Confession, and believed only a spiritual presence and perception of the body and blood of Christ, by faith in the eucharist, and this limited, of course, to the believer; and especially was this the doctrinal position of Mr. Schober, who was the leading and most active spirit in that body, and personally carried on a controversy with David Henkel, partly on this very doctrine.

But still farther, to show the real doctrinal position of Mr.

(1) See Transactions of the Lutheran Synod of North Carolina and adjacent States for 1820 printed at Raleigh p. 18.

Schober and his Synod, at the organization of the General Synod, we add another extract from the same minutes, (p. 6,) in which Mr. Schober, as Secretary, gives a statement of a discussion which occurred at that meeting, between several, Messrs. Henkels, and the Synod. Mr. Schober says: "They accused us of not teaching water baptism to be regeneration, and that *we did not accept the elements in the eucharist as the true body and blood of the Lord, corporeally,* and therefore, and because the plan for a general union of our church, (that is, the General Synod,) which they feared we would adopt, *was against the Augsburg Confession;* they could not unite with us." These Messrs. Henkels, who had for years been associated with Mr. Schober in the same Synod, and well knew his views, seem to have had little expectation, that the General Synod, which Mr. Schober was so anxious to establish, would have the least desire strictly to enforce the Augsburg Confession; on the contrary, their standing charge against him and his associates was, that they did not hold the doctrines of that Confession.

It has indeed been supposed that a pledge to the unaltered Augsburg Confession bound its subjects to the whole system, taught also in all the other symbols!! This opinion is utterly unfounded. Nor can any authority be adduced for it. No historian has ever asserted, that an understanding existed in Europe, that whoever signed the unaltered Augsburg Confession, thereby bound himself to adhere to the entire system taught in all the other books. If such an understanding had existed, how absurd, then, was the custom of binding ministers explicitly to the other books also, which prevailed for several hundred years, until the beginning of this century? If the matter was so understood, why did Sweden, and Denmark, and Prussia, and a number of other portions of the Lutheran church refuse to receive the Apology to the Confession? And why did the more rigid Lutherans complain of those countries, which received the unaltered Augsburg Confession, but rejected one or more of the other books, if the reception of that one bound them to all? Why does even Guericke complain that they did not attain symbolic manhood? In short, we cannot make the supposition tally with history at all, and therefore, are compelled to regard it, in fact, as unreasonable and unfounded, as it, at first view, appears to be. Guericke does indeed attempt to show, if we recollect rightly, that those who received the unaltered Augsburg Confession were under a *logical* obligation to adhere to the others, which we shall prove unfounded; but the question before us is entirely different, namely, whether our fathers did not relinquish the practice of requiring a pledge to the other symbolical books, and confine themselves to the Augsburg Confession, which is a fact to be established by historical evidence.

But may it not also be maintained, that the other symbolical books, the Catechisms of Luther excepted, were written to explain the Augsburg Confession, and do not teach any different doctrines, but only define the position of the church towards the Calvinists, &c., and therefore, all who receive the latter should receive the former also. To this we reply, if the other books did not touch on any additional doctrine, (which is, however, not the case,) but only dilated on those more generically stated in the Augsburg Confession, they would be objectionable as binding creeds; because, whilst men might agree on the few general specifications of doctrine, delineated in the Augsburg Confession, they might, and would differ on many of the explanations, ramifications and amplifications of them, contained in the other books. As well might we affirm, that all who can agree to pledge themselves to the few generic specifications of the Augsburg Confession, could just as well adopt, as their confession of faith, that excellent and voluminous work, "*Reinbeck's* (Betrachtungen) *Reflections on the Augsbury Confession,*" in nine ponderous quarto vols.; for they are all written professedly and actually in explanation of that symbol. Or, to illustrate the point still more clearly, as well might we assert, that all who adopt the American Constitution, as all our citizens do, can just as well also adopt the many volumes containing explanations of the provisions of that constitution, written by authors of our several political parties. The thing is impossible. Who does not know that these different authors, like the several parties to which they belong, deduce very different, yea, directly contradictory views from that same instrument, and that they could not possibly agree? And is it not equally notorious matter of history, that different writers, who have all agreed in assenting to the generic statements of the Augsburg Confession, have entertained a multitude of different opinions in regard to the minor specifications, the explanations, the circumstances and relations of those doctrines.

The *proton pseudos*, the radical error, of the ultra-Lutherans on this point, is this, that they *lose sight of the difference between generic and specific truths*. Religious, as well as other truths, are encircled by a vast multitude of relations and circumstances. Now these truths may be stated more or less generically, that is, in stating them, we may introduce more or fewer of those minor relations and circumstances. And such is the constitution of mind conferred on us by the Creator, that whilst the great mass of men agree in a generic statement of truths, in political or religious science, even of truths derived from the Bible; the more you enter into an enumeration of specific details, or supposed relations, the smaller the number of those, who can agree in them all. Thus, all denominations of Christians, agree to the few generic truths stated in the so-called Apostles' Creed, the only one used by Christians during the first three centuries. Yet, when we take up a creed of ten or twenty times its length, such as the Augsburg Confession, the 39 Articles of the Church of England, or the Heidelberg Catechism, we find these same Christians differing concerning the detailed statements of these several symbols on the subject of the very doctrines generically stated in the Apostles' Creed. And just in proportion as we extend the creed by adding more specifications and relations, do we also increase the difficulty of its reception by others. The grand reason of this fact is, that these minor circumstances and relations are less clearly revealed in scripture, and in some instances, are mere human inferences from what is revealed, and also, because the human mind can apprehend some of these minor relations less clearly than it does the cardinal facts and doctrines of the gospel. From these considerations, we trust our readers will easily perceive the fallacy of the supposition, that whoever can assent to the more generic statement of doctrine in the Augsburg Confession, a pamphlet of something like the size of Matthew's gospel, can also necessarily adopt all the minor specifications of relations and circumstances, which are contained in the whole mass of the former symbolic books, amounting to twice the size of the whole New Testament!

But in order, if possible, to illustrate this point still more clearly, we will select an example taken from the symbolical books themselves. Thus, the Augsburg Confession, in its third article, *consisting of about twenty lines*, contains a historical and *generic* statement *concerning the Person of the Saviour*, affirming his divinity, his incarnation or birth of the Virgin Mary, the union of his divine and human nature into one person, who is true God and man, his sufferings, crucifixion and death as a propitiatory sacrifice, not only for hereditary depravity, but also for all actual transgressions; his descent into hell, resurrection, ascension to heaven, his session at the right hand of God, his everlasting dominion over all creatures, his sanctification of believers through the Spirit, and protection of them against sin and satan, as also his final appearance to judge the quick and the dead. Now, to all these statements, given in very few more words than we have here employed, all evangelical Christians can cordially assent, except the descent into hell, (which was not in the earliest form of the creed,) and that they would only wish to have changed into the *world of spirits*, which might or might not be hell. But for these twenty lines, the other symbolic books give us discussions under various captions, to the amount of from fifty to a hundred pages, in which they not only several times repeat these general positions, but also add about fifty specifications, and related topics which are not in the Augsburg Confession. The major part of them were regarded as true, but others as erroneous. Among them are such topics as the following: 1. That *God is man and man is God.* 2. That the Virgin Mary did not conceive and bring forth *a mere man but the true Son of God*, and therefore, she is *the Mother of God.* 3. That it is right to say, that God suffered and died for us. 4. That it was not the mere humanity of Christ that suffered. 5. That the divine and human natures of Christ *communicate their attributes and properties to each other*. 6. That there are three species of this communication. 7. That Christ, in his *human* nature also, is *omniscient, omnipotent*, and *omnipresent.* 8. That he acquired omnipotent power in his mother's womb. 9. That the *flesh* of Christ is a life-giving food, (also, ist das Fleisch

Christi eine lebendigmachende Speise.) 10. That the body of Christ received a certain glorification and majesty, not only after his resurrection, and at his ascension to heaven, but at the time when he was conceived in the womb. 11. That the one *body* of Christ can be present at any place in three different ways. We are prepared to support all these topics by explicit quotations from the several symbolical books; but they would occupy more space than can be allowed. Now, if our readers will examine these specifications, they will find that *not one of them is contained in the Augsburg Confession* above quoted. So we might pass over all the articles of the Augsburg Confession, and show that a vast multitude of specifications is found in the other books, which are not contained in the Augsburg Confession. It will be seen, too, that some of these specifications are, to say the least, very doubtful; and others obviously erroneous and unscriptural. How it should follow, that whoever receives the Augsburg Confession, either ought or can also receive or bind himself to this host of additional tenets, we confess ourselves at a loss to perceive. We freely acknowledge that we can neither see nor feel any such obligation, either logical, or theological, or ecclesiastical, or moral.

But admitting that there is no obligation of any kind to receive all these books, and bind ourselves to believe their contents; is it expedient, would it conduce to the glory of God, would it advance the interests of our church? *Most certainly not.* As the difficulty of all assenting to any creed is increased just as we augment the number of minor and less important specifications in it; and as even the Augsburg Confession contains a few minor items, which the great mass of our ministers and laymen do not believe; it would be evident folly to attempt to bind us to books containing ten times as many more such minor and doubtful points. The attempt would unavoidably give rise to endless contentions, and must necessarily terminate in divisions of the church. Moreover, as our church has been signally blessed of God with doctrinal purity and doctrinal harmony under the General Synod's doctrinal basis, for more than a quarter of a century; why should we not adhere to it, and devote our energies to supplying the destitute of our church over the land with the preached gospel? If desired, let us add the Maryland Synod's explanation of the pledge, by enumerating what articles are fundamental; which expresses exactly what the pledge was intended to convey. The discord and diversity which have in some regions marred the peace of our Zion, had no reference to doctrine, and admit of no doctrinal remedy. They originated and consisted in particular *measures*, and especially in violations of our Formula of Government and discipline, *which strictly forbids all noise and disorder in the worship of God.* The remedy for these is already provided by the General Synod in her Formula; let the attention of those who lament these disorders, where any prevail, be directed to enforcing the provisions of the Formula, and all will be well. At the same time, let them demonstrate to the disorderly, that their zeal for order does not arise from want of zeal for religion, by redoubling their efforts to promote *orderly prayer meetings, and orderly Special Conferences*, for the purpose of awakening and converting sinners and edifying believers, and thus winning souls to Christ. Let the *catechetical instruction* of the rising generation be more faithfully attended to, wherever it has been neglected; and children be taught to love the institutions of the church as administered in our own denomination. Let them be taught to love the biblical, liberal, spiritual features of our Lutheran Zion, and the days of peace and harmony among pious Lutherans, the days of conversions and orderly genuine revivals, where they have disappeared, will again return to bless us.

CHAPTER III.

THE SYMBOLICAL BOOKS OF OUR CHURCH IN GERMANY NEVER FORMALLY ADOPTED IN THIS COUNTRY, THOUGH PRACTICALLY USED IN DIFFERENT CASES TILL NEAR THE CLOSE OF THE LAST CENTURY.

THE next position claiming our attention is, *That our church in America has never formally adopted the symbolical books of the Lutheran church of the sixteenth century;* though individual congregations had acknowledged the Augsburg Confession at the erection of their churches, and in some cases assent to the symbols, and especially to the Augsburg Confession, had been required at licensure and ordination.

By this we mean that no considerable or respectable Lutheran Synod or convention of Lutheran ministers in this country ever passed a resolution and published it, acknowledging the authority of the former symbolical books of our church in Germany, or of any of them as binding on them and on all who would unite with their body, until it was done within the last few years by several German Synods of the West.

1. It is true that the Governor and Directors of New Amsterdam, (New York,) then a Dutch colony, had concluded that the doctrines of the Augsburg Confession might be tolerated there, and therefore that the Lutherans might worship in private till they could obtain a minister. But, were these grave dignitaries, the Governor and Directors of New York, the "Lutheran church" in America, when they did not even belong to the Lutheran congregation? And was their action the action of "our church?" And if they had even been Lutherans, was their resolution to tolerate worship according to the Augsburg Confession, a resolution to make the whole mass of the symbolical books binding? Nor does the fact that the members of that church styled themselves "United members of the unaltered Augsburg Confession" prove any more. It shows that those members professed to believe the Augsburg Confession, a *part* of the symbolical books, one out of half a dozen of them, but not that even they received the whole of these books, much less was their giving themselves this name the action of the church, or of a part of it, formally adopting the symbolical books as binding.

2. Again, the Saltzburg emigrants also professed the doctrines of the Augsburg Confession in Germany, and whilst there contracted with the Trustees of the colony, that several ministers should be maintained among them, to preach to them the word of God "according to the purport of their own confession," and that they should "protect them in the free exercise of their religion according to the import of the *Augsburg Confession and other symbolical books of the Evangelical church.*" Now, although this latter phrase, and "*other symbolical books*" of the Evangelical church, was not of their

own selection, but was contained verbatim in the offer or invitation sent *from England* to Rev. Ursperger to induce emigrants to go to Georgia, and accepted by them; still admitting that these emigrants who were nearly all "farmers or mechanics, day-laborers or domestics," had all seen and read all the symbolic books, which is certainly a very liberal concession, what does it prove ? It establishes the fact that these emigrants professed the doctrines of the symbolical books in Germany, and intended to adhere to the same faith in this country, a point which we have already asserted of the early Lutherans in general. But were these Saltzburgers, when in Germany, the Lutheran church in this country, or even as yet a part of it? And could this contract, which they formed there, with any propriety be adduced to prove that our church *in this country*, or even that they, when they subsequently became a part of it, passed a resolution, or took any public step *formally* adopting the symbolic books as binding on their churches here ? Certainly not.

3. In regard to the founders of our church in Pennsylvania, the facts in the case incontestably prove that "our church never *formally adopted*" the symbolic books, that is, that no synod or convention ever passed an act declaring the symbolical books binding on themselves, and to be required of all who wished to unite with them. The question, whether the patriarchs of our church adopted these symbols formally, or substantially, is immaterial in reference to our present duties. The obligation of the present generation of our ministers, both in honor and religion, depends simply on the question, whether they individually bound themselves at their licensure or ordination, to receive any other symbol than the Bible. If not, then, by no course of legitimate reasoning can a mass of human productions, twice as large as the whole New Testament, be imposed upon them, as binding on their consciences.

4. As to the little handful of Swedish Lutheran churches, —they have long since been swallowed up by the Episcopalians, and there is not even a single congregation of them that has retained its Lutheran profession. However pious, and noble-minded and liberal, some of their ministers were, they were the servants of their ecclesiastical superiors in Sweden, from whom they derived their subsistence and under whose instructions they acted, to which they no doubt

conformed. But they *never had the right* formally to resolve to accept or reject the symbolical books, unless they wished to lose their support, which was paid from Sweden, and be dismissed from the Swedish churches. It is undoubtedly true, that the instructions sent from Sweden, to Governor Printz, directed that the worship of the church of the colony should be conducted, according to the symbolical books and usages of the Swedish church. But we certainly need not inform the reader, that their ecclesiastical superiors in Sweden were not the Lutheran church in America; nor is it supposable that these Swedish ministers after their arrival in this country, ever *formally* adopted a resolution that the symbolic books should be regarded as binding on them, for that was a matter of course. Still, it should not be forgotten, that the Swedish church in Europe did not receive any other Lutheran symbol than the Augsburg Confession, and Luther's Smaller Catechism: so that these Swedish churches on the Delaware also certainly rejected all the other books. On the whole, then, it appears that not one of all these cases bears on the point, whether the Lutheran church in this country ever formally adopted the symbolical books or not, excepting the several individual cases of ordination, in which a pledge was in fact required. And in several of these the specific contents of the pledge are not known, though they doubtless embraced the Augsburg Confession, and possibly also the other symbolical books. These cases prove the *practical* adoption of at least a part of the symbolical books; but do not touch the *formal* adoption of either a part or the whole by our American church.

In corroboration of this position, we add a few remarks. It is reasonable to suppose, that if the founders of our American church, had formally adopted even the Augsburg Confession alone, or all the symbolic books, at any synod or convention, they would have recognized these books as symbolic in some part or other of their liturgies or synodical constitutions. But in their liturgy of 1786, even the Augsburg Confession is no where mentioned, much less the other symbolic books; excepting a direction that Catechumens should study Luther's Catechism. In the liturgy of 1818, there is a formulary for ordination, containing the prayers, address, and even the questions proposed to the candidates; but neither the Augsburg Confession nor any other symbolic book is even named in it. Only in the form for the consecration of churches is the Augsburg Confession referred to. But the study of the Catechism is enjoined, as was also the case in the former edition, and at Confirmation, in one of the formularies, the subjects profess fidelity to the doctrines of Jesus, according to the professed views or confession of the Evangelical church, though neither of the symbolical books is named.

Again, if a synod or convention of the early ministers of our church, had ever passed a resolution formally to adopt the symbolical books, and to require assent to them, at licensure or ordination, would it not necessarily be seen in the constitution of the Synod subsequently published, in which the rights, *duties*, &c., of *licentiates* and *ordained pastors*, as well as the rules for Synodical and ministerial business are contained? We have two editions of the constitution of the Synod of Pennsylvania, ("Ministerial Ordnung.") The oldest is a reprint of an earlier copy, and was published in 1813; but that from which it is copied, probably belongs to the former century. At all events, it seems to belong to the period prior to 1805; for it contains a resolution appended, passed June 12th, 1805, and "ordered to be incorporated with the constitution," which must therefore have existed before it. No notice is given in this edition that any alterations had been made in the constitution itself, nor is it styled a revised edition. Yet in this early constitution, *not a word* is said of requiring a pledge, oral or written, to all or any one of the symbolical books. Since then not one of the symbolical books is even named in the detailed formulary for ordination in the liturgy of 1818, though the questions to be answered by candidates are there given, and nothing is said on the subject of ordination in that of 1786, and since the same is the case in the constitution (Ministerial Ordnung) of the Synod of Pennsylvania, dating back at least to within five years of the last century, although the rights, duties, &c., of licentiates and ordained ministers, as well as the rules for synodical and ministerial business, are contained in it, it seems certain from the present state of the evidence, that this respectable, ancient and mother Synod of our church *never did formally adopt* any of the symbolical books, as a test of licensure or ordination; and that their actually having required such a pledge in various cases in practice, was done by the tacit consent of all parties, it being conceded by all that the symbolical books, and especially the Augsburg Confession, contained, with the exception of a few minor articles, a correct expose of the doctrines which they held.

CHAPTER IV.

Actual abandonment of all symbolic requisition at the commencement of this century, and virtual recognition only of the Augsburg Confession as to the fundamentals of God's Word.

We pass on to our *fourth* position:

4. *That, about the beginning of this century the fathers of our church ceased, in fact, to require assent even to the Augsburg Confession at licensure and ordination, and demanded only faith in the word of God, thus practically rejecting (as they had a right to do) all the symbolical books as tests; though still respecting and occasionally referring to the Augsburg Confession as a substantial expose of the doctrines which they taught.*

The literal truth of this position, that all requisition of assent to any creed but that one furnished by the Holy Ghost, in the Scriptures given by his inspiration, was abandoned about fifty years ago, is not denied. That, about the beginning of this century the custom of requiring assent even to the Augsburg Confession, which had been observed in several instances, was wholly relinquished, is just as certain as that General Washington died near the close of last century, or that Thomas Jefferson was elected President in the first year of the present one. Numerous living witnesses yet remain to attest the fact, and it cannot be successfully denied.

But, it has been supposed by some, that the abandonment of the practice of requiring a pledge of assent to these books, does not remove our church from the *historical basis of these symbols!*

A shrewd observer of human nature once remarked, that "*names are things;*" and things they doubtless are in the importance of their results, although in the language of the schools, they are but signs of our ideas. It cannot be denied, a large portion of mankind, learned and unlearned, are often deceived by the mere indefinite or figurative use of words. Of this we have a striking example in the opinion under consideration, namely, that our church was founded on the historical basis of these symbols, and therefore the practical rejection of them by the church subsequently, cannot remove her from this basis. A brief analysis of this opinion will demonstrate its fallacy. By our church is meant the *members* who constituted it at any particular time, and by our church at the period of its foundation, is to be understood the mass of its members at the time of their organization into a regular ecclesiastical society in this Western world, and not their successors in any other age. To be *historically* founded, signifies to be founded in history, that is, to be proved by events which are matters of historic record. What, then, are the historical facts connected with the organization of our church as recorded in history? They have constituted the topics of a large portion of the discussions in this essay and are briefly these: That the founders of our church, who probably had assented to the symbolical books in Germany, also in various informal ways avowed their belief of those doctrines here—that in several cases they required assent to one or all of these books at licensure and ordination, and at the erection of church edifices,—but that they never formally, that is, by a resolution of Synod, adopted any of these books as symbolical or binding, as tests of admission or discipline—and that subsequently, about the close of last century, whilst some of the earlier ministers were yet lingering on the stage of action, and mingling in their counsels, they wholly relinquished the practice of requiring assent to any thing but the Bible. Now was there any thing in these events binding future ages? Nay, did not these devoted men practically decide, by ceasing to use and thus practically rejecting the symbolic authority of these books, that they themselves were not bound by their own previous action, after they ceased to regard it as proper? In short, there is a difference between history and prophecy.

The one relates only the past, the other the future. A historical basis involves no obligation on future ages, other than they approve and voluntarily assume. Thus did Luther reason. He well knew that the errors and superstitions of Rome were "historically founded" in the decrees of councils, bulls of popes, the Romish missal, &c. But did he say, "therefore I must not oppose them? Or, if I wish to advocate other views, I must withdraw from the church thus historically founded on these errors?" Every tyro in history will answer no. He began to inveigh against these corruptions because he regarded them unscriptural, and he persevered in doing so for years, without the least thought of withdrawing from the church, until he saw that he was to be excommunicated, and then he committed the papal bull to the flames, and renounced all connexion with the church of Rome. As genuine disciples of Luther, we, therefore, recognize no binding authority in the "historical foundation" referred to, as depriving us, in any degree, of our natural and individual obligations and rights.

CHAPTER V.

The voluntary and personal nature of ecclesiastical obligations: and the obligation of the church in every successive age to conform her confession to the word of God.

The position now claiming our attention is the fifth in the series, as formerly enunciated:

5. *That ecclesiastical obligations are voluntary and personal; and not either hereditary or compulsory. Hence the church, that is, the ministry and laity of every age, have as good a right, and are as much under obligation to oppose, and, if possible, to change what they believe wrong in the religious practice of their predecessors and to conform it to the word of God, as were Luther and the other christians of the sixteenth century.*

In order fully to appreciate the truth and force of this position, we must recur to first principles. What, then, is the church, whose obligations we are discussing? In a former chapter we showed, that in the view of the inspired Paul, the "Church" consisted of *persons*, not of things; and of individuals, not of an abstract, ideal, corporate personality. He describes it as embracing "those that are sanctified in Christ Jesus, called to be saints, with all that in every place call upon the name of Jesus Christ our Lord." 1 Cor. i. 2. In full accordance with this is the view of Luther, who defines the church to be "the congregation, number or assemblage of all christians in all the world, who are the only bride of Christ and his spiritual body."[1] Melancthon says the visible church is the "cœtus vocatorum seu profitentium evangelium," the assemblage of the called, or of those who profess the Gospel. The New Testament introduces us to a number of such churches, as that at Jerusalem, at Corinth, at Ephesus, at Rome, &c. From all that is said of these churches, the following points are indisputably established, as well as by other evidence from Scripture and reason:

1. That *the church is no where spoken of as an abstract, corporate mass*, or an *ideal body possessing substantive personality apart from the members* at any time constituting it, according to the Puseyite or Romish notion; nor as serving as a reservoir to contain all the spiritual influences vouchsafed by God to his children, and dispensing them through her officers and sacraments to the applicants. Nor do they speak of the church as possessing or being capable of possessing any character such as being faithful or unfaithful, orthodox or heterodox, that is sound or unsound in the faith; except as these attributes are applicable to the persons then constituting the Church. Nor do they tell us that the church at Jerusalem had one confession of faith, and the church at Antioch, or Rome, another and a different one. Much less do they utter the remotest intimation that if the persons constituting the church in any particular age or country see fit to devise a human system of organization,

(1) Ich glaube dasz eine heilige christliche Kirche sei auf Erden, "das ist die Gemeine und Zahl oder Versammlung aller Christen in aller Welt, die einge Braut Christi und sein geistlicher Leib."

consisting of confessions, liturgy, discipline, &c., as was first generally done by the successors of Luther, about fifty years after the publication of the Augsburg Confession; that their doing so places the church, that is, professing christians, in after ages, under the least obligation to adopt such human system, unless they believe it accordant with the principles and instructions of God's word. And as to any such creed being established by civil government, and enforced by civil disabilities, it is an outrage alike upon the rights of man and the character of the Protestant church.

2. *We find each of these churches spoken of as a church of Christ, not as part of a church,* or as having only a part of the privileges and duties belonging to his church on earth. Nor do we find that those churches were bound together by any external stated bond of union; nor that in the apostolic age the churches were connected together into any synodical associations as at present, much less into different denominations on the grounds of differences in doctrine or forms of government and worship. Hence, if the inspired apostles knew what is essential to the valid organization of a church of Christ as well as their uninspired successors do, it is obviously preposterous to suppose that any thing essential was left wanting by them; or that churches by associating into synods or denominations, are in any sense more perfectly churches of Christ than was each such individual local church in the apostolic age; or that they in the sight of God possess any higher privileges or authority. Still, on the ground of human expediency, Synods and General Synods may be and are highly useful; if they do not impose a yoke on individual churches, but as in our American Lutheran system of government, act chiefly as advisory bodies. The principle of such union for advisory counsel and co-operation, is given us in the primitive council held at Jerusalem; and the churches in every age are at liberty to employ it, as far as experience proves it useful and safe.

3. *Each individual member of the Church is bound to search the Scriptures, and to believe and act for himself.* It was for pursuing this course that the apostle Paul applauded the Bereans; and it was not only to the apostles, but to his hearers generally that the Saviour addressed the command, "Search the scriptures, for in them ye think ye have eternal life, and they are they which testify of me." In short,

reason and scripture combine to teach us that God deals with every individual as a moral agent, possessed of certain inalienable rights, and obligated to certain inalienable duties; and the right and duty of private judgment in matters of religion are so universally conceded *as essential principles of Protestantism,* that it were superfluous to spend time in establishing them.

But this principle of individual responsibility and of obligation to individual action is still further established by the fact, that in the day of retribution, when we shall all appear before the judgment-seat of Christ, He will judge and dispense his retributions to *every one* according to the deeds done in *his* body. Nor is the principle of personal imputation admitted at this grand assize. Here our *temporal* situation is often affected by the conduct of our parents, and in this way the sins of parents are often visited on their children to the third and fourth generation. But there, when the Son of Man shall come in the glory of his Father, he will reward every individual "according to *his* works." "The son shall not bear the iniquity of the father, neither shall the father bear the iniquity of the son. But the soul that sinneth, *it* shall die." *It therefore follows unavoidably, that our ecclesiastical, as well as other obligations,* from the observance or neglect of which these rewards and punishments result, *are also personal and not hereditary, are voluntary and not compulsory,* which is the point of our proposition.

4. *As every church is but a collection of such professed believers, each of whom is under immediate responsibility to God to make the word of God the paramount and only infallible rule of his faith and practice, it follows, that as a church, they are all under precisely the same obligations, in the discharge of all associated religious or ecclesiastical duties.* Hence, if the members of a church find a human creed, professed by their predecessors, it is their duty individually and collectively to compare it with the scriptures, and if found erroneous, or of injurious length, to have it corrected by the infallible standard.

Again, though the churches may co-operate in any arrangement or association, not inconsistent with the precepts and spirit of the scriptures, such as synods, councils, societies, &c., if experience proves them favorable to the advancement of religion; yet must they always be watchful, not to forget or renounce any of their individual and inalienable rights. Thus churches may adopt an expose of their scriptural faith, long enough to exclude fundamental errorists, as did the christians of the second, third and fourth centuries, in receiving the so-called Apostles' Creed and the Nicene Creed. But we cannot believe it justifiable in any church, to adopt such extended creeds as include numerous articles of doctrine not necessary to harmonious co-operation among acknowledged christians, and as rob the members and ministers of the church of that individual liberty in searching the scriptures, which is our inalienable right. If our predecessors in the church, with which we are providentially connected, have adopted creeds, some parts of which we cannot believe to be scriptural, it is our duty to publish our dissent from such creeds, as well as our agreement; and if we differ on points which we regard fundamental, to reject such creeds altogether. This is the view of duty entertained and pursued by that highly respectable and active portion of our American Zion, the Congregationalists of New England, in the reception of the Westminster Assembly's Catechism and Confession of Faith. Says the Rev. Dr. Woods, late Professor of Theology in Andover Seminary, in his letters to Unitarians, "As it is one object of these letters to make you acquainted with the real opinions of the Orthodox in New England, I would here say with the utmost frankness, that we are not perfectly satisfied with the language used on this subject in the Assembly's Catechism. Though we hold that Catechism, taken as a whole, in the highest estimation, we could not with a good conscience subscribe to every expression it contains, in relation to the doctrine of original sin. Hence, it is common for us, when we declare our assent to the Catechism, to do it with an express or implied restriction. We receive the Catechism *generally*, as containing a summary of the principles of Christianity. Again, the imputation of Adam's sin to his posterity, in any sense which those words naturally and properly convey, *is a doctrine which we do not believe*," (though taught in that creed,)—pp. 44, 45. Thus the New School Presbyterians also disbelieve the limited extent of the atonement, agreeing with the Lutherans and Congregationalists in the belief of its universality; and they also freely profess their dissent on this point from their Confession of Faith. Exactly the same is the manner in which the churches of the General Synod receive the Augsburg Confession, namely: with the express restriction of its binding authority to the fundamentals of the gospel, and the admission of difference on unfundamental points. So far from our case being in this respect unprecedented, it is sustained by the example of the two most respectable sister denominations of our land. And this is as it should be. The church, that is professing believers, should alter, limit, or reject what is in their judgment unscriptural in the creed, and not the unscriptural creed eject the members from the church. Or in other words, in the language of our proposition, *it is the duty of the church in every other age as much as in that of the Reformation, to reform or reject what they believe unscriptural in the religious practices of their ancestors, and to conform their own to the infallible word of God.*"

Our *sixth* proposition naturally flows from the preceding:

6. *Whatever moral obligation the practical requisition of assent to the Augsburg Confession by our fathers, may have imposed on themselves and those thus admitted by them, it was annulled, when, by common consent, they revoked that practice.*

Our duties are not created by our opinions of them, but arise from the nature of things, and from the relations we sustain to the various beings in the universe. Hence, whilst it is reasonable to expect us to retain a practice, so long as in our opinion it is obligatory; if we change our opinion, it is equally proper, that we should relinquish it. It is also admitted, that good men ordinarily do what they regard as obligatory on them; hence their habitual conduct is a fair index of their views of duty. When, therefore, our fathers under the influence of the views they brought from Europe, at first practically required assent to the Augsburg Confession, it is a just inference that they believed it their duty to do so. With these views of duty, they and those to whom they administered this pledge, were under obligations to adhere in the ministrations of the sacred desk, to all the contents of this symbol. This course the christian public had a right to expect them to pursue, until they professed a change of opinion. But it is equally certain, and for exactly the same reasons, that whenever they did change their opinion of the propriety of such a course, not commanded in scripture, and did in fact publicly abandon the practice of requiring any other test than the word of God; they in like manner thus published to the world their altered conviction of duty, which change absolved them and all persons subsequently admitted, from any such obligation in the view of the public, on the ground of consistency. The reasons in both cases are found in the positions above established, that it is the duty of the church, that is, of christians, in every age, to search the scriptures, and to act out the honest convictions in which such investigation results. To suppose that the practical observance of a custom, not enjoined in scripture, could impose obligations, which a change of opinion in the same persons, or in those succeeding them, could not annul, and from the observance of which an equally public practical rejection of it, would not release us in the eyes of the christian community, is contrary to all sound reason, as well as the ethical principles of scripture.

7. In perfect accordance with the principles here evolved, was the practice of the Great Reformer. He was trained up in the doctrines and usages of the church of Rome, he found them sanctioned by the authority of popes and councils, and confirmed by the practice of many centuries. To crown the whole, he had voluntarily obligated himself by an oath, when he was created Doctor of Divinity, "*to obey the church of Rome, and not to teach any doctrines condemned by her.*" Nevertheless, when in the providence of God he became acquainted with the Scriptures, and his continued study of them taught him the errors of Rome, he fearlessly began the work of Reformation, and in disregard of councils, popes and the holy mother church, and even of his own oath, which he now regarded as null and void, he prosecuted the work of reform within the church, and when he found this a hopeless enterprise, finally anticipated his excommunication by renouncing the church, and commenced an independent organization. Numerous passages might be cited in which he avows the principles involved in this course of action, and necessary to its justification.

Nor was Luther guilty of the inconsistency of desiring to impose upon others the yoke which he had indignantly cast off. Never did he wish any human composition, either of his own or others, to be made symbolical, or binding on the church. Nor was the symbolic system introduced into the church during his lifetime, nor until more than a quarter of a century after his translation to a better world. But, has not the contrary been supposed to be the case? It has, and therefore it may not be amiss to correct the error. The true origin of the symbolic system of servitude is thus fairly stated by Dr. Kœllner, in his Symbolik, (Vol. I. pp. 106, 107:) "The symbolical books, (as they were afterward styled,) were first merely an expression of what *was* believed; afterwards they became the rule of what *must* be be believed. But where and how this was first done by public authority, it is very difficult to determine. The traces and evidences of it are often fallacious; because cases in which such subscription to a creed was merely requested and voluntarily given, may easily be adduced as cases in which the subscription was commanded. It, however, appears to be true, that some individual symbols had so much authority attributed to them, as to be recommended as rules of faith and of instruction, and in some instances also commanded, long before the formation of the Form of Concord, (which was half a century after the publication of the Augsburg Confession.) Nevertheless this does not appear everywhere to have occurred at the same time, and in the same manner; nor does the principle of binding men to the symbols, seem to have been a universal and prevailing one, prior to the formation of the Form of Concord, (i. e. 1580,) or before the prevalence of the controversies which originated from its formation. But a change took place about the time the Form of Concord was composed, and on account of its formation, and after it. Prior to this time, some cases had occurred, of oppressive coercion in matters of faith, and of compulsory adoption of the symbols as a rule of faith and instruction; but afterward they became more numerous." These positions he sustains by numerous authorities, which even fix the precise times, when, at different places, the custom of demanding assent to these symbols was first introduced. That distinguished historian, Dr. Schrœck, bears the following testimony as to the time when the custom of requiring assent to the symbolical books was *generally* introduced in the electorate of Saxony. "This oath, (says he,) was not prescribed in electoral Saxony until AFTER THE TIME OF THE FORM OF CONCORD, when Christian II., in 1602, (more than half a century after Luther's death,) prescribed it. Subsequently, in 1661, (more than fifty years later still,) the civil government required it so generally, that throughout the electorate of Saxony all preachers, schoolmasters and officers at court or elsewhere, were required to assume this obligation." Here we perceive that although theological professors had been required to pledge themselves to the Augsburg Confession at an early day, as we stated on a former occasion, yet no such pledge was required of the ministry in general, until half a century after the Augsburg Confession was practically acknowledged as the expose of Lutheran doctrine, even in the electorate of Saxony itself, the residence of Luther, and the head-quarters of the church. Schrœck, sup. cit. vol. IV., pp. 470, 471.

It seems evident, then, that the habit of ascribing normative or binding authority to these books, though, in a few instances, it was done at an early day, was of gradual growth, and did not become general *for half a century after the Augsburg Confession was published* and used as a profession or expose of faith, and *many years after the death of Luther*. But could this be the case if Luther had from the beginning, or at any time during his life, desired that these books should possess this binding authority? Or if this had been his wish, as it was so partially done, would he not have expressed his desire on this subject? Yet his works contain no passage of such import. On the contrary, Luther repeatedly expressed his opposition to having his works regarded as binding upon the consciences of others. In his instructions to the visitors in the Electorate of Saxony, he uses this noble language: "Nevertheless, we cannot suffer this, (book of instructions,) to go forth as rigid commands that we may not issue new Popish decretals, (auf daz wir nicht neue Pæpstliche Decretales aufwerfen,) but only as a historic description, and also as a testimony and *Confesssion of our faith*," not mere ceremonies and forms of worship.) In his well-known passage, protesting against his followers being called Lutherans, he expressly declares: "*I will be no one's master*, (Ich will keines Meister seyn.)" In his "Preface to the first part of his German works," written in 1539, only seven years before his death, (vol. 14, p. 420, Walch's ed.,) he says: "Gladly would I have seen all my books neglected and lost." "This was also my opinion (or design meinung) when I began the translation of the scriptures themselves, that I hoped there would be less writing done, and more studying and reading of the Scriptures. For all other writings (or publications) should lead us to the Bible, as St. John to Christ, (John iii. 30,) in order *that each one might for himself drink out of the pure* (or fresh) *fountain.* For neither the councils, nor the fathers, *nor we ourselves*, can, by our best and most successful efforts, make as good work as the Scriptures, as God himself has made."

"Well, then, (since, as he had just said, he could not prevent the republication of his works,) I make the friendly request, that whoever desires, at present, to possess my works, (and he makes no exceptions of those which have since been made symbolic,) shall by no means allow them to hinder him from studying the Scriptures themselves, *but shall regard them as I regard the decrees and decisions of the popes and the books of the sophists;* that is, occasionally to examine them and see what they have done, or to calculate the history of the times; *not that I regard it a duty to study them, or to practice what they taught.*" Other passages of similar import might be added, but these we would fain hope are sufficient to confirm the positions of Kœllner. and to show that Luther never wished any of his books to "be binding on others." That he desired his catechisms to be used as books of instruction, is natural and proper. It was for this purpose that he composed them. But, that he wished them to be regarded as symbolical, as binding on all who should belong to the same religious denomination, is quite another thing, and requires very different, yea, positive evidence.

But, if all the above evidence, so satisfactory in itself, were obliterated from the pages of history, the very language of Luther in his preface to the Smaller Catechism, should, we think, settle it forever. Not only does it not contain a syllable about his wish, that it should be regarded as binding; but the reverse. In this preface, (Baumgarten's Concordeinbuch, pp. 614, 615,) he deplores the ignorance of the people, urges the importance of elementary instruction, and begs those ministers *who could not make better ones themselves*, to use these forms and tables, i. e. the catechisms which he had prepared. (*Bitte ich euch—welche es nicht besser vermaegen, diese Tafeln und Form vor sich zu nehmen.*) And urging the importance of adhering to the very same words in teaching the populace the decalogue, the Lord's prayer, the Apostles' creed, the sacraments, &c., he says: Therefore *select what form you choose*, and adhere to it perpetually, (Darum erwæhle welche Form du wilt, und blieb' dabey ewiglich.) Again, after the pupils have committed to memory the text, as he terms it, that is, the decalogue, Lord's prayer, &c., he urges the ministers to explain the import of them, and for this purpose, he says: "Take again before you, (that is use,) these tables, *or some other short method, whichever you please*, and adhere to it, (Nimm abermal vor dich, dieser Tafeln Weise, *oder sonst ein kurze einige Weise, welche du wilt*, und bleib dabey.) Now all these quotations are Luther's own declarations, prefixed to the very catechism in question, and if they do not, especially in connexion with the mass of other evidence here adduced, utterly preclude the idea of his having wished his catechism to be regarded as symbolical, and as binding on the Lutheran church, we confess our inability to estimate the force of evidence.

That our estimate of the facts and evidence in the case is correct, is admitted by the ultra-Lutherans themselves, as we will prove by a quotation from Professor Guericke, showing that even he does not suppose that Luther designed his catechisms to be symbolical.

"As Luther's catechisms (says he) were not prepared in consequence of any public resolution, so also they did not attain symbolical authority by formal subscription to them, but rather by tacit consent. They introduced themselves into use every where, especially the smaller one, by their pure and animated simplicity and unsurpassable practical concreteness. Moreover, the Form of Concord, also, formally and unequivocally avows them, after they had previously been received into several Corpora Doctrinæ (or collections of Confessions of Faith)." Symb. p. 102. Now if Guericke had supposed that Luther had designed these catechisms to be symbolic, would he not have said so when he was speaking of their origin and the manner in which they acquired symbolic authority, and admitting that they were not declared symbolic by any ecclesiastical authority, prior to that of the Form of Concord, fifty-two years after they were written. In perfect accordance with this view is the testimony of Kœllner. "Therefore, in just acknowledgment of their importance both for doctrine and religious practice, they were received into the Corpora Doctrinæ; and this importance and existing general use also received the public sanction of the church, inasmuch as symbolic authority was given them in the Form of Concord, and thus secured to them." Symbolik, I. p. 511. It seems therefore evident that the symbolic authority, even of these catechisms, was not acknowledged by any act of the church, till the time of the Form of Concord, long after Luther's death.

CHAPTER VI.

The actual doctrinal position of our church at the time of the formation of the General Synod, was that of adherence to the fundamentals of scripture as substantially taught in the Augsburg Confession, with acknowledged and professed dissent on non-essential aspects of doctrine.

That the position here affirmed, namely, that of agreement in fundamentals with the Augsburg Confession, together with acknowledged dissent on some minor points, fairly represents the doctrinal position of our principal Synods, especially of the mother Synod of Pennsylvania, and of those connected with the General Synod, we know from extensive intercourse with them, both personal and epistolary. We believe there are a very few ministers in the Synod of Pennsylvania who hold the doctrine of the bodily presence, &c.; but we have yet to hear of one that desires to force these views upon his brethren. In corroboration of our opinion, we shall, I. Present general statements concerning the doctrinal position of our church during the last quarter of a century. II. Adduce more specific testimony in regard to individual synods and persons, especially the Synod of North Carolina and Rev. Shober and Storke. III. Prove by the declaration and acts of the General Synod herself that she has always held the same position. We begin with the testimony of one of our most aged and respected divines, Dr.

Hazelius, whose partiality for church history is well known, and who has enjoyed unusually favorable opportunities of acquaintance with the views of our church in the Northern, Middle and Southern States.

1. *Dr. Hazelius.* In the Annotations on the Augsburg Confession, prefixed to the "Discipline, &c., of the Synod of South Carolina," (pp. 20–23,) Dr. Hazelius says: "That Luther and the Reformers who labored with him, entertained the idea of the real presence of Christ in the Eucharist, is undeniable; but it is also well known, that the sentiments of Luther concerning the real presence of Christ in the Supper have not always been fully received in the Lutheran Church. Melancthon departed from them, and many of our divines of the seventeenth century, otherwise strict adherents to the doctrines of Luther, moderated the expressions of the great Reformer in such a manner that few Protestant christians of any other denomination could well find fault with their explanation of the manner in which they represented to themselves and taught the presence of Christ in the Eucharist."

"*The opinions,* (continues Dr. Hazelius,) *now entertained in the Lutheran church as to the nature of the sacrcment of the Lord's Supper, differ in no material point from those entertained by the other Protestant churches on the subject.* We believe that Christ instituted this sacrament as a means of spiritual communion with him, as the invisible head of the church, and which is to be statedly observed, until the saints are admitted to personal communion with him in heaven. In it, the christian commemorates with devout feelings the sufferings and death of Christ. By means of this ordinance the christian renews his faith, and receives the *spiritual* blessing which the Saviour has promised to impart to all *worthy* communicants. The body and blood of Christ are set forth in this ordinance, as the *spiritual* food of the soul," &c.

"If, however, (proceeds the Doctor,) any of our brethren should entertain sentiments apparently more conformable to the views and language held forth by the Augsburg Confession, and other writings of the first Reformers, we do not desire to disturb them in that opinion, inasmuch as we know that the main point in this, as in every other religious observance, is the heart," &c. "At the table of Christ, they (Christians differing on minor points,) may forget their minor differences and commune in sweet and endearing fellowship with each other and their Lord." In this quotation the italics are our own; and we doubt not the interest of its matter will fully justify its length.

These sentiments, to which we cordially assent, are fully endorsed by the Synod of South Carolina, by whom the volume containing them is officially published for public use in their churches. The action of the Synod also shows the fallacy of the inference, that the publication of the Augsburg Confession by the Hartwick Synod, or one of its ministers, implies a belief of all its contents, or a desire or even willingness to make it binding in any other manner than we contend for, and than is secured by the General Synod in her Constitution for Synods. For the same volume which furnishes us the above extract, also contains the Constitution of that Synod, in which the Augsburg Confession is avowed as the bond of union in the following terms:

Art. II. "The Augsburg Confession of Faith shall be the point of union in our churches, inasmuch as we believe that the *fundamental* doctrines of the Word of God are taught in a manner substantially correct in the doctrinal articles of said Confession." In this sense all the Synods belonging to the General Synod, have received this Confession, and in this sense alone, we confidently believe, would any one of these bodies be willing to accept it.

It has been conjectured by some that there has of late years been a recession from the more rigid confessional ground assumed by that body at its formation. Now, it so happens, that we were present in Baltimore in 1819, when the Rev. Schober first proposed his plan for a General Synod, which was very much like that of the Presbyterian General Assembly. We were present at Hagerstown in 1820, when the Constitution was definitely formed and adopted; and we heard with much attention all the debates in both meetings. We have been present, either as member or visitor, and for many years as chairman of the Hymn Book Committee, at the meeting of every General Synod, save one, that has ever been held; we were intimately acquainted with those elder members of that body who have since been called to their rest, such as Drs. Endress, Lochman, Geissenhainer, and Mr. Schober, and we think we ought to understand the real views and plans of that Synod, as fully as any man in our church. Now we can assure our readers, that instead of a retrograde movement, actual progress has been made in an opposite direction. Our own views coincided, in general, with those of Mr. Schober. We regretted the failure of his efforts to have the Augsburg Confession substantially recognized, or even named in the Constitution of that body; and after the lapse of some years we ourselves accomplished the very thing, by introducing it into the Constitution for Synods. To this substantial recognition of the mother symbol of Protestantism, the General Synod still adheres. *It is all her most zealous friends ever desired,* and I trust that is all that the enlightened friends of religion and of our church will ever admit. Our own views of this subject have never changed. And the Professorial oath of office in our Seminary, though written by us as early as 1825, is in exact conformity with this position. We made it express exactly what we thought right, and what we still think every Professor of a Lutheran Seminary ought to be pledged to; and it is substantially the same that is required by the Constitution for Synods at licensure and ordination. Instead, therefore, of retrogression, there has been approximation to the Augsburg Confession, in the General Synod since her formation. And the alleged recent growth of a more lax system among the members of the General Synod, is a gross misapprehension of the truth, as is well known to those who personally participated in the transactions of that body from the beginning.

And why should we, after the additional experience and light of more than three centuries, feel any reluctance in departing from some of the minor doctrines of the Augsburg Confession; when it is certain that its very author, Melancthon himself, did so; yea, that Luther, the great founder, not of our religion indeed, for which we look to Christ, but of our organization as a denomination, did the same? For, in his Smalcald articles he denounces the *mass* as "the most horrible abomination of popery," though it had been "in a measure defended in the Confession," especially in the abuses mutati, or articles concerning the corruptions of the church. Why should we feel any reluctance, when even the secular authorities, the Protestant princes themselves, directed their theologians to re-examine the Augsburg

Confession by the inspired word of God, and alter anything that might be found inconsistent with that only infallible rule; and all this seven years after that Confession had been published and translated into various languages, and circulated over all Europe?

"If, therefore, (we again quote the judicious and appropriate words of Dr. Hazelius,) every departure from the literal sense of the Augsburg Confession, amounts to a dereliction of Lutheranism, it is certainly a source of congratulation and joy to those who have thus departed, that Luther and Melancthon have set them the example. Those heroes of the Reformation never intended that christians should follow them in all respects, for even they differed among themselves in regard to some opinions concerning the Lord's Supper; but they demanded that christians should prayerfully study the Bible and consider the authority of that book as paramount to all human wisdom and philosophy."

"On this broad basis of Protestantism the American Lutheran churches are still standing; charitable and liberal in matters of minor importance, they are willing to aid in leveling down the partition walls, which are now separating Protestant from Protestant." This latter sentiment, so congenial to the millennial glory of the church, is fully expressed in the General Synod's Constitution, and itself dissipates the contracted delusion, that the founders of that noble institution desired to recall to prominent attention, the sectarian peculiarities of our church, by restoring the obsolete authority of her enormous symbols. "The General Synod shall apply all their powers, their prayers and their means toward the prevention of schisms among us, to be sedulously and incessantly regardful of the circumstances of the times, and *of every casual rise and progress of unity of sentiment among christians in general,* in order that the blessed opportunities *to promote concord and unity, and the interest of the Redeemer's kingdom,* may not pass by neglected and unavailing." Art. III, § 8. Such was the exalted, the truly apostolic design of our General Synod, and it were easy to demonstrate that her action in the promotion of Christian union in general, as well as unity in our own church, has been perfectly accordant with the principle thus avowed.

2. *Dr. C. Endress.* Our next proof is taken from a very interesting, though extended letter of the *Rev. Dr. Endress,*

one of the ablest, most distinguished and influential among our oldest divines. He entered the ministry about the year 1794, and wielded an important influence in our church as one of its leading spirits until his decease in 1827. He was an able expounder of the word of God, a learned and enlightened theologian. He also richly merits the grateful remembrance of our church as one of the most active and controlling founders of the General Synod. As the letter, which was addressed to Rev. J. P. Schindel, senr., Lancaster, dated July 25th, 1821, is somewhat miscellaneous in its contents, we shall barely allude to some of its topics and then cite the portion more directly bearing on our subject. Dr. E. speaks with the highest respect of the different forms or symbols of the Lutheran church, as theological compositions, excepting the Form of Concord, concerning which his sentiments cannot well be mistaken: "We have the Formula Concordiæ, in which expulsion, condemnation, anathema were, in the most liberal manner, pronounced and poured forth against all those who were of a different opinion, which, however, thank God, was never received *universally* by the Lutheran church. *I would suffer both my hands to be burned off before I would subscribe that instrument.*"

The Dr. also asserts what we have repeatedly affirmed, that the Augsburg Confession, like the other symbols, (except the Formula Concordiæ,) was never intended by its authors to be used as symbols to bind the consciences of others, says "the Lutheran church existed in parts of Germany for thirteen years, and was established throughout Saxony six years, and in Prussia, Moravia, Sweden and Denmark, several years before even the Augsburg Confession was written"—"During this time they distinguished themselves as Lutherans by peremptorily and absolutely refusing to receive or acknowledge, as a confession of faith, the writings and dictates of *man*." This book alone (the Bible) should be and should remain the foundation of their faith."

Dr. Endress then quotes the opinion first of Melancthon, and secondly, of Luther, as follows:

"Here they say: Shall there be no visible judge in the church, and what avails the judgment if it have no power from the judge? "To this we give this sufficient answer: It is God's will that there should be visible courts in the church, that they should be truly upheld, as it is written:

De Ecclesia, and it is not God's will that blasphemy or any erroneous doctrines should be suffered to be propagated."

"And this visible judge is the *church,* i. e. pious ministers and others; this visible judge is, however, strictly bound to God's Word, for these are things from God, and are contained in the writings of the Prophets and Apostles. Therefore shall no creature—no angel—no man—no pope—bishop—minister, &c., set up articles of faith or confessions against God's Word or separated from God's Word—nothing new nor different from the Holy Word of God."

"Against *this* the philosophers and wise men of the world say, the Scriptures are uncertain, and are interpreted and explained by one portion in one way and by others in a different way: for this reason the visible judge should have persons to decide."

I could not have expressed Melancthon's opinion better in his own words, than I have done in mine, before the Synod, without seeing the above. What he says further in his long dissertation, amounts to this: That councils and synods may confess for themselves. Their confession, however, is not binding upon others; but the Scriptures are binding upon all, and that they should oppose false doctrines; but should not judge them according to the opinion of councils, synods, or confessions of faith, but according to Holy Writ.

You shall now hear Luther's opinion, for fear you might think this was only Melancthon's, although *that* would be sufficient for the attainment of my object, because he wrote the Augsburg Confession. Luther himself says:

"On the other hand, to judge of doctrinal matters, &c., we must not care for precepts of men, i. e., for things set up by men, for laws, antiquity, custom and usage, whether it be of the pope or the emperor, or prescribed by the princes or bishops, and approved by the half or whole of the world, &c. For the soul is an immortal thing, and must be governed only by the Eternal Word, and for that reason we must act agreeably to God's Word. If then the Word of God and the doctrines of men are to govern the soul together, then will they unquestionably fight and war against each other. This we will abundantly prove by the following: The word and doctrines which men have set and ordered, we should leave to the judgment of bishops and learned men and councils, (synods?) what they say should be considered by all the world as law and articles of faith. Behold what honor! how indecent and foolish! It operates against the law and word of God."

"For Christ establishes plainly the contrary, and takes this right and power to judge of doctrine from the bishops, the learned men and councils, and gives it to every one and all christians in common. John x. 4, 5, 8. "The sheep follow him; for they know his voice. And a stranger will they not follow—for they know not the voice of strangers. All that ever came before me are thieves and robbers; but the sheep did not hear them." Here you see plainly who has the right to judge of doctrine. Bishops, popes, learned men and all others have power to teach; but the *sheep* shall judge whether it be the voice of Christ or that of a stranger. Friend, what can these water-bubbles say who continually cry, Councils! Councils! You must hear the learned! and you must look to old customs and established ways! Do you suppose that the word of God shall give way to your old customs? No—never! For that reason we leave bishops and councils to conclude and set up what they please; but where we have the word of God we shall stand with that and not with them—they must give way to us and to our word."

Here you see Luther's opinion. Did he not then show the difference between him and the Romanists sufficiently? At that time there was no confession written—but only the Scriptures. Dear brethren, if we hold to the Bible truly, sincerely, and conscientiously, we will not be Romish, nor Calvinistic, nor Zwinglians, nor Socinians, nor Quakers, nor Methodists; we shall distinguish ourselves from them all; nor will we condemn any one on account of mere opinion; we shall, to be sure, find with us and among us tares and that until the harvest comes. The Lord will, however, never permit the true church to go down by misinterpretations of the Bible—" for the foundation of God will stand sure and has this inscription: "The Lord knoweth them that are his."

"As we have (says Dr. Endress) hitherto received the Augsburg Confession, and Luther's Catechism, and Melancthon's Apology, so I have no objection that they should be kept in the same reverence and respect as *our peculiar documents; but not to overrule the Bible.* For by *this* shall the Lutheran church for ever distinguish itself from all other religious connections, that the *Bible*—the *Bible* alone shall remain the only sun in Christ Jesus, and that we rest upon human declarations of faith only in so far as they receive their light more or less from that great light.'

Dr. E. then speaks with the utmost respect of the different symbolic books; and closes in these words:

"What shall I answer on the question: What is the confession of faith of the Lutheran church? Answer: I will not dictate to you what you should say; but if I should be asked, I would say, *first, and principally, and solely, and alone, the Holy Word of God* contained in the writings of the Prophets and Apostles. The confessions of faith by the church, of the first four centuries, we hold in conformity with the Bible, and receive them, as far as I know, universally in the Lutheran church. The confession of the princes of the German empire, presented at the Diet of Augsburg, is held by all in honor and respect, and *when we compare it with other human confessions, we give it a decided preference.* Luther's Catechism is used in all Lutheran churches, and no catechism of other religious denominations has that honor. The so called apology is in possession of very few Lutheran ministers; but whether they have read it or not, they consider it a good book. The Smalkald Articles I have often read. In Germany they are taken up among the synods. I know not whether any other divine in the Lutheran church in America ever read it except Muhlenberg and Lochman. In short we hold firmly and steadfastly to our beloved Bible, when the one holds to Calvin, the other to Zwingel, a third to the Heidelberg Catechism, a fourth to the Confesssion of the Synod of Dort, a fifth to the Westminster Catechism, a sixth to the common-prayer book, a seventh to the solemn league and covenant, and the eighth to the darkened and depraved reason, per se, the ninth to reason, under the name of Holy Spirit, and the tenth to the devil himself in the form of an angel of light. But I will cleave to my beloved Bible, and hereby it shall remain. Amen."

3. *Rev. Dr. Bachman*, in his excellent discourse on the Doctrines and Discipline of the Lutheran church, preached in 1837, by appointment, before the Synod of S. Carolina, and published by said body, says "The articles of the Augsburg Confession, contain the *fundamental* principles of our faith." p. 10.

"In fact, the Lutheran Church has, for a century past, ceased to agitate this question, (i. e. concerning the presence and reception of the body and blood of Christ at the eucharist—leaving its members to follow the dictates of conscience agreeably to the light of Scripture. This we are authorized to do *without a departure from the creed of our church;* since, at our ordination, in this country especially, we only profess to believe "that the *fundamental* articles of the word of God, are taught in a manner *substantially* correct, in the doctrinal articles of the Augsburg Confession." p. 24. By publishing this discourse, which the committee of Synod justly style, "able, lucid and learned," the brethren of that Synod naturally designed to publish to the world their approval of its views, which are precisely accordant with what we have pronounced to be the standpoint of our American Lutheran Church, *fundamental agreement* with the Augsburg Confession, with *acknowledged difference* on *minor* or *non-fundamental points.*

4. *Rev. Dr. Lintner,* of Hartwick Synod, New York, together with Rev. Messrs. Crownse and D. Eyster, and Messrs. Borst and Springer, as a committee of said Synod, in the preface to their edition of the Augsburg Confession, published 1837, say: "The Evangelical Lutheran Church in the United States, profess to adhere to the Augsburg Confession. The General Synod has adopted it as a doctrinal standard; although it does not require the ministers and churches in its connection, to believe every sentiment it contains on those unessential points, which caused so much contention when it was first adopted." From the pledge which the Constitution requires at licensure and ordination, (which is then reported,) "It will appear, that we are not bound to receive the *unessential points* of the Confession. All that is required is, an acknowledgment, that on *essential points of doctrine,* it agrees with the word of God. And this we *do* believe. We hold, that the *fundamental* truths of the gospel, and the *essential* doctrines of salvation, are correctly set forth in the Augsburg Confession; and in this declaration *the committee know that they agree with the body of the Lutheran Church in the United States.*"—p. 3, 4.[1]

(1) This respected brother has recently published an article exhibiting the advantages of having a creed in opposition to some few persons in his

5. *Rev. Dr. Krauth*, about the year 1830, when residing in Philadelphia, prepared for a new edition of Buck's Theological Dictionary, an accurate and impartial, though very brief sketch of the Evangelical Lutheran Church in the United States, in which he gives precisely the same view of our church. "The doctrines of the Evangelical Lutheran Church (says he) are *substantially* those of the Confession of Augsburg. The doctrine of the Trinity, as held by those who differ from Arians and Socinians, a vicarious atonement made by the passion and death of Jesus Christ, the depravity of human nature, the necessity of conversion produced by the Holy Spirit, the resurrection of the body, and a future state of rewards and punishments, eternal in their duration, *may be specified as the cardinal doctrines of this creed.*" Here the reader will perceive the same general view of our doctrinal position; and the doctrine of the bodily presence of the Saviour in the eucharist is very properly not included among the articles regarded as "cardinal" or fundamental. See Luth. Observer for 1831, p. 86.

6. *Rev. Dr. B. Kurtz*, when entering on his duties as editor of the Observer in 1833, in his introductory expose of his principles, after affirming the Evangelical Lutheran Church to be the church of his choice, adds the following views of his duties as a Lutheran: "While, therefore, he (the editor) regards the sacred Scriptures without note or comment, as the only infallible rule of faith and morals, he at the same time holds the prominent doctrines of the Reformation, as *substantially* set forth in the Augsburg Confession, and will consider himself bound, according to his best abilities, to defend and promote them." See Observer for August 24, 1833.

7. *Rev. Dr. G. B. Miller*, Professor of Theology in Hartwick Seminary, New York, in his discourse preached before the Evangelical Lutheran Ministerium of the State of New York, in 1831, uses the following language: "No one, competent to judge, will deny, that it (the Augsburg Confession) contains the two following propositions: That no one who should die without having received baptism, can be saved;

vicinity. who oppose any, even the most temperate use of creeds. That article, taken in connection with his opinions here expressed, exhibit the Dr. as an enlightened friend of a creed of fundamentals, which is the ground of the General Synod.

and that in the Lord's Supper, we actually, not symbolically, or figuratively, but *actually* receive the body and blood of Christ; the same body that was slain, the same blood that was shed on the cross. *Now, few of our ministers, and few of our people, I am bold to say, in this country at least, hold such a belief.*"—p. 8. Here again, one of the oldest and most respectable ministers of our church testifies, that the great mass of our ministers and laymen, have abandoned several prominent doctrines of the Augsburg Confession, one of which was formerly ranked among the distinguishing doctrines of the Lutheran Church. A very few of our ministers have gone so far as to advocate the propriety of rejecting all human creeds. Among these is our esteemed friend, Professor H. I. Smith, of New York, then of Hartwick Seminary. In a discourse, delivered before the Synod of New York, in 1834, he says: "The authority of the New Testament is sufficient for me, without requiring the sanction of either Lutheran or other creeds," &c., &c. Yet this sentiment has never obtained much currency among the ministers of the General Synod.[1] They at once fixed on the medium position as desirable, *fundamental* agreement with the Augsburg Confession, with liberty of difference from it in non-fundamentals, and to this almost the whole mass of our ministers and churches are wisely determined to adhere.

8. *Rev. Dr. Reynolds.* Our last individual testimony on the general aspect of our subject is from an interesting and excellent letter of Dr. Reynolds, penned ten years ago for the Lutheran Observer, when he forwarded to the editor his translation of the letter of Dr. Endress, an extract from which we presented on a previous page. We take pleasure in adding that Dr. R. now agrees with us in regarding the Augsburg Confession as a necessary symbol of our church, and we trust his continued reflections on the subject will also lead him to favor such a liberal use of it as Dr. Endress recommends. On this scriptural, and rational and primi-

(1) It is but justice to Dr. Smith, to state that, more mature reflection led him to forsake this latitudinarian ground, and to place a high value on the use of symbols. It is true, he has now gone further than is in our judgment consistent with true christian and apostolic liberty of conscience; yet we doubt not the generous impulses of his heart, and the further investigation of the subject will lead him to the *juste milien*, to the liberal ground of the inspired apostle, "A brother that is weak in the faith receive thou, but not to doubtful disputations."

tively Lutheran ground our entire American Lutheran Church could be happily united. "The formation of the General Synod (says Dr. R.) marks an epoch in the history of the American Lutheran Church, for it was there she first fairly declared her distinctive character. Hitherto she had been slowly growing up, in individual congregations and in separate synods, in accordance with her original genius and with the free spirit of the institutions of that country to which she had now, for more than half a century, been so happily transplanted. Now, however, she came together, as one body, animated by one spirit, to enter upon and labor in that wide sphere allotted to her. I say *she came together*, for although two synods still stood aloof, the great mass of the church in America was there united, and a moral union was formed even with those fragments which could not at once be blended into one harmonious whole. And although two synods soon after withdrew, in obedience to the blind impulse of a powerful element admitted into the new system, but not then, nor even now, perfectly assimilated to it, or put into its proper relation to it; I mean the popular principle, or congregationalism, yet these two bodies continued in heart integral parts of the union, as was shown by the speedy return of the one, and the frequent efforts of the other to do the same thing. But when in their separation from the General Synod the great mass of the brethren have still co-operated with it and made it a virtual bond of union.

Dr. Endress' letter and the constitution of the General Synod tell us the form which the Lutheran church assumed at this important period. She did not cut herself loose from her Germanic stock and form—the one faith of the church of all ages, by a schismatical separation from it and rejection of its doctrines. Neither, on the other hand, did she slavishly bind herself to the doctrines and discipline, the liturgy or the symbols of any particular branch of the church, whether national or provincial. She duly appreciated the freedom which she had attained by being emancipated from the thraldom of the state by which even the bold spirit of *Luther* himself, much more that of his successors, in every part of Europe, had been fettered and arrested in its onward career. We might verify this in every part of the American church organization, but for the present we confine ourselves to her action in regard to the *symbolical books.* These she neither rejected nor received as an absolute rule of faith. Hence we find in the constitution of the General Synod no action whatever in regard to them, although Art. III., Sec. 3, takes it for granted that our doctrinal views are based upon them, when it requires synods uniting with it to *"hold the fundamental doctrines of the Bible as taught by our church."* So when the General Synod afterward drew up a *constitution for Synods,* it merely required ministers to declare their belief that *"the fundamental doctrines of the Bible were set forth in a manner substantially correct in the Augsburg Confession.* Nor did the delegates who formed the General Synod misrepresent *their constituents.* On the contrary these were then and still continue to be the sentiments of the Pennsylvania and New York Synods, which then embraced the great mass of our ministers and churches. The Pennsylvania Synod, particularly, never required subscription or assent to the symbolical books, nor was the least disposition manifested by it to change its ground when, in 1841, it revised its *Ministerial Ordnung.* But what is still more remarkable and significant in this matter is, that in the liturgy drawn up by a joint committee of the Pennsylvania, New York and Ohio Synods and adopted by those bodies, as also by the Synods of East and West Pennsylvania, and recommended by the General Synod to all the Synods in its connection, *there is no reference either in the formula for licensure or in that for ordination to any obligation of the ministry to teach according to the symbolical books.*

Has the American church then ceased to be Lutheran because she does not subscribe to the Augsburg Confession and other symbolical books? God forbid! for then would she have denied the truth that *Luther* revived and confessed, viz., the *Bible* as the only infallible exposition of God's will and *faith* in our Lord Jesus Christ, as the sole ground of justification. But I need not dwell upon this, as it is the object of *Dr. Endress'* letter to show what it is that specifically distinguishes Lutherans from all other branches of the church. No one, I think, can doubt that he has clearly shown that the symbolical books are not necessary for this end.

There is one idea that seems to have been before *Dr. Endress'* mind, which, however, he has not brought out as clearly as he might have done, and no doubt would have done, had any one impugned his views—I mean the power of the church in all ages to make and publish her own confession of faith. Luther and his compatriots were perfectly right in proclaiming their faith as they have done in the Augsburg Confession and the other symbols. It is a noble testimony which they bore and do still bear to the truth. But they could not—they did not confess for us, their successors. It is true there is a communion of faith among the saints of all ages, but that does not consist in these written creeds, however true and excellent they may be. It is a living principle which may exist under various external forms and may speak itself forth in very different language. And there is likewise a historic connection between the church of all ages, and in reference to this we are prepared to show that the *American* is a true daughter of the *German* church, as reformed by *Luther* himself."

CHAPTER VII.

SPECIFIC TESTIMONY CONCERNING INDIVIDUAL SYNODS AND DIVINES OF THE GENERAL SYNOD, SHOWING THEIR DOCTRINAL POSITION TO BE THAT OF AGREEMENT WITH THE AUGSBURG CONFESSION IN FUNDAMENTALS, AND ACKNOWLEDGED DISSENT ON SOME MINOR POINTS.

WE promised to adduce additional, specific testimony, in regard especially to the Synod of North Carolina and Rev. Messrs. Stork, Shober, the Messrs. Sherers and J. Reck, who were among its principal members. As Mr. Shober was confessedly prominent in desiring some recognition of the Augsburg Confession at the organization of the General Synod, it has been erroneously inferred, that at least he and his Synod, received that symbol without restriction, and desired its unrestricted recognition by the General Synod. This we proved to be all fabulous in our former series; yet as it is an important point in the argument, we add other irresistible proof. So far from yielding implicit assent to the

Augsburg Confession, much less to the other former symbolical books of our church in Germany, Mr. Shober for years carried on a controversy with the Henkelites, who confessedly received every thing found within the lids of the whole Concordeinbuch. In 1821, the very year of the first meeting of the General Synod, Mr. Shober published a work against David Henkel, who was the leader and principal writer as well as disputant of the Tennessee Conference, under the title of "Review of a pamphlet published by David Henkel," &c., containing 64 pages, 8vo, from which we extract the following passages, showing the light in which Mr. Shober, Stork, &c., viewed the doctrines of the ubiquity of Christ's glorified body, taught in the Form of Concord, and the doctrine of the presence and reception of the body and blood of Christ in the Lord's Supper, contained in the Augsburg Confession:

1. From Mr. Shober's Review.

P. 4. Mr. Shober says: "That the body of Christ fills all space, none but *idiots* can believe."

P. 28. Mr. S. remarks: "If every body who partook of the elements, partook of the flesh and blood of the Saviour, all those would remain in Christ and Christ in them." Again: "If this mortal body partook of the *humanity* of Jesus, (as D. Henkel asserted,) in the eucharist, the first enjoyment would make that body incorruptible, and if it partook of the *glorified* humanity, it would make the same like his glorified body."

P. 33. Mr. S. observes: "But his (D. Henkel's) attempts to convince the reader, that the humanity of Christ is enjoyed, (received in the eucharist,) are so far-fetched that common sense cannot comprehend them, and they are abhorrent to the understanding."

P. 34. Mr. S. says: "Let me only repeat again that if all who partook of the Lord's Supper, eat and drink Jesus bodily, they cannot see corruption, they cannot die."

P. 38. Here Mr. S. charges D. Henkel with endeavoring "to make the people believe, that the Rev. Mr. Stork was heterodox," because he had said "that one hundred bibles would not convince him that the humanity of Christ was taken into the Godhead, and that therefore Christ obtained all divine perfection." But the Rev. Stork informed Mr.

Shober, that the conversation referred to was not about the humanity of Christ, but specifically "about the omnipresence of the *body* of Christ," and the expression occurred in a friendly conversation, for, (says Mr. Stork,) the *idea was so absurd that a body could be everywhere present*, that the expression, though unguarded, was hastily made."

P. 39. Mr. S. remarks: "Such is your crafty way to make people believe, that we, (particularly Mr. Stork,) do not teach right, and this only to lead them, if possible, to believe that the body of Christ is everywhere in immensity of space at the same moment." And then Mr. S. subjoins the remark in refutation of Henkel's view, "After his resurrection Jesus was not at the grave, at Emmaus, and with his other disciples at the same moment." From these extracts we think our readers will find no difficulty in deciding whether Mr. Shober could have desired the unrestricted recognition of the Augsburg Confession by the General Synod, or not.

But we proceed. That Mr. Shober and his Synod, did not adhere implicitly to the Augsburg Confession, is further evident from the declaration and official action of,

2. THE TENNESSEE CONFERENCE,

Which confessedly did so adhere, and which was the only ecclesiastical body in America at that time which received that symbol without reserve. Of these men, Dr. Bachman, in his Discourse before cited, (p. 12,) gives the following characteristic: "Some years ago several individuals residing in North Carolina, who had previously been members of our church, on account of some dissatisfaction separated themselves from our communion. They chose as a leader an individual by the name of (David) Henkel, (hence they are called Henkelites,) a weak and illiterate man, whose ground of dissent, as far as can be gathered from the crude, visionary and inflammatory publications, which have from time appeared, either under his name or that of his sect, was, that the Evangelical Church had departed from the true doctrines of the Reformation, which he and his church had attempted to restore." At a meeting of this Tennessee Conference, held in Augusta county, Va., in 1824, a proposition was made to appoint a committee of conference, to meet a similar committee of the North Carolina Synod, to confer on the doctrinal differences between the two bodies. They also instructed a committee "to place the doctrines of the North Carolina Synod in one column, and those of the Tennessee Conference in another, extracted from their published writings of both, and *then the public can judge which of the two teaches according to the Augsburg Confession.*"

In the same year, (1824,) David Henkel addressed a letter to the Synod of Maryland and Virginia, in which he asserts, "The doctrines on which the said ministers of North Carolina have deviated from the doctrines of the Lutheran church, are these: They teach, 1. That baptized or not baptized, faith saves us. 2. That the real humanity of Christ is not *omnipresent,* and that none but *idiots* can believe that his body fills all space. 3. Consequently that the real *body and blood are not present, administered* and *received* in the Lord's Supper." See p. 4 of his printed memorial.

The same is evident from the letter of D. Henkel and eighteen of his adherents, addressed to Rev. Messrs. Stork, Shober, J. and D. Sherer,[1] charging them with *teaching doctrines inconsistent with the Augsburg Confession,* and *Luther's Catechism,* "and inviting them to a public disputation at the time and place of their next synodical meeting." p. 2 of said letter.

The minutes of this Conference for 1827 furnish abundance of evidence of the same kind. Page 33: "The Tennessee Synod impeach them, (the ministers of North Carolina Synod,) with having deviated from the Lutheran Confession of Faith, and propagating doctrines under the covert of Lutheranism, which are erroneous." "One of the charges against them is that they have *deviated from the Lutheran doctrines.*" p. 35. Again: "The ministers of the North Carolina Synod call themselves Lutherans; but, as we believe, that they propagate doctrines contrary to the Augustan Confession, we consider it necessary to require of them to stand an examination. It is necessary to correct a wrong opinion, which is: that Lutheran ministers are at liberty to deviate from the Augustan Confession whereinsoever they conceive it to be erroneous. Some ministers,

(1) It is proper to remark that the Rev. Mr. Sherer had publicly denied this charge, and defined his position.

(namely, of North Carolina Synod,) have *declared that th y did not care what the Augustan Confession teaches*, that they simply taught the doctrines of *the Scriptures*. Further, that Luther was only *a man and liable to err*."

Finally, that the North Carolina Synod were known to teach doctrines on minor points different from the Augsburg Confession, is proved by the fact, that when a Mr. Seechrist left the North Carolina Synod, and applied for admission in the Tennessee Conference, they examined him, and made him renounce the supposed errors of the Synod of North Carolina and avow his belief in *baptismal regeneration* and *the presence and reception of the body and blood of Christ in the eucharist*. See pages 8 and 9 of their Minutes for 1823.

3. From the Testimony of Rev. D. F. Schæffer, D. D.

In the Lutheran Intelligencer for 1827, we find an article from the pen of the editor, on the state of the church in North Carolina. On p. 74 he says: "From these, (several recent letters from North Carolina,) we learn, "that those who represented themselves as Lutherans, (the Henkelites,) but taught doctrines diametrically opposite to those which the church approves, are sinking in the estimation of all who know by experience and from the sacred scriptures, (*our only guide in matters of faith*,) that to be born again and made meet unto salvation, is *more than to be baptized*." Nay, others "are induced to inquire into those matters, and acknowledge that the doctrines taught by our regularly authorized ministers are *scriptural*, and that those who have arrogated to themselves the authority to teach without submitting to an examination or ordination by one or other Synod, (alluding to David Henkel,) have departed from the true faith."

4. From Rev. John Reck.

In a report of a committee on the state of religion in North Carolina, of which this esteemed brother was chairman, he remarks: "The doctrines of the Bible, as published by the Great Reformer of Saxony, and echoed by the *Augsburg Confession*, are *substantially* taught by us, (that is, by the North Carolina Synod.") Having thus proved that the North Carolina Synod did not receive the Augsburg Confession unrestrictedly, from the testimony of their enemies who went out from their midst, from the declarations of her prominent ministers themselves, we now close the evidence in regard to them by showing that they had not only as individuals exercised the right of differing from the Augsburg Confession when they believed it to differ from the word of God, but that when in 1832, they as a Synod collectively and officially adopted as

5. THEIR CONSTITUTION,

the Constitution for Synods, recommended by the General Synod, they avowed their assent to the Confession in the following usual and *qualified* terms: "*We believe that the scriptures are the* ONLY INFALLIBLE *rule of faith and practice, and that the* FUNDAMENTAL *doctrines of the scriptures are taught in a manner* SUBSTANTIALLY *correct in the doctrinal articles of the Augsburg Confession.*" See their Minutes for 1832, German copy, p. 20.

OUR OWN POSITION IN REFERENCE TO HENKELISM.

As this has sometimes been misunderstood, and may be unknown to our younger brethren generally, it may here not be irrelevant to remark that nearly one half of this Tennessee Conference, which for some years consisted chiefly of David Henkel, his father, and several of his brothers, resided in our pastoral district in Virginia between 1820 and 1825, and during the whole time carried on the same warfare against us, charging us with upholding the General Synod and with not adhering to the doctrines of the Augsburg Confession. Hundreds of our parishioners yet live to testify that we never pretended to deny the differences between us, and that in whatever defence we felt called on to make, we represented their peculiarities either as misapprehensions of the Augsburg Confession, or especially the doctrine of the bodily presence as being remnants of Romanism, retained indeed in the Confession, but universally rejected by our church in the present age.

Having now established beyond all contradiction the merely fundamental adhesion of the North Carolina Synod to the Augsburg Confession, we may now add a few words concerning several other Synods. We begin with the ancient

SYNOD OF PENNSYLVANIA.

Although it is a well known fact that this respectable body has not, for about half a century, required assent to any thing more than the Bible, not one of the former symbolical books being ever named at licensure or ordination, as may be seen even from the new Liturgy; and although her merely fundamental accordance in fact with the Augsburg Confession is included in the general testimony of Drs. Hazelius, Bachman, Lochman, Krauth, Lintner, &c., presented in former articles, it will be interesting to hear additional evidence.

1. *Rev. Probst,* who was a member of that Synod from 1813 until his recent death, and well acquainted with the sentiments of his brethren, in a work published in 1826, for the express purpose of promoting a formal and complete union of the German Reformed and Lutheran churches in America, entitled, "Reunion of the Lutherans and Reformed," argues throughout on the supposition that there was no material difference of doctrinal views between them, the Lutherans having relinquished the *bodily presence* and the Reformed unconditional election. Speaking of the supposed obstacles to such union, he remarks: "The doctrine of unconditional election cannot be in the way. This doctrine has long since been abandoned; for there can scarcely be a single German Reformed preacher found who regards it as his duty to defend this doctrine. Zwingli's more liberal, rational and scriptural view of this doctrine, *as well as of the Lord's Supper,* has become the *prevailing one among Lutherans* and Reformed, and it has been deemed proper to abandon the view of both Luther and Calvin on the subject of both these doctrines." p. 74.

Again: "The whole mass of the old Confessions was occasioned by the peculiar circumstances of those troublous times, has become obsolete by the lapse of ages, and is yet valuable only as matter of *history.* Those times and circumstances have passed away, and our situation both in regard to political and ecclesiastical relations, is entirely changed. We are therefore not bound to these books, but only to the Bible. For what do the unlearned know of the Augsburg Confession, or the Form of Concord, of the Synod of Dort," &c. p. 76.

Again: "Both churches (the Lutheran and Reformed) advocate the evangelical liberty of judging for themselves, and have one and the same ground of their faith, the Bible. Accordingly, both regard the Gospel as their exclusive rule of faith and practice, and are forever opposed to all violations of the liberty of conscience." p. 76.

Finally: "All enlightened and intelligent preachers of both churches agree, that there is much in the former symbolical books (or confessions of faith) that must be stricken out as antiquated and contrary to common sense, and be made conformable with the Bible, and that we have no right to pledge ourselves to the mere human opinions of Luther, or Calvin, or Zwingli, and that we have but one master, Christ. Nor is any evangelical Christian bound to the interpretations which Luther or Calvin, or any other person may place on the words of Christ; but each one has the right to interpret them according to the dictates of his own conscience." p. 80. "Inasmuch as all educated ministers of the Lutheran and Reformed churches now entertain more reasonable and more scriptural views on those doctrines which were *formerly* the subjects of controversy, what necessity is there of a continued separation?" p. 81.

2. *Testimony of Dr. Lochman,* confessedly one of the most active, distinguished and pious divines of our church, in the preface to his *Catechism,* published in 1822, after stating that the proper name of our church is Evangelical, and not Lutheran, thus defines

The leading Principles of our Church.

1) "That the *Holy Scriptures and not human authority,* are the only source whence we are to draw our religious sentiments, whether they relate to faith or practice."

2) "That Christians are accountable to God alone for their religious principles," and therefore no man should be punished by civil governments for his opinion's sake, &c.

3) As Christ has left no express directions for church government, &c., therefore every society may follow its own judgment, and the Lutheran Church in different countries has adopted different forms of government, &c. *But not a word is said about adherence to the Augsburg Confession as belonging to the principles of our Church.* Moreover, that

the Dr. himself, in common with the majority of his associates, did not believe the doctrine of the

PRESENCE AND RECEPTION OF THE BODY AND BLOOD OF CHRIST IN THE EUCHARIST,

is evident from his Catechism on that subject, p. 33, where the question, "For what purpose did Christ institute this sacrament?" is answered thus:

"Not only to *put us in mind of his great love* for sinners, but also to offer us *an interest in his sacrifice,* and to assure us that all *penitent* and *believing* souls should be partakers of it, as surely as they partook the consecrated bread and wine. Bread and wine are the pledges to assure us of our interest in the sacrifice of Christ." But not a word is said about the Saviour's body and blood being present or received by all or any communicant; and the spiritual benefit affirmed is confined to *penitent* and *believing* souls. And in his work, entitled, History, Doctrine and Discipline of the Lutheran Church, published in 1818, p. 106, he explains the terms "receiving the body and blood of Christ," as follows: "As sure as the penitent communicant receives the bread and wine, so surely does he receive the body and blood of the Lord Jesus—OR IN OTHER WORDS, THE BENEFITS OF REDEMPTION."

That the *Rev. Dr. Endress,* also one of our most distinguished divines, entertained the same views on this subject was well known during his lifetime, and is evident from a note to his articles in the Lutheran Intelligencer for 1827, p. 255. Unfortunately, although he wrote much and well, he published very little. Yet on the subject under consideration, the extract from his letter given above among the testimonies on the general state of our American church, affords sufficient proof; for, in describing our church in general, he of course describes one of its prominent portions, the synod to which he belonged.

A UNITED LUTHERAN AND REFORMED THEOLOGICAL SEMINARY.

3. In accordance with these views the synod of Pennsylvania, in 1819, "appointed the Rev. Drs. Schmucker, Lochman, Muhlenberg and Ernst, as a committee to confer with a similar committee of the German Reformed Synod, and devise a plan for a united Theological Seminary for the

two denominations." If the Pennsylvania Synod had differed materially from the views of the German Reformed would they have desired to unite with them in erecting a joint Seminary?

AN ENTIRE UNION OF BOTH CHURCHES PROPOSED.

4. In 1822, at the meeting in Germantown, the Pennsylvania Synod *unanimously* adopted the following resolution, on motion of Drs. Endress and Muhlenberg:

"*Resolved,* That a committee be appointed by this Synod to deliberate in the fear of God on the propriety of a proposition for a general union of our Church in this country with the Evangelical Reformed Church, and also on the possibility and most suitable method of carrying this resolution into effect." p. 16 of their Minutes for 1822.

UNANIMOUS DECLARATION OF PENNSYLVANIA SYNOD.

5. When the Synod of Pennsylvania, at the meeting of 1823, at Lebanon, felt it a duty to yield to the popular clamor excited for selfish purposes by some political demagogues and a renegade German layman, who, it is believed, fled from justice in his native country, and here published a slanderous book against the synod, and hawked it about from house to house, that body, by an almost unanimous vote, adopted the following declaration of sentiments in the preamble to their resolutions: "We beheld large and beautiful congregations of brethren (the Reformed) who labor with us in the same spirit and with the same view in proclaiming the doctrines of Jesus, and discharging the duties of the office of reconciliation, who often in the same house labor, teach and worship the same Lord in the same manner and for the same purpose. We gave utterance, as it were, from afar to the wish, dictated by love, to enter into a closer union with these our German Evangelical Protestant brethren, and termed it *a union of the German Protestant Church.* But our own brethren (members) have misapprehended us," &c. p. 15 of their minutes for 1823. If then the members of this respectable body know their own doctrinal views, these words contain a declaration that they agreed substantially with those of the Reformed, who never received the peculiarities of the Augsburg Confession, such as the presence of the body and blood of the Saviour in the Eucharist,

&c., and thus they confirm the declaration of Rev. Probst, that the members of the Pennsylvania Synod generally had rejected this doctrine.

Synod and Ministerium of New York.

Of this respectable body, which formerly embraced all the Lutheran ministers in that state, we will merely present the *explicit* and *conclusive* testimony of one of its oldest, most learned and respectable ministers, contained in a private communication to us: "In the earlier days of our Ministerium, it did require an assent to the Augsburg Confession; but how far qualified, or whether qualified at all, I cannot say. Nor do I know whether the requirement was uniformly insisted on. That it was not contained in the *first constitution* of that Synod *I am confident,* and equally so that a majority of its members were disinclined to any such rule. In the Constitution *afterwards unanimously* adopted, every thing of this sort was not only omitted, *but forbidden;* and no attempt to unsettle the long practice of our Ministerium in this respect has been made, or could be made with any hope of success." The Synod of New York has, therefore, certainly long since rejected the binding authority of the former symbolical books.

The Synods of West Pennsylvania, Maryland, and Virginia.

In regard to these several bodies, it is a well known and undisputed fact, that neither of them ever required any pledge at all, except to the word of God, not even to the Augsburg Confession, until the General Synod proposed the acknowledgment of that Confession as to fundamentals. The liberal, yet truly scriptural spirit which pervaded both of them, is echoed by the President of the latter body in his address to a number of candidates for ordination in 1828: "Wherever we cast our eyes, we see the Christian community actively engaged. The Bible, the Bible appears to be the watchword, and the dissemination of its heaven-born truths the motto of the Protestant world." Urging them particularly to *take heed to their doctrines,* he utters the following language: "Let the Gospel of Christ, therefore, be the fountain whence you derive all your religious views, and according to that standard test and decide upon every doctrine of religion that is presented to you for acceptance. Then we are sure that "Christ and him crucified," will be the burden of your ministerial performances, and the theme of all your discourses, and that, like the Apostle, you will be "determined to glory only in the cross of our Lord Jesus Christ." But not a word is said about any human creed. Lutheran Intelligencer, vol. III. p. 228. Even the children of the church are taught to regard the *mode of the Saviour's presence* in the Eucharist as a subject which should be left to the free judgment of each individual, as may be seen from the Catechism of *Dr. Morris*, published in 1844, and extensively used in these Synods, as well as in the church generally, in which work, also, this presence is pronounced to be a *spiritual* one. pp. 100, 101.

The Rev. Dr. Baugher, in his excellent report on the *Doctrines and Usages of the Synod of Maryland*, prepared by order of said body about the year 1840, fully confirms our account of the doctrinal position of this respectable body

"ON REGENERATION.—We believe that the Scriptures teach that regeneration is the act of God, the Holy Ghost, by which, through the truth, the sinner is persuaded to abandon his sins and submit to God, on the terms made known in the gospel. This change, we are taught, is radical, and is essential to present peace and eternal happiness. Consequently, it is possible, and is the privilege of the regenerated person to know and rejoice in the change produced in him."

"OF THE SACRAMENTS.—We believe that the Scriptures teach, that there are but two sacraments, viz.: Baptism and the Lord's Supper, in each of which, truths essential to salvation are symbolically represented. We do not believe that they exert any influence '*ex opere operato*,' but only through the faith of the believer. Neither do the scriptures warrant the belief, that Christ is present in the Lord's Supper in any other than a spiritual manner."

"OF THE SYMBOLICAL BOOKS.—Luther's Larger and Smaller Catechisms, the Formula Concordiæ, Augsburg Confession, Apology, and Smalkald Articles are called in Germany the Symbolical Books of the church. We regard them as good and useful exhibitions of truth, but do not receive them as binding on the conscience, except so far as they agree with the word of God."

It will be seen, that the position of that body on the subject of *baptismal* regeneration, the *real or bodily* presence, and the obligation of the former symbolical books, is clearly expressed.

We have thus proved, from the express published declarations of some half dozen of our most respectable divines, that the doctrinal position of our American church in general, about the time of the origin of the General Synod and thereafter, was that of fundamental agreement with the Augsburg Confession, with acknowledged difference in minor points. We have proved the same fact concerning the Synod of North Carolina, of Pennsylvania, of West Pennsylvania, of Maryland and Virginia, and of New York in particular; and as there is not a single author who, within this period, has published any thing either affirming or proving the contrary, we should suppose this point must be regarded as settled in all time to come.

CHAPTER VIII.

THE GENERAL SYNOD HERSELF.

WE shall now proceed to show that the same doctrinal position was also assumed and perpetuated to this time, by the General Synod herself. That these were the doctrinal views which she was understood to profess and hold, we prove,

a) By the testimony of her most violent opponents, the members of the Tennessee Conference, who made it a standing objection to the General Synod, that she was not *Lutheran*, and had *not adopted* and *"did not adhere to the Augsburg Confession."* In the Minutes of said Conference for 1822, p. 8, (of German copy) we find the substance given of a letter from a minister of their own body, in which he affirms "that the General Synod is *not Lutheran*, but much rather the contrary." In their Minutes of 1823, p. 6, they publish a communication from one of their churches in Virginia, stating that they will accept no minister connected with the General Synod, but desire to have one belonging to their Conference, "because they *do yet adhere to the Augsburg Confession.*" On p. 7 we find a similar letter from a church formerly belonging to the pastoral district of which I had charge in Virginia, stating, "that as they had no opportunity to obtain the services of any minister, except such as belong to the General Synod, they beg to be supplied by said Conference, as it yet adheres to the *Augsburg Confession.*"

At a meeting of a Conference held in Nelson county, Ky., and consisting chiefly of several members of the Tennessee Conference, on p. 5, of their Minutes, we read: "Every article thereof (of the General Synod's Constitution) was minutely examined; whereupon the session (Conference) unanimously declared the Constitution of the General Synod to be contrary to the Holy Scriptures and the *Augsburg Confession* of faith, and subversive to (of) Christian liberty." Again, on p. 6: "It was unanimously resolved, that we by no means sanction the General Synod, as we have sufficient reason to believe that the *General Synod have departed from the Lutheran doctrine.*"

2. We shall prove that the General Synod did not adhere to all the tenets of the Augsburg Confession, from *her own acts and declarations.*

a) The Augsburg Confession is *never once so much as named* in the Constitution of the General Synod, and yet if the members framing that Constitution had designed to require an implicit conformity to it, would they not at least have mentioned that Confession in some way?

b) LUTHER'S CATECHISM NOT APPROVED AS SYMBOLIC OR PERFECT.

In 1821, the very first General Synod ever convened passed the following resolution:

"*Resolved,* That the present state of our church requiring it, a committee be appointed to *compose* an English catechism, and to offer it for the consideration of the next General Synod."

The Rev. Drs. Endress, J. G. Schmucker, Lochman, and Messrs. Shober and D. F. Schæffer were appointed, all of whom, (confessedly among our very first divines,) regarded it as necessary to make various improvements in Luther's Catechism to adapt it to what was "*required by the present state of our church*," or to compose a new one. One of their number, Dr. Lochman, had actually made preparations for such a work, which he published on his own responsibility the succeeding year, 1822, before the meeting of the next General Synod. In 1823 this committee submitted their report, together with the materials for a *new* catechism. As these materials were not ready for the press, and the General Synod wished to act deliberately in this matter, the materials were committed to another committee, consisting of Rev. Messrs. Shober, D. F. Shæffer, Herbst, and ourself, "to examine and report thereon with additions." This committee, principally through our own efforts, resolved to retain Luther's Catechism for the present, and to report an improved translation of the questions, What is your state by nature? &c., with explanatory additions on the decalogue, infant baptism and the eucharist, which were furnished by ourself, were adopted by the next General Synod and published by their order. See Minutes for 1821, p. 5; for 1823, p. 5; and for 1825, p. 9. Now if the General Synod had regarded Luther's Catechism as symbolical, or had desired to require every minister to use it in the instruction of the young, would they have appointed a committee to *supercede it by another?*

e) But the General Synod did explicitly declare her relation to the Augsburg Confession at a very early day. At the meeting of the third General Synod in 1825, that body feeling the necessity and duty of providing their numerous destitute churches with competent ministers of the Gospel, took action on the subject of establishing a

Theological Seminary.

And here certainly, if anywhere, when fixing the principles on which the institution was to be conducted, and determining the doctrines which should be taught to those who were to minister in holy things in time to come, the members of the General Synod would certainly feel it their duty to fix the doctrinal standard which they desired to have inculcated on their future associates and their successors in office. And did they neglect this solemn duty? No, verily, the very first resolution they adopted was devoted to this sacred obligation, and is couched in the following words:

"Whereas, the General Synod regard it as a solemn duty imposed on them by their Constitution, and due from them to their God and to the Church, to provide for the proper education of men of piety and talents for the Gospel ministry; therefore,

"*Resolved*, 1. That the General Synod will forthwith commence, in the name of the Triune God, and in humble reliance on his aid, the establishment of a Theological Seminary, which shall be exclusively devoted to the glory of our Divine Redeemer, Jesus Christ, who is God over all blessed forever. And that in this Seminary shall be taught, in the German and English languages, *the* FUNDAMENTAL *doctrines* of the sacred scriptures as contained in the Augsburg Confession."

Here, then, the question is settled forever as to what was to be the doctrinal basis of the Seminary. The Augsburg Confession was to be used as well to exclude Socinians, and other fundamental errorists, as out of respect to that ancient symbol of our church. Yet that Confession was not to be implicitly followed, its binding authority was *explicitly limited to fundamental doctrines;* not to the fundamental doctrines or features of ancient Lutheranism, amongst which the so-called old Lutherans of the present day would class some of Luther's peculiarities, such as the doctrine of the bodily presence, &c., but its binding authority extends only to the fundamental doctrines of *Scripture*, among which no theologian of any standing will rank the peculiar doctrines of his sect. For every enlightened divine will cordially respond to the noble sentiment of the venerable Dr. Miller, of Princeton, but recently translated to a better world: "Though I am a decided Calvinist, (says the Dr.,) yet it would never occur to me to place the peculiarities of the Calvinistic creed among the *fundamentals* of our common Christianity." Thus felt and thus acted the members of our General Synod, and we rejoice that we were among them.

PERSONAL CHARGE OF THE "LUTHERANER," OF MISSOURI, REBUTTED.

Here it may not be improper to add a few words touching the course of "Der Lutheraner," a paper representing the

Old Lutherans of the West, whose editor not only denounces all the late efforts of European nations to cast off that oppression from which he and so many thousands have found a happy asylum in the Western world, as unjustifiable rebellion, but openly advocates the duty of passive obedience to kings amid the most flagrant oppression. That paper is but consistent with itself when advocating similar absolute submission to creeds—for the foundations of civil and religious liberty are the same. This paper recently published an article flatly charging us with perjury and dishonesty, because we professedly reject some minor tenets of the Augsburg Confession, to which the article affirms, our oath as Professor in the Theological Seminary bound us. Now this oath of office is similar to the resolution of the General Synod above quoted, *expressly limiting our obligation to the Augsburg Confession "to the fundamental doctrines of Scripture."* We wrote it ourself, and ought to understand its import. These men are ignorant of the doctrinal history of our American church, and if they are christians ought not so precipitately to pass judgment on what they but imperfectly understand. They should know that our American church, exercising her inherent right to judge and act for herself, had, a quarter of a century before the origin of the General Synod, rejected the binding authority of the Augsburg Confession, and of all other human creeds; and had in fact rejected some of the minor tenets of the Augsburg Confession: that the founders of the General Synod approving the state of doctrine existing among themselves, did not once name the Augsburg Confession in their Constitution, and whenever in subsequent years that Confession was referred to in any of their acts, it was invariably accompanied with a restriction to the *fundamental* doctrines of scripture. On exactly the same basis the Theological Seminary founded by them was placed; and that we have been true to this basis and have occupied exactly the same ground in our theological instructions and our publications is admitted. Our Popular Theology, containing our doctrinal system, was universally received as a fair exhibition of the *prevailing* doctrines of the great mass of our American churches. From various commendatory articles we cite only what refers to this point. In the Lutheran Observer for July 1, 1833, then edited by him, the Rev. Dr. Morris, whose extensive acquaintance with the church cannot be doubted, says: "This work is characterized by all that logical precision and clearness of thought, which distinguish the writings of that gentleman, and it will really be a valuable addition to the literature of our church. We take pleasure in recommending it to all who desire to see the fundamental doctrines of the church plainly stated and triumphantly proved," &c. And in his introduction to Dr. Kurtz's work, entitled, "*Why are you a Lutheran?*" he remarks: "Dr. Schmucker's valuable Popular Theology has contributed much to remove wrong impressions from the minds of many intelligent readers." In the Observer for January 9, 1835, a highly respectable writer affirms: "We think that in presenting this work to the public, Dr. S. has conferred a distinguished favor upon the members of *our Church*, &c. The public has already judged his book. The highest encomium, we apprehend, which it can receive has been bestowed in the eagerness with which it was received," &c. February 6, the able editor of the Observer, Dr. Kurtz, says: "Regarding as we do the Popular Theology not only as an ably written work, exhibiting much learning and a vast amount of lucid and conclusive argument on subjects of paramount interest and vital importance, but *also as a correct representation of the doctrinal and ecclesiastical views entertained by our ministers and people generally*, we are happy," &c. And Dr. Lintner and the committee of Hartwick Synod, affirm in their notes on the Augsburg Confession, in 1837: "Dr. S.'s Popular Theology is *a standard work in our church.*" It is evident then that we agree with the prevailing doctrinal views of the churches of the General Synod, which are those of fundamental agreement with the Augsburg Confession, with acknowledged differences on minor points, and as this is what is required by the Professor's oath in the Seminary, we are at a loss to see any ground for the charge against us in the "Lutheraner." The Popular Theology has of late sometimes been censured as not giving a correct view of the doctrines of the Lutheran symbols. Such censure is, however, both unmanly and unchristian, not to say unscientific. We nowhere profess to present the symbolic theology of the church in Europe. On the contrary, our preface and the introductory chapter on the history of the Augsburg Confession, and the qualified manner in which it is received in this country, distinctly state the standpoint which we occupy; and to censure a work for not containing what it does not profess to present, is unworthy of a respectable critic, or an honorable man.

d) Pastoral Addresses of the General Synod.

Even the second General Synod ever convened, (in 1823,) in their Pastoral Address to the churches, distinguished between fundamental and non-fundamental aberrations or deviations from the scriptures or from the Augsburg Confession, affirming that the former we should view with charity, but fundamental errorists or "heretics" we should cast out." p. 14. But in the address of the General Synod of 1829, that body has given as explicit a declaration as language can convey, which must forever remove all doubt as to the doctrinal position she occupies:

"Amid these circumstances we rejoice anew in the grand design of the General Synod of our church. This design *is not* to produce an *absolute uniformity in minor points of doctrine,* for we have no reason to believe that this existed even in the primitive church; and we are decidedly of opinion, that whilst the *grand doctrines of the Reformation* are absolutely *insisted on,* every minister and layman should have full liberty to approach the study of his Bible untrammeled by the shackles of human creeds. *The General Synod therefore only requires of those who are attached to her connexion, that they hold the* FUNDAMENTAL *doctrines of the Gospel, as taught in the Augsburg Confession, and in all minor points leaves them* UNRESTRICTED. On the one hand we are not able to go with those who renounce unconditionally all creeds and confessions, because, we cannot see how Socinians could be effectually excluded from the church without them. But we feel well assured that the great majority of creeds in the Christian church, by entering far too much into minor ramifications of doctrine, and attaching too great importance to subordinate and even doubtful points, have cherished in the most direct manner, and from their very nature must cherish the unhallowed spirit of bigotry and sectarianism. It cannot, we think, be doubted by any one who has paid attention to this subject, that there are in each of the several orthodox denominations, and often in the individual congregation, persons differing from each other as much as the several (denominational) creeds do. Why then should not all the Synods which bear the name of the immortal *Luther*, and still retain the *cardinal views* of that illustrious Reformer, be associated together by the very slender bond of our General Synod, *though they may not agree in some points not touching the fundamental doctrines of the Augsburg Confession?*" Minutes for 1829, pp. 15, 16.

An invitation by the General Synod to all Lutheran Synods holding the fundamental doctrines of the Bible as taught by our church, to unite with them, was adopted in 1835, (see Min., pp. 23, 24,) as part of their Constitution.

Explicit recommendation of the General Synod to bind only to the fundamentals.

In the Constitution for Synods prepared by the General Synod and recommended to all District Synods, in 1829, it is directed that candidates for licensure and ordination be pledged *absolutely to the Bible*, but only to the fundamentals as taught in the *Augsburg Confession*. It is in these words:

1. "Do you believe the Scriptures of the Old and New Testaments to be the word of God, and the *only infallible rule* of faith and practice?

2. Do you believe the *fundamental* doctrines of the word of God are taught in a *manner substantially correct* in the doctrinal articles of the Augsburg Confession?" See Minutes for 1829, p. 38–9.

In addition to this accumulated mass of evidence, and to show its perfectly conclusive character, we confidently affirm, that for a quarter of a century after the foundation of the General Synod, no writer *connected with* that Synod has published a single page inconsistent with the above testimony, and no writer *out of* the General Synod has represented the prevailing opinions of the churches and ministers of the General Synod, to be different from what the above testimonies affirm.

CHAPTER IX.

Features of the American Lutheran Church.

We claim that the American Lutheran Church is a *free, integral, independent* part of the church of Christ, possessing all the privileges and acting under all the obligations pertaining to any other branch of Christ's kingdom, and therefore possessing the full right to settle its own standards of doctrine, discipline, and worship. On the proof of this almost self-evident principle, we deem it unnecessary at present to enter. And why should there not be an *American* Lutheran church, as well as any other? There is a German, a Danish, a Swedish Lutheran church, each possessing its distinctive peculiarities, arising from their different civil governments, and the different views of those who founded them, to say nothing of the differences between our church in the several kingdoms and principalities of Germany. Then why should not American Lutherans be permitted to organize their church, in accordance with the principles of their own glorious civil institutions, in conformity to the dictates of their own consciences and their views of the inspired word of God? Are they less able to search the Scriptures with fidelity and success, than their brethren of other countries? Are we less competent to judge of what suits our peculiar circumstances, and the peculiar age of the world, and the signs of the eventful times in which we live than others? Are we less able than others, to apply the great principle of Lutheranism, that the Scriptures are the only infallible guide and rule of faith and practice, that noble principle without which the immortal Reformer could never have accomplished the great work of Reformation, and to which he with Melancthon and the greater part of their coadjutors remained faithful to the end of his life; but which many of his less noble and less enlightened followers gradually abandoned? It is a well known fact, that by continuing to search the Scriptures, Luther continued to improve his views till near the end of his life. Nor were the opinions rejected by him merely the corruptions of Romanism. During a large part of his life he was a rigid Augustinian, or as we would now term it, a rigid *Calvinist*, on the distinguishing features of that system; although Melancthon had commenced to change his opinions on that subject, as early as the publication of the second edition of his *Loci*. Having thus felt compelled, by the light of God's word, to continue changing and improving his views, Luther was so far from wishing his attainments to be regarded as the *ne plus ultra* of doctrinal purity, that he dissuades men from reading his works, and urges them to drink from the infallible fountain itself. We have, therefore, no right to renounce the privileges, or to neglect the duty of adhering to his principle, and of rejecting those of his opinions which we find contrary to Scripture as well as also of conforming our government, discipline and worship to the precepts and spirit of the New Testament, and the peculiar circumstances of our age and country.

And are not the peculiar circumstances of our situation, social, geographical and political, at least as characteristic, striking and potential, as those which gave diversity to the church in the different countries of Europe? A moment's glance at the contrast must convince every unbiased mind.

In Europe, the unhappy union of church and state, commenced by Constantine in the fourth century, and continued in Europe till the present day, has hampered the energies and corrupted the purity of the church: this country, on the other hand, is the chosen theatre of God for the free, unbiased development of humanity, and the settlement of the highest questions regarding its privileges, capacities and duties, in social, political and religious life. There the civil government restrains the activity of private christians within legalized limits, giving a crippled form and an enfeebled aspect to the body of Christ: here the laity are left to exert their full influence, and to sustain their important part in all the enterprises for the advancement of the Redeemer's kingdom. There, ministers are not allowed to preach oftener than their instructions from their government prescribe, namely, once a Sabbath. Preaching at night or in the week, is wholly unusual, protracted meetings for continued preaching, &c., are utterly unknown, and ministers of similar views and congenial feelings never, so far as we could learn, exchange pulpits, though they may spend a lifetime within a few miles of each other! Here the servant of Christ can preach as often as his strength admits, and the exigencies of his charge seem to require; when requisite he can invite the aid of a neighboring brother, and can reciprocate the favor by occupying his pulpit in return. There, revivals of religion and special efforts to obtain them of God, are almost wholly unknown; here these gracious showers of divine influence are constantly refreshing one or other part of the vineyard of the Lord. There, synodical meetings of ministers and lay elders as representatives of the churches, to deliberate on the interests of the church, and enact rules for her government, are unknown. In one or two portions of the church we hear of occasional synods; but they do not consist of the ministry in general, but only of select dignitaries of the church; nor of any laymen elected by the churches, but only of a few political officers of the government! Here, the ministers and lay representatives of a given district, all meet on terms of equality to deliberate and devise measures for the advancement of the kingdom of Christ, subject to no other rules than such as they themselves adopt. There, even in Wittenberg itself, in the venerable halls once electrified by the fearless eloquence of Luther, theological students are not now permitted to investigate and discuss untrammeled the various questions of human duty and interest in the light of Scripture, history and reason; but an officer of government, forsooth, must be present at their debates, noting down the tenor of their discussions, especially if they bear on civil governments, or the duties or conduct of civil rulers! And woe to the prospects of preferment of that student, who should be found guilty of a tendency to liberal institutions. Here, theological students are permitted freely to discuss any question within the entire range of human interests and duties in the light of Scripture, reason and history, none daring to molest them or make them afraid. And for the selection of their ministers, our congregations need not apply to ungodly politicians; they themselves possess the power, and exercise it according to their own judgment.

In presenting these statements, we wish it distinctly understood, that we do not charge any one with approving these European peculiarities, which we condemn. Nay, we doubt not that the majority of our European brethren (constituting, if we include those Synods not connected with the General Synod, about the half of our ministry) will cordially unite in this condemnation. Those belonging to the General Synod and to the mother Synod of Pennsylvania, will all do so, and we trust also the major part of the others. But we present these views to prove, that if ever the peculiarities of any Christians called for an original, independent re-organization, our fathers were justly summoned to this work, which they also nobly accomplished. Cast by the hand of Providence into these Western wilds, separated by the vast Atlantic from the mother country, they felt this to be a peculiar and favorable time to revert to the first principles of the apostles, and taking lessons from the civil bondage of the church for more than a thousand years, to return to the simplicity of the gospel, and adapt their organization to the peculiar situation of their adopted country. This organization was at first practically begun, and gradually fixed by her liturgies and Synodical constitutions, and finally completed by the establishment and action of the General Synod.

What are the characteristics of the American Lutheran Church?

I. *Feature is the practical rejection of the binding authority of all the former symbolical books, except the Augsburg Confession.*

As practical rejection signifies rejection in practice; and as those who do not in practice acknowledge the binding authority of a book, do necessarily practically reject such authority; it follows that as our fathers during the first quarter of this century acknowledged the binding character of no human symbol at all, and we since then have acknowledged none except the Augsburg Confession, they practically did reject all those books, and we reject all except the Confession of Augsburg.

II. *Feature is the rejection of several tenets formerly held by our Church in Europe, and taught in some of her former symbolical books.*

a) *Exorcism,* which is taught in the Taufbuchlein (Tract on Baptism) of Luther, and was formerly annexed to his Smaller Catechism.

Let the reader, who is in doubt, examine Luther's Smaller Catechism, in the edition of the symbolical books, published by Mr. Ludwig, of New York, a year or two ago, and now patronized by the old Lutherans of the West, he will find this Taufbuchlein in full, containing the identical directions for Exorcism, which we presented in the first chapter of this essay. If he will examine that very extensively circulated edition of the Symbolical Books, edited by the learned Dr. Baumgarten, of Halle, published in 1747, he will find the very same directions on p. 467; and also in the Leipsic edition of 1790, p. 610. If he will examine the very first edition of the Concordienbuch, or Authentic Collection of the Symbolic Books ever published, printed at Dresden, in 1580, he will find it there, on p. 170–173. And that Luther is its author, is not denied by any one who has examined the subject. He first translated it from a previously existing Romish Latin directory in 1523, (Funk's Kirchenordnungen, p. 124.) In this form it is found in the Jen. ed. of his work, vol. II., p. 248–252. In 1524 or 1526, he re-wrote it in the form in which it was added to the Catechism edited by himself in 1529, (Muller Symbolic books, p. 88, 89 of Introduction,) and is found in the Altenb. ed. of his works, Fom. II., fol. 327. See Kollner, vol. I., p. 501, 502, and Baumgarten's Introduction to the Symbolic books, p. 166.

If then a book derives its symbolic authority, in any degree, from the fact that Luther wrote it, this was symbolical; or if, as may more properly be contended, it derives this character by being received into the authentic edition of the Concordienbuch, or official Collection of Symbolical books, then also must this character be conceded to it. But directions for exorcism were also inserted into some of the Kirchenordnungen or directories for worship in the different provinces of Germany. Luther and Melancthon always retained exorcism, as did a large portion of the Lutheran Church in Germany, and *the entire Church in Sweden.* Yea, during the 17th century, a rigid adherence to this superstitious rite was regarded in many portions of the Church, as a special mark of fidelity to Lutheranism; whilst its rejection was denounced as a symptom of Crypto-Calvinism. But it was more generally regarded as a symbolic inculcation of natural depravity of the subjects of baptism. Yet it is true, and we rejoice that it is so, that a large part of the Lutheran Church was at an early day ashamed of this remnant of papal superstition, and rejected it. Especially in the Latin copies destined for the learned, it was most generally omitted. It was excluded from the second edition of the Concordienbuch, also printed in 1580, out of regard to the Churches of the Electoral Palitinate, which had rejected the practice; and a recent writer, Muller, has asserted that it was not received among the Symbolical Books at the beginning, which is evidently a mistake. It was received into the very first edition, but omitted from the sec-end, as above stated, on the authority of Baumgarten and Kollner. And even previously to that, it had been received into the Corpus doctrinæ Thuring, or Collection of Confessions, &c., and into that of Brandenburg and others. In Saxony exorcism was relinquished in 1591, but again restored a few years after, and retained until the last century, when it was made optional with the parents, and in some cases was actually practised as late as 1836. In Hamburg the practice was retained till 1786, and in *Sweden* until 1811!! Siegel's Handbuch, vol. II. p. 67. This may suffice to show, that this book which inculcates exorcism, was not only written and sanctioned by Luther himself, but actually received into several collections of Creeds and Confessions, before the Concordienbuch existed, and when that was formed, was also received into it; although the good sense of a large portion of the Church at all times raised a strong party opposed to it, and led to the publication of different editions of the Symbolical Books, from which it was excluded. Still, it did originally belong to the Symbolical Books, as it is still found in some of the latest editions, and we are, therefore, perfectly right in quoting exorcism as one of the former and now obsolete doctrines of the Lutheran Church.

b) The next error rejected by us is *Private confession and absolution.* The necessity of enumerating all our particular sins to the priest at Confession, termed Auricular Confession, Luther and his adherents rejected, but *Private Confession*, at which the individual confessed his sinfulness and penitence in general, together with absolution, was retained in the Lutheran church. "In regard to confession, (says the Augsburg Confession, Art. XI,) they (the churches) teach, that private absolution ought to be retained in the churches; but that an enumeration of all our transgressions is not requisite in confession. See the elucidations on the subject in Popular Theology, p 308–310, 5th ed. In Art. XXV, of Augsburg Confession, the Reformers say: "*Confession is not abolished*, but that according to custom, *no one is admitted to the supper without haviug previously confessed and received absolution.*" p. 74–75, of Baumgarten's Concordienbuch. "The words of absolution are to be regarded *as the very words of God, &c.* We are to believe the priest's absolution *as certainly as if we heard the voice from heaven.*"

p. 75. "Confession is not commanded in Scripture ; yet it is to be retained on account of the absolution, which is the principal thing in it," &c., p. 77.

Art. XXVIII, of Augsburg Confession, says: "*Ministers possess the power to forgive and to retain sins.*" p. 111, of Baumgarten. "That everlasting righteousness, the Holy Spirit, and eternal life cannot be obtained, except through the office of preaching and the reception of the sacraments." p. 110. "Absolution was received privately *by each one individually,* kneeling before the confessional, the confessor imposing his hands at the time." See Funk's Kirchenordnung, &c., p. 189–190. "Private Confession was to be given *only in the church,* in which the confessional was so located near the pulpit, that no other person *could be near, or hear what was said,* by the penitent." Idem. p. 190.

That this practice is almost universally rejected in Germany, except by the few old Lutherans, is certain, and in this country universally, except by the old Lutherans of the West. As this will not be denied, it is unnecessary to present proof that private confession is not practiced in the American Lutheran Church.

c) The doctrine that *the true body and blood of Christ are received with the bread and wine by the mouth of every communicant.* In reference to this doctrine, the following, amongst many other specifications, are made in the different symbolical books, to which we refer as found in Muller's edition. 1) "The words of the institution, 'this is my body,' &c., *are to be understood literally,* (wie sie nach dem Buchstaben lauten,) p. 539–647. 2) That both the worthy and *unworthy* communicants receive the *true body and blood of Christ,* (und werde nichtalliengereicht und empfangen von frommen, sondern auch von bosen christen,) p. 320, 540, 649, 660, 650. 3) That it is the omnipotence of Christ, which causes the presence of his body and blood in the eucharist, (und allein der allmachtigen Kraft unseres Herrn Jesu Christe zugeschrieben werden soll.") 4) That we receive the *real body and blood* of Christ. Apol. to Confession, Art. X. "The tenth article (of the Augsburg Confession) our opponents, the Papists, do not object to, in which we confess, that our Lord's body and blood are *truly* present in the eucharist, and are offered and received with the visible articles, bread and wine, *as has heretofore been believed in the* (Romish) *church.*" p. 164. They believed as fully as did the Romanists, in receiving the real body and blood of Christ; only they denied that the *bread and wine were changed* into such body and blood. 5) That we receive the body of Christ, not only spiritually but *orally.* p. 647–653. 6) That when Luther speaks of receiving the body of Christ "*spiritually,*" he does not use the term in the sense of the Sacramentarians (or Zwinglians.) p. 668.

On the subject of this doctrine, Melancthon himself subsequently changed his views, and in a former chapter we proved by the testimony of Prof. Guericke, that before 1817 the great mass of Lutheran divines had relinquished this doctrine; as also by other testimony, that it had been generally abandoned in our church in this country. Our own father is regarded as among the few who yet retain something of this view, yet he disclaims the belief of the real presence of the body and blood of Christ altogether, and believes only in a *special spiritual presence and influence;* and greatly deplores the movements of those who desire to make binding the old Lutheran view of this or any other non-fundamental doctrine, and thus to disturb the doctrinal basis of the General Synod, namely, fundamental adherence to the Augsburg Confession, with acknowledged liberty of difference on minor points.

d) Baptismal regeneration, or the opinion that baptism is necessarily accompanied by spiritual regeneration, and *the unconditional necessity of baptism to salvation,* are views of baptism, which are taught in the Augsburg Confession, Art. II, IX. "This natural depravity is really sin, and still condemns and causes eternal death to those who are not regenerated by baptism and the Holy Spirit." But they are not entertained in this country, as we proved by the testimony of Dr. Miller, of Hartwick, p. 9, of his discourse on the Reformation, of Dr. Lintner, in his notes on Augsburg Confession, p. 15, and of Dr. Bachman, in his sermon on the doctrines and discipline of the Lutheran church, p. 15, &c.

e) The mass, that is, *the name and some of the ceremonies of the Romish mass,* were retained in the Augsburg Confession; although the errors in doctrine, by which the Romish mass grew out of the scripture doctrine of the Lord's Supper, were rejected in that as well as subsequent symbols. "Our churches (says the Augsburg Confession, Art. XXIV.)

are unjustly charged with having rejected the mass, (man legt den Unsern mit Unrecht auf, dasz sie die messe sollen abgethan haben.) For it is publicly known, that the mass is celebrated amongst us with greater devotion and earnestness than among our opponents." "Nor has there been any perceptible *change made in the public ceremonies of the mass*, except that at several places, German hymns are sung along with the Latin ones." "Our custom is on holy days (and at other times also if there be communicants) to say a mass, and those who desire it, receive the Lord's Supper." Subsequently, however, great changes were made in the public ceremonies attendant on the Lord's Supper; and Luther, in his Smalkald Articles, rejects the mass entirely, both the name and accompanying ceremonies. And soon after the whole Lutheran church followed him. Still, if the Augsburg Confession were strictly binding on us, we should be under the necessity of adopting on sacramental occasions all the public ceremonies then and now usual in the Romish church in celebrating public mass!

f.) *The imputation to us as personal and damning guilt of that natural depravity, which has come upon us in consequence of Adam's transgression.* Luther and Melancthon both taught the immediate imputation of Adam's transgression to his descendants, and the language of Luther in his Smalkald Articles (Art. I.) falls very little if any thing short of it. He says: "We must here confess, as St. Paul says, Rom. v: 12, That sin is derived *from one man, Adam, through whose disobedience all men became sinners, and were subjected to death and the devil.*" Still, the Augsburg Confession only represents our natural depravity as the cause of our condemnation. That this doctrine has been rejected we proved in parts of this work.

We might add to this list a number of other topics taught by the symbolic books, and such as Luther's peculiar views on the mode of baptism, in his Larger Catechism, which were never generally adopted in the Lutheran church, even in Germany; the omnipresence of the human *body* of Christ, the *omniscience* of his human nature, and in general the actual reciprocal transfer of the attributes of his human and divine natures to each other; that the virgin Mary conceived and brought forth not a mere human being, but the veritable Son of God, and therefore actually is and may properly be called the mother of God; the sin-forgiving power of the ministers, (Art. XXVIII. of Augsburg Confession;) the lax notions of the Augsburg Confession concerning the Christian Sabbath, &c., &c.; but their discussion is unnecessary.

III. *Feature is the reception of the Bible, as the only infallible rule of faith and practice, and the acknowledgment of the Augsburg Confession as the recognized expression only of the cardinal doctrines of the Bible.* This is fully established by the action of the General Synod, in adopting the Constitution for District Synods, in which this form of obligation is explicitly adopted for licensure and ordination.

IV. *Feature, Luther's Smaller Catechism,* (except the questions on exorcism,) not as a symbolical book, but as the authorised book for the catechetical instruction of the young, yet without any prohibition of other similar works. This feature is proved by the action of the General Synod in directing its publication.

V. *Feature, the Formula for Government and Discipline,* also proved by the action of the General Synod in preparing and publishing it.

VI. *Feature, A Hymn Book*—proved in like manner.

VII. *Feature, A Liturgy, both German and English,* ditto; the use of which is optional.

VIII. *Feature, Catechetical Instruction of the Young;* proved by her providing the Catechism for this express purpose, by the specific injunction of this duty in chapter III, sec. 6; IV, sec. 5, and sec. 10. "It shall be the duty of the church council to watch over the religious education of the children of the church, and to see that they be occasionally collected for the purpose of being taught the *Catechism* of the church, and instructed in the duties and principles of the Christian Religion."

IX. *Feature, The admission of those who had been baptized in infancy, to sacramental communion, by confirmation.* Chap. IV, sec. 5, of Formula.

X. *Feature, Holding of prayer meetings and family worship.* Formula, Chapter VII, sec. 1. "Therefore it is earnestly recommended to the different churches in our connexion, to establish and promote them (prayer meetings) among our members,—their object is the spiritual edification of the persons present; but the utmost precaution must ever be observed, that God, who is a Spirit, be worshipped in spirit and in truth—that these meetings be characterized by that solemnity and decorum, which ought ever to attend divine worship; that no disorder be tolerated or any thing that is calculated to interrupt the devotions of those who are convened, or to prevent their giving the fullest attention to him who is engaged in leading the meeting; in short, that according to the injunction of the Apostle, all things be done decently and in order."

"It is solemnly recommended to all church members, and more especially to the members of the council, to make daily worship in their family a sacred duty."

XI. *Feature is Special Conferences,* each containing from five to ten ministers, ordinarily to continue two days, and "the chief business to be performed at them is, to awaken and convert sinners, and to edify believers by close, practical preaching of the gospel." Formula, chap. xvi, § 1, 2, 3.

XIII. *The promotion of a spirit of liberality and Christian union on scriptural principles,* among the different portions of our own church, and among evangelical Christian denominations in general. Formula, chap. xxi, Constitution of General Synod, Art. iii, § 8. A system of Christian union, not proposing to amalgamate the different denominations of Christians, but to establish more fraternal relations between them by correspondence and occasional delegates, was adopted and recommended by the General Synod, and we trust will be adhered to.

Having now clearly established, if we mistake not, the several positions propounded in the beginning of this essay, and especially that the great mass of our churches had at the origin of the General Synod, rejected all those tenets of the former symbolical books, which they now reject, and that the General Synod established as her doctrinal basis *fundamental* agreement with the Augsburg Confession, *with acknowledged liberty of difference on minor points;* we close this essay with the earnest hope, that our ministers and laity will vindicate their rights as American Lutherans, and not suffer themselves to be deprived of their Protestant liberties, by the influence of old Lutherans, who have not yet been amongst us long enough to appreciate either our civil or religious institutions. *American* Lutheranism grew out of the Lutheran predilections of our fathers, the unrestricted liberty of following the scriptures, which they enjoyed in this Western world, and the influence of our free civil institutions. Under this joint influence they gradually rejected the symbolical bondage of Germany, and restored the original liberty in fundamentals, which Christ and his apostles bequeathed to us. They bought this liberty at the price of great sacrifices; and shall their American sons, that were "born free," suffer it to be taken from them? As the elder fathers who participated in the organization of the General Synod, have nearly all passed from the stage, we regarded it due to them and to the interests of truth, to contribute our mite to prevent the future misapprehension of their doctrinal position, as well as their views and motives in organizing the General Synod. Many of the relevant documents also have become exceedingly rare, and a few years more will sweep many of these into oblivion. As we have for thirty years done in regard to the Lutheran church, what the earliest Christian historian, Eusebius, tells us, he did in regard to the church of the earlier ages, namely, collected all the documents we could find; it seemed desirable that the testimony contained in them on the points at issue, should be made available to the present generation of Lutherans. We have, therefore, spread before the church all the principal facts in the case, and some of the reasons which led the General Synod to assume the enlightened and liberal, apostolic ground which she occupies; and our confidence in the intelligence and enlightened piety of our ministers and laity is too strong to countenance a doubt, that under the guidance of the good Spirit of our God, they will manfully maintain their ground. If our old Lutheran brethren are willing to regard their peculiarities as non-essential, and live in peace with us, they are welcome to take part with us in our ministry and ecclesiastical organizations; but if they cannot refrain from either regarding or denouncing us as dishonest, and pseudo Lutherans, and perjured, because we do not believe every thing contained in confessions which we never adopted, and because we will not adopt books as symbolical, which contain numerous errors and Romish superstitions; for ourselves, whilst we wish them well as individuals, we desire no ecclesiastical communion with them, either in our Synods, or General Synod; and believe it will be for the furtherance of the Gospel of Christ, that they should be associated with those who share their intolerance and bigotry. In less than twenty years they will themselves see their error, and change their position, and their children will be worthy members of our *American Lutheran Church.*

VI. DISCOURSE.

VOCATION OF THE AMERICAN LUTHERAN CHURCH.

THE term *vocation* (vocatio) has, from time immemorial, occupied a position in the nomenclature of Systematic Theology, in application to individual sinners, to designate that invitation given to the unconverted, by the Holy Spirit through the means of grace, to repent of their sins, and accept the offers of mercy on the conditions prescribed in the gospel.[1] But what do we understand by the vocation of a *church?* To this question we shall, in the premises, endeavor to present a generic solution, and then carry out our idea to its specific details, giving a tangible and visible form to the abstract conception.

On another occasion, we published our convictions on the subject of Church Development in general; and arrived at the following results: *That those points of doctrine, experience, and duty in the Christian religion, are unchangeable, which, in the judgment of the great mass of the Protestant churches, are clearly revealed in God's word, and as far as thus revealed; whilst all not thus clearly determined, all in regard to which a diversity of opinion exists between the different Evangelical churches, are less certain, and are proper subjects for amicable, fraternal discussion, and progressive development.* The points which this rule furnished as fundamental and unchangeable, are those enunciated by the Evangelical Alliance of all Protestant churches, held at London in 1846,

(1) Thus *Calovius:* Vocatio ad ecclesiam est infidelium extra ecclesiam positorum ad ecclesiam per verbum et sacramenta a Deo ex gratia dispensata, efficax adductio.

and re-affirmed by the Synod of our church in Maryland, namely: 1, The divine inspiration, authority, and sufficiency of the Holy Scriptures; 2, the right and duty of private judgment in the interpretation of the Scriptures; 3, the unity of the Godhead and the Trinity of Persons therein; 4, the utter depravity of human nature in consequence of the fall; 5, the incarnation of the Son of God, his work of atonement for sinners of mankind, and his mediatorial intercession and reign; 6, the justification of the sinner by faith alone; 7, the work of the Holy Spirit, in the conversion and sanctification of the sinner; 8, the divine institution of the Christian ministry, and the obligation and perpetuity of Baptism and the Lord's Supper; and 9, the immortality of the soul, and the judgment of the world by our Lord Jesus Christ, with the eternal blessedness of the righteous, and eternal punishment of the wicked. These fundamentals stand acknowledged by Protestant Christendom, as so many imperishable pillars of the church. They constitute a zone of light encircling this glorious edifice, seen and admired by all, who do not close their eyes on its benignant rays. On the other hand, we maintained, that the appropriate and *extensive field for church development, lies only in nonfundamentals*, in points not clearly determined in the records of inspiration; and that within these bounds the church is developed numerically, geographically, ritually, juridically, exegetically, theologically, and economically.

As the development of the church is confined to nonfundamental aspects of truth, and to points not clearly settled in Scripture, it follows that the special vocation of every portion of the church, must lie in the same field, and be circumscribed by the same metes. It is only in regard to points left undecided in revelation, that we can expect to find the lessons of instruction in the book of Providence, inculcating the propriety of change or amendment. In the progress of this development in nonfundamentals, the particular circumstances and incidents of the phenomenal experience of different churches, will be found to vary. The character of the population, belonging to a particular branch of Christ's visible kingdom, may elevate or reduce the intellectual and literary standard of her ministry, and by consequence, that of the ministrations of her sanctuaries. The institutions with which any particular church started in her career, may have derived a peculiar character from the government under which they were adopted, and from the historic influences amid which she was formed. Where arbitrary power has for ages ruled the civil destinies of a people, the management of her ecclesiastical, and even domestic affairs, will exhibit a correspondent impress. Even the constitutional peculiarities of particular controlling individuals, who organized the elements thrown into chaotic disorder by the commotions of ecclesiastical revolution, may be traced in the creations to which they give being. Who does not recognize the rigid disciplinarian tendency of Wesley's mind, in the entire system of government and discipline still retained by that efficient and extended portion of the church of Christ? Or the regal origin and aristocratic bias of the Church of England, in the strict gradations, and conservative tendencies of her episcopal hierarchy; or the lingering habits of subjection to civil superiors, in the consistories and superintendencies of Germany, notwithstanding the strong Congregational convictions of her leaders as to primitive Christianity?

Whilst, therefore, the grand vocation of all portions of the Christian church, is to conform their institutions to the word of God, and to "let their light so shine before men, that they may see their good works, and glorify their Father who is in heaven," the history of each individual cluster or denomination of churches, may be peculiarly adapted to inculcate some special lessons of instruction. The general vocation of the Lutheran church, in which all other churches participate with her, we at present pass over, and direct our attention to special duties inculcated by Providence, not on our friends in Europe, but on the *American Lutheran Church.* And when we speak of the American Lutheran Church, we intend not only those Synods now connected with our General Synod, together with the mother Synod of Pennsylvania, by which the General Synod was mainly formed, and to whose influence, numerical and theological, the Constitution of that Synod chiefly owes its enlightened and apostolic features; but also all other Synods and individuals, who have acquired a proper consciousness of their concrete existence in this free country, and who sympathize with the circumstances of our times and free institutions. Nor is this designation applicable only to those born in our midst, although they constitute the great mass of our church. We are proud also to number in our ranks many excellent and enlightened, and some learned men, who left the land of our fathers, dissatisfied with the civil and ecclesiastical condition of things, and having been conducted by the hand of Providence to this Western world, have not only learned to love the freedom and wisdom of our well-balanced civil institutions; but have also attained a consciousness of the fact, that one grand part of the vocation of the American churches is, to throw off the shackles of traditionary, patristic, and symbolic servitude; and availing themselves of the liberty secured by the divorce of church and state, to review the ground of Protestant organization, and to resume the Scripture lineaments of Christianity. Yea, we number men of high standing amongst us, who, under the evangelical influence of our liberal ecclesiastical arrangements, have gradually cast off the impressions of a perverted and neological education, and cordially adopting the grand fundamentals of Gospel truth, stand forth in defence of evangelical but enlightened Christianity: men, who aim to improve our church, not merely by a recurrence to the principles of the Reformation, but also by going higher, and drawing from the very fountains of sacred truth and love, whence the reformers themselves derived those streams that refreshed and enlightened the benighted and priest-ridden nations of Europe; men, too enlightened and well acquainted with the whole field of theological science, to suppose that the three eventful centuries since the Reformation, had made no progress in knowledge, had reflected no light upon the path, on which the church is to travel onward to her appointed destiny.

In Germany the church is still hampered by her relation to the State, to which the majority of the truly pious unwisely cling. She has thus been prevented from settling down on the improved results of a scriptural development, which would have dictated the separation of the fundamentally orthodox from every species of neologians. Had the church in Germany been separated from the State, and all the pious united into one church, adopting merely the three ancient creeds, the Apostolical, the Nicene, and the Athanasian, and required a rigid bona fide assent to them, with a scriptural system of church discipline; the divine power of the Gospel would not only have soon given preponderance to this emancipated and apostolic church, and spread her influence over the whole land; but she would actually have possessed far more doctrinal purity than at present; for now every form of heresy, from the mildest Semipelagianism to the rankest Socinianism and Deism, Communism and Pantheism, are found within her pale. And should even the Augsburg Confession and Heidelburg Catechism have been added, with the express proviso, that any person holding the tenets of either of these symbols, or a selection from both, should be regarded in good standing in the renovated church, all insuperable difficulties would have been removed. A separation would thus be effected between the neologians and orthodox, distinct churches would be organized, and experience would soon prove, that the neological religious consciousness sits too loosely on the mind, to urge its subjects to a voluntary support of their ministry; whilst the friends of Jesus would there, as in our own country, in England, and Scotland, give a moderate, though adequate support to those ministrations of the sanctuary, with which they believe their salvation closely connected. But, hitherto, the attachment to state establishments, conflicting pecuniary interests, and the lingering spirit of sectarianism, have frustrated this happy result. From the bottom of our hearts we say, both in regard to Germany and our own country, *Faxit Deus feliciter*!

But in our own happy land, in which all can worship God unmolested, under their own vine and fig tree; in this asylum for the oppressed of all nations, this heaven-appointed theatre for the free development of man in his social, civil, and religious interests, our church, standing on her high vantage ground, should review the past, carefully ponder the lessons it teaches, and maintain a position, which, whilst it is firmly based on the fundamentals of the Gospel, adds only those peculiarities of our ecclesiastical ancestors, which have generally commended themselves to the enlightened, orthodox, and pious portions of our church, and vindicates a rational liberty on all other points. What are the great landmarks of this position, how it can best be secured, and in how far it has been attained by our General Synod, are points which will be more clearly perceived in the progress of our discussion.

I. *Since, as eldest sister of the Reformation, our church was first to express the grand Protestant principle of exclusive, infallible authority of the Bible, in antithesis to tradition and human authority, and yet was prevented from carrying it out to its legitimate sequences; it is part of her vocation to complete the work so happily begun.*

The sufficiency of a revelation from Heaven, without the auxiliary light of tradition, is the natural corollary of its divinity itself. The very reason which rendered the one necessary, implies the invalidity of the other. If uninspired human teachings had been reliable, as sources of new truth, a revelation would have been superfluous. Hence the fact, that God inspired holy men of old to speak as the Spirit guided them, seems to establish the insufficiency of mere uninspired human deduction. But this word of revelation being admitted as divine, its own declarations must forever settle this point. The same inspired Apostle who declared all Scripture to be divinely inspired, (θεόπνευςος) and able not only to subserve some purposes of the man of God, but to make him "*perfect,*" thoroughly furnished, not only for some, but "for all good works;" has also explicitly pronounced the Holy Scriptures competent to teach us the supreme and vital interests of man, "able to make us wise unto salvation." Whilst he warns us to beware of any and every teacher, even if it were an angel from heaven, who should preach any other doctrine than that taught by himself, (and contained in his epistles,) and whilst he pronounces the curse of God upon him; the disciple whom Jesus loved, in the book placed last in the canonical collection, whether last written or not, adds the fearful menace: "if any one shall add unto these things, God shall add unto him the plagues that are written in this book." Since, then, it is evident that God designed his revelation to be as complete as it is infallible, to be the standing and only certain guide to his church in all ages; we urge the inquiry upon every ingenuous mind, upon every true disciple of our blessed Master, and especially upon ministers of the Gospel, what should be our unflinching determination on this subject? Certainly, that which the noble minded Luther and his Spartan band of coadjutors adopted, to adhere to the word of God, in opposition not only to angels and devils, but to popes, cardinals and councils, whenever, in our judgment, they come in conflict with this divinely authenticated voice of Heaven. "No man (said Luther) can or ought to doubt, that every thing contrary to the commands of God, whether it be living or dying, taking a vow or becoming free, speaking or remaining silent, is to be condemned, and by all means to be abandoned, changed and avoided. For the will of God must be supreme, and must be done in heaven and on earth. Matth. 6 : 10." And if the professions of any man were ever put to the test, Luther's were at the memorable diet of Worms, when summoned to recant his doctrines before that august court of the empire. His truly sublime answer, synonymous with that of the apostle's to the Jewish Sanhedrim, and given when he expected it would cost his life, has for three centuries been the subject of admiration to the civilized world: "Except I can be convinced by clear and conclusive reasoning, or by proofs taken from the Holy Scriptures, I neither can nor will recant; because it is neither safe nor advisable to do any thing which is against my conscience. Here I stand, I cannot do otherwise, God help me! Amen." The same principle he has expressed in various parts of his works. One or two passages must suffice. "Hitherto," says he, "all cases which arose concerning true and false doctrine, were referred to a council, or to the Pope at Rome, or to the universities, which were to be umpires. But these are not Gilead, they have misled and deceived us. But the Holy Scriptures pronounce the decision, as to whose instructions are correct or erroneous. For although the Holy Ghost instructs every one in his heart, so that he knows what is right; it is still necessary to resort to the Scriptures, in order to prove the accuracy of our views. It is the Scriptures which decide whether our faith is correct or not. Therefore, we can look for no farther evidence, either of the fathers or councils; but must adhere exclusively to the clear declaratious of Scripture."[1] Again, "God's word is the only certain rule which cannot deceive us."[2] Once more: "The right of free judgment we must retain, so as not to suffer ourselves to be bound indiscriminately by what

(1) Luther's Works, Walch's edit. vol. 3, p. 754.
(2) Vol. 1, p. 1854.

the councils or fathers have taught; but we must make this difference: if they have decided and appointed any thing according to God's word, we also receive it, not on their account, but on account of the same divine word, on which they rest, and to which they refer us."[1] Here, then, we have a distinct avowal of the paramount and exclusively infallible authority of the Scriptures, an avowal in direct conflict with the oath which he had taken when he was created Doctor of Divinity, in which he had solemnly *sworn* "*to obey the church of Rome, and not to teach any doctrines condemned by her.*"[2]

And shall it be supposed that he, whose sublime principles thus elevated him above the fate of emperors and kings, and cardinals and popes, contended against popes and bishops only to occupy their station himself, and wield a similar authority? That he who was so evidently guided by the fear of God, when contending against the decrees of councils, the authority of the fathers, and the bulls of popes, did so in order that men should bow to his opinions and make him the subject of similar idolatry? No, he neither did so himself, nor did others attempt it during his lifetime. It was not until more than a quarter of a century after his death, that *not the church* or body of believers; but some *secular princes* usurping authority not confided to them by God, together with some learned and excellent, but mistaken theologians, undertook to prescribe a doctrinal test to ministers in general, and thus dictate to them not only the general and fundamental doctrines of Christianity, but an extended detail of particulars, in one case at least, commanding the belief

---

(1) Idem, vol. ix. p. 631.

(2) As this oath is a literary curiosity, we subjoin it in the original, for the gratification of our learned readers: "Ego juro Domino Decano et Magistris Facultatis Theologiæ obedientiam et reverentiam debitam. et in quocunque statu utilitatem universitatis. et maxime Facultatis Theologicæ, pro virili mea procurabo, et omnes actus theologicos exercebo in mitra, (nisi fuerit religiosus) vanas peregrinas *doctrinas, ab ecclesia damnatas, et piarum aurium offensivas non dogmatisabo*, sed dogmatisantem Dn. Decano denunciabo intra octendium, et manutenebo consuetudines libertates et privilegia Theologicæ Facultatis pro virili mea, ut me Deus adjuvet, et Sanctorum evangeliorum conditores. *Juro etiam Romanæ ecclesiæ obedientiam* et procurabo pacem inter Magistros et Scholasticos seculares et religiosos. et biretum in nullo alio gymnasio recipiam." Lib. Statutorum facultatis theol. Academiæ Wittemberg. Cap. 7.

of a doctrine from which Luther had receded, the ubiquity or omnipresence of Christ's body! Yes, let it ever be remembered that Luther himself was no symbolic Lutheran, and that this whole system of minute confessional servitude, was riveted on the church long after Luther and Melancthon had been translated to a better world.

But although these two distinguished servants of Christ, guided by their supreme reverence for the Bible, accomplished wonders in casting off the major part of the errors and prejudices of their Romish education; they did not live to complete the work, nor had they power to introduce all the reforms, the necessity of which had become clear to their vision. They were therefore alike too wise and too humble, to desire the stadium of their attainments to be the *ne plus ultra* of reform. Against the practice of designating the church of the Reformation by his name, Luther protested in the most energetic manner, alledging it to be a repetition of Corinthian sectarianism, condemned by Paul. "The Papists," says he, "may well have party names, because they are not satisfied with the doctrines and names of Christ, and desire also to be popish. Then let them be called after the Pope, who is their master. *But I am not and will not be any one's master.*" Yet it was not only against this abuse of his name, that the noble-hearted Luther protested; it was far from his desire that his writings should be invested with binding authority on his successors. "If any person," said he in the latter part of his life, (1539,) "desires to have my writings, let him by all means not suffer them to interfere with his study of the scriptures themselves, but treat them as I do the papal decrees, and the works of the sophists, that is, though I occasionally look into them to see what they have done, or to take an account of the history of the times, it is not for the purpose of studying them, as though I must act according to their views."[1] "I have no catalogue of my works, and not even all the books themselves, and I would much rather that men would read the Bible alone, instead of my works."[2] And finally he says, "Read my books, compare them with the writings of our opponents, and both with the scriptures, and then judge them according to this touchstone."[3]

(1) Preface to his German Works. (2) Letter to Ursinus.
(3) Luther's Works, 3d vol., p. 256.

It is therefore the duty of Christians of the present day, and especially of this favored country, where liberty of conscience is our birthright, to act on the noble principles adopted by these reformers, and to reduce them to practice in those cases also, in which their Romish education prevented them from doing so. It is the special vocation of the American Lutheran church to forsake, as she has done, those remnants of Romanism and also those anti-papal superstitions which the church of Rome had borrowed from the earlier fathers, and which the first reformers failed to renounce. It is our vocation to cast off all regard for the authority of the fathers, Nicene and Anti-Nicene, Romish and Protestant, excepting what justly attaches to them on account of the intrinsic force of their arguments, or their character and opportunities as witnesses of facts; for no point in patristic theology is more fully established than the numerous and serious aberrations of even some of the earliest so-called fathers from the truth of God. Yea, it is certain, that the whole of them as a body are not more reliable as expositors of scripture than the same number of respectable authors in the different evangelical churches of our day. It is our duty to do as Luther did, to look up through the long vista of antiquity to the era of the apostles, and from that high standpoint to form a scriptural judgment not only of the corruptions of Rome, but of the doctrines and practice of all past ages. Had Luther acted on the principles of many now bearing his name, he would have founded his Christianity and the organization of his church on the basis of his great theological favorite, *Augustine*. He would have selected one or more of his works, either that entitled "*De Civitate Dei,*" in which he defends the Christian religion against the heathen, or more probably his "*Enchiridion* (or Manual) *ad Laurentium, sive de fide, spe et caritate liber,*" in which he gives an account of his doctrinal views and those of the church. This he would have made symbolical, pledging himself to abide by its contents for life, and binding all who united with his ministry to the same production. And this church he would have baptized as the *Augustinian church.* But no, Luther had not so learned Christ. He could discriminate between inspired and uninspired writings, between the books of God and those of men. Whilst, therefore, he avowed his assent to the three ecumenical creeds, the Apostolic, the Nicene and the Athanasian, which are confined to fundamentals, and are very short, he never adopted as binding any extended creed, nor suffered any human productions to deprive him of that liberty conceded by the word of God. He continued through life to improve his views of doctrine and duty, by the light of scripture, and in the most emphatic language inculcated on others the obligation to do likewise. That he was intolerant to Zwingli, and his followers, belongs to the imperfections of the age and of the man, not to his general principles of action. *Temporum culpa fuit, non ejus.* And were he still living we doubt not, he would hurl his denunciation at the intolerant ultra-Lutherans of our day, as he did at Carlstadt and Zwingli of old, only, by this time, in milder phrase.

How completely our General Synod has fulfilled her vocation in this respect, is evident from the fact that she makes no reference to the fathers, ancient or modern, thus leaving them all to stand on their intrinsic merits as theological authority, and as witnesses to historical facts; whilst the former symbolical books, after having pronounced the fathers fallible, nevertheless cite their views and arguments in multitudes of cases.

II. *As she has experienced the baneful effects of transfundamental and very extended creeds, it is her vocation to correct the evil.*

We have seen that Luther never desired any of his publications to be binding on others. Still farther was any disposition of this kind, removed from the mind of the unassuming Melancthon. All those publications of theirs, which were afterwards made symbolical, were composed and published for other puposes. How then did it happen, that these publications assumed so unexpected a character? The true state of the facts in the case is, we think, given by Dr. Kœllner, in his Symbolik.[1] "The symbolical books, (as they are afterwards styled,) were at first merely an expression of what *was* believed, and afterwards they became the rule of what *must* be believed. But when, and how this was first done, by public authority, it is very difficult to determine. The traces and evidences of it are often fallacious;

(1) Vol. I, p. 106, 107.

because cases in which such a subscription to a creed was merely requested and voluntarily given, may easily be adduced as cases in which the subscription was commanded. It however appears to be true, that some individual symbols had so much authority attributed to them, as to be recommended as rules of faith and of instruction, and in some instances also commanded, long before the formation of the Form of Concord," (which was *half a century* after the publication of the Augsburg Confession.) "Nevertheless this does not appear to have occurred everywhere at the same time, nor in the same manner; nor does the principle of binding men to the symbols, seem to have been a universal and prevailing one, prior to the formation of the Form of Concord in 1580, or before the prevalence of the controversies which originated from its formation. But a change took place about the time the Form of Concord was composed, and on account of its formation and after it. Prior to this time, some cases had occurred of oppressive coercion in matters of faith, and of compulsory adoption of the symbols as a rule of faith and instruction; but afterwards they became more numerous." These positions Dr. Kœllner sustains by numerous authorities, which even fix the precise time, when, at different places, the custom of demanding assent to these symbols was first introduced. It seems evident, therefore, that the habit of ascribing normative or binding authority to these books, though in a few instances it was done at an early day, was of gradual growth, and did not become general for *half a century after the Augsburg Confession was published* and used as an expose or profession of faith, and *many years after the death of Luther*.

It was the mistaken impression, that a general introduction and more stringent exaction of assent to these books, and the fabrication of another determining the several disputed points left free in them, would secure peace, that led to the formation of the Form of Concord, and to the imposition on the church; of the whole system of symbolic oppression. Whilst we deny the wisdom and dispute the Scripture authority of the political rulers of a country to impose any, much less such extended confessions of faith on their subjects; we, nevertheless, do not doubt the upright and benevolent intention of the Elector Augustus of Saxony, and of John William, Duke of Weimar, in ordering their principal theologians to Altenburg, to deliberate on the best method of terminating these disputes; nor of the Duke of Wurtemberg, and of Julius, Duke of Brunswick, in imposing on the distinguished James Andreæ of Tubingen and his associates, the duty of preparing the Form of Concord, which was finally adopted, and together with all the other symbolical books, made binding in their territory, June 25th, 1580. Nor do we hesitate to concede the purity of those distinguished divines, who cordially co-operated in this work. That diversity of opinion existed among the followers of Luther, on different points of nonfundamental importance, is historically certain; and when his death removed that restraint, which his personal influence and energy of character had imposed on them, they gave free utterance to their opinions. A very large proportion of the divines rejected Luther's view of the bodily presence in the Lord's Supper, and coincided more or less with that of Melanchthon. It is also certain, that their wily enemies, the Catholics, were employing these differences as arguments to urge upon the Emperor the revocation of the treaty of peace of 1555, which limited toleration to those, who worshipped according to the Augsburgh Confession.[1] This was, however, only a pretext, and would not have induced the Emperor to venture on such a step, until political reasons inclined him to it. When this contingency actually did arise, about forty years afterward, the forcible extinction of Protestantism was attempted by fire and sword, although the Form of Concord had driven from the bosom of the Lutheran church, the great mass of those who could not embrace all the peculiarities of the Augsburg Confession. We strongly favor the opinion, that the adoption of a liberal platform, by uniting the two great branches of the Protestant church, or rather by preventing in a great degree the schism itself, would have presented so formidable a front, as to have prevented the "Thirty years' War."

But that the adoption of the Form of Concord, and with it that unreasonably extended symbolic system, however

(1) The fourth article of the treaty was in these words: "Attamen ceteri omnes, qui alteri prænominatarum harum binarum religionum (that is, the Lutheran and Catholic) non sint adhærerentes, sub hac pace non comprehensi sed plane exclusi esse debant." For Zwinglians and Calvinists there was no toleration in this treaty.

well-intended, was a mistaken step, is evident from various considerations. It may justly be objected that the Scriptures have furnished us no confession of faith, an omission that was certainly not accidental, if their inspiration be conceded. Nor have they conferred authority on any one, to impose such a yoke upon the church, or to abridge her liberty in nonessentials. The only grounds which justify the adoption of even a short creed, are to exclude fundamental errorists, those who deny that Jesus is the Christ, or reject any other vital truth of the Gospel, and to produce uniformity sufficient for harmonious co-operation. Accordingly, during the golden age of Christianity, under the guidance of the apostles and their successors, the church for three centuries had no other creed than that termed the Apostolic and then the Nicene Creed. It was the opinion of the Nicene fathers who framed that creed, that its specifications were sufficiently ample for all practical purposes. Athanasius himself the Coryphæus of the orthodox party in that council, thus unequivocally expresses their conviction: ''Η γάρ ἐν ἀυτη παρά τῶν πατέρων κατα τὰς θείας γραφὰς ὁμολογηθεῖσα πίςις, ἀυτάρκης ἐςὶ προς ἀνατροπην μεν πάσης ἀσεβείας, συςασιν δε τῆς εὐσεβειας ἐν Χριςω πίςέως.[1] (For the faith avowed in it by those fathers in conformity to the word of God, is sufficient for the subversion of all impiety and for the establishment of all godliness, and of the faith in Christ.) The Emperor Zeno also wrote an epistle, urging all the discordant parties to unite on this creed, promising in that event to hold communion with them, and added that *the church should never receive any other symbol than that framed by the Nicene fathers.*[2] But whilst the above named considerations justify these brief summaries of faith, and a moderate extension of them, so as to exclude all subsequent fundamental errorists; they by no means establish the propriety of that vastly extended collection of symbols adopted by the Lutheran princes some time after Luther's death, which deprived that church of all reasonable liberty in points of minor importance.

That our view of the inexpediency of such extended creeds is just, may also be inferred from the circumstance that the major part of all these Lutheran symbols was rejected by

(1) Evag. Lib. III. c. 14. (2) Taylor's Liberty of Prophecying, p. 72.

one or more of the Lutheran kingdoms, even when they did not in all cases dissent from the doctrines taught in them. Indeed, as *Dr. Hase* justly remarks: "*The Augsburg Confession is the only one of them all, that was received thoughout the entire Lutheran Church.*" Yet strange to tell, some of our native Americans exhibit less love for their liberty of conscience, than the subjects of the regal and despotic governments of the old world! I. The *Form of Concord* was rejected by the *kingdom of Denmark.* "The king, though invited to adopt it, refused to do so, by advice of his clergy, who disapproved of it, because peace and unity of doctrine prevailed in his dominions, and he feared its introduction would *create strife aud divisions.* So bitterly was the king himself opposed to it, that he took the copy (decorated with pearls and gold) which had been sent to him from Germany, and cast it into the fire."[1] It subsequently acquired more popularity, but was never publicly acknowledged as symbolical.[2] The *kingdom of Sweden* did not receive the form of Concord, nor concede proper symbolic authority to the other symbolical books, except the Augsburg Confession.[3] Still at a later period, (1593) the Form of Concord received a tolerably formal acknowledgment, (ziemlich formlich Anerkennung).[4] It was also rejected by *Hessia, Pomerania, Holstein,* (for more than half a century), *Anhalt,* and the cities *Frankfort, Speier, Worms, Nurnberg, Madgeburg, Bremen, Danzig,* &c.[5] II. *The Smalcald Articles* were rejected by the Lutheran church in Sweden and Denmark. In Sweden the symbolic books generally are now regarded as an authorized explanation of the Lutheran faith; yet the symbolical books of the Danish church, lately published, like those of the Swedish church in 1644, (entitled Confession of the *Swedish* faith, approved by the council of Upsal in 1593,) contains only the so-called Apostles' Creed, the Nicene and Athanasian Creeds, and the Augsburg Confession, to which the Danish Confession adds the Smaller Catechism of Luther. Both these collections exclude the Smalcald Articles. Guericke's Symb. p. 67, and his History,

(1) Kollner's Symbolik, vol. I. p. 575, 576.

(2) Baumgarten's Concordien-buch, p. 184–185. Mosh. Eccles. Hist. vol. III. p. 155, Dr. Murdock's edit.

(3) Hutterus Redivivus. p. 116.

(4) Guericke's Symb. 2d ed. p. 112-113. (5) Kollner, p. 577.

first ed. p. 807. III. *The Apology to the Augsburg Confession* was denied official symbolic authority, by Sweden and Denmark. Guericke sup. cit. IV. *The Larger Catechism* of Luther was denied formal symbolic authority in Sweden and Denmark. Yet in both these kingdoms these Catechisms are highly prized, and the Smaller, if we mistake not, is used for the instruction of youth. Guericke, p. 113. Here, then, we behold the judgment of about one half of the different Lutheran kingdoms and principalities of Europe, announced in the most unequivocal and emphatic manner, in opposition to this extensive system of symbolic restriction; given too when these parties were fresh from the scenes of the Reformation, and warm in the principles by which that glorious moral revolution had been achieved. Surely these lessons of instruction ought to be heeded by the friends of reviving Lutheranism in Germany, and still more by those in this country who were "born free," but some of whom, from a zeal for Lutheranism, sincere we doubt not, but mistaken, seem disposed to sell their birthright.

Again, the infelicity of this Procustean symbolic system, which was completed by the Form of Concord, is demonstrated from its having *cost the Lutheran church a large portion of her ecclesiastical territory,* estimated at *about one-fourth of all her churches in Germany!* It drove off two numerous classes of persons, those who believed in the real presence as Luther did, but with him also rejected the ubiquity of the Saviour's glorified body; and those who agreed with Melanchthon on the Lord's Supper, as well as on some other topics, but wished to remain in the Lutheran church, as Melanchthon had done.

Had the civil rulers and their theologians been satisfied with the Augsburg Confession, and conceded liberty on all points, left undecided that symbol, the Reformed church would probably never have gained a foothold in Germany. In 1580, when the Form of Concord was proclaimed, there were but two Reformed congregations in all Germany, namely those of Bremen and Neustadt. But such was the unpopularity of this book, that in consequence of it and other related causes, in thirty years about one-fourth of the Lutheran churches in Germany had gone over to the Reformed communion. If it be objected, that the peculiar views of Luther on some points would have been abandoned, if they had not been stereotyped in a creed, and conformity to them been exacted by the civil authority; we reply, this would not have been the case to any considerable extent. But if any of the peculiar views of Luther should prove unable to sustain themselves in fair and equal conflict on the ground of reason and Scripture, the presumption would arise, that they are destitute of scriptural foundation, and on Luther's own principles, ought to be abandoned. The exaction of the Form of Concord, however, robbed the church of her liberty on many points not decided in the Confession of Augsburg, and thus drove thousands away from the Lutheran communion, either because they could not conscientiously adopt all the specifications of the new symbol, or if they did believe them, regarded it as unjust to condemn their brethren, and eject them from the church, because of non-essential differences of opinion. Indeed, had Luther and Melanchthon lived at that time, they would both have been excluded by this creed from the church which they founded, the former for not believing the ubiquity of the Saviour's body, and the latter for rejecting that and several other opinions affirmed in it; for as the distinguished historian, Dr. Staudlin justly observes: "This creed made binding the doctrinal system of the rigid Lutherans, which *went beyond the doctrines of Luther himself*, (welche selbst uber Luther's Lehren hinausgegangen waren), and took cognizance of all the controverted points, which had previously been discussed."[1]

In confirmation of our position we shall advance the testimony of but two historians. Touching the effects of the Form of Concord, Dr. Henke says: "But the most lamentable consequence of the book of Concord was, that whilst the number of *new Reformed churches was constantly increasing in Germany*, (for previously there were but two, namely in Bremen and in Neustadt on the Hardt), the mutual sectarian hatred of both Protestant parties was visibly increased, their interests were divided, and their mutual security jeoparded."[2] And the celebrated Lutheran historian, Dr. Plank, in his excellent and able History of Protestant

(1) Staudlin's Universal Geschichte der Christlichen Kirche, p. 308.
(2) Henke, vol. III. p. 464.

Theology, thus distinctly sustains our position: "This alone could be the result, and this alone was the result (namely of the adoption of the Form of Concord), that not only a number of individual theologians, but also a number of whole churches, which had hitherto belonged to the Lutheran party, gradually approximated nearer to the Calvinists, and soon formally and fully united with them. In the year 1580, at the time of the publication of the Formula, there were but two churches in Germany that had positively declared themselves for the Calvinistic doctrine on the Lord's Supper. At the close of the century, however, and therefore within the next twenty or thirty years, perhaps *fully one-fourth* of all the Protestant churches in the empire, had given in their full adhesion to this party. This was such a natural consequence, that it could not fail to follow. Already during the preliminary negotiations which had been conducted before the publication of the Formula, on the subject of its adoption, the ministers of a number of churches, as for instance of Hesse Cassel, of Nassau, of Anhalt, and of Zweibrucken, had declared in the most positive manner, that they never would submit to having the hypothesis of Christ's ubiquity forced upon them, either as a collateral idea in the doctrine of the Supper, or as a distinctive idea of the doctrine of the person of Christ. Yet these very churches in part declared just as decidedly, that they had every disposition to retain and profess the true Lutheran presence of Christ, as contained in the language of the Augsburg Confession and that of the unaltered edition. It thus happened, and that too in the natural course of things, that the very party which they had desired more particularly to suppress by means of the Form of Concord, that the Calvinistic party, now for the first time obtained such a footing, that the continuance of its existence was secured forever in Germany."

Assuredly, then, the fact that this extended symbolic system drove from the Lutheran church in Germany one-fourth of all her congregations, and was rejected by one-half of the kingdoms and principalities constituting the great Lutheran brotherhood, whose history fills so large a space in the annals of Europe during the last three centuries, should lead those amongst us, who have, without the most careful and extensive examination of the subject, eulogised this Form of Concord, to reflect. We know the impartiality of Dr. Plank has been called in question, but it is in vain. The undeniable facts of history establish his positions. It will not be supposed, that all those kingdoms and principalities rejected those books out of love to them, and refused to concede to them symbolic authority because they thought them fully deserving of it. And that they did reject them cannot and will not be denied. The testimony of Dr. Plank is, therefore, true, and facts will bear out the distinguished historian, Dr. Shroeck, in his honorable tribute to the merits of Dr. Plank: "The history of the Form of Concord, published by Anthon, deacon at Schmiedberg, in Electoral Saxony, is elaborated from the best of sources with much industry and accuracy. But here, also, as in the history of the antecedent controversies, *Dr. Plank has surpassed his predecessors* in acute penetration and impartial judgment."[1]

That this extended symbolic system was a mistaken one, is further evident from the fact, that it *failed to exclude disputes and differences from the church,* even where fully adopted; and infused greater acerbity of spirit into those controversies which occurred. Who that is acquainted with the history of those times, does not know, that whilst the adoption and enforcement of the Form of Concord and other confessions, decided what should thenceforth be regarded as authorized Lutheranism on many minor points, which had before been left free, thus giving greater fixedness and detail to the symbolical system; it nevertheless failed to alter the convictions of those, whose views it condemned. Some of the very princes and theologians who had advocated its formation, were dissatisfied with it when finished. Such was the case of Julius, Duke of Brunswick, and his theologians. "In Saxony itself," says Dr. Mosheim, "not a few detested in their hearts, that Formula which they subscribed with their hands, holding fast the doctrines

(1) Schroeck's Kirchengeschichte, Vol. iv, pp. 648, 649. "Aber auch hier wie in der Geschichte der vorhergehenden Streitigkeiten hat Herr Consist. Rath Plank, durch eindringende Scharfsicht und unparteiische Wurdigung seine Vorganger ubertroffen."

which they had received from Melancthon and his friends." On the accession of Christian I, they aimed at the rejection of the Form of Concord, the omission of exorcism in the Form of Baptism, and in general, the dissemination of Melancthonian views. As to the century immediately following the adoption of this extended symbolical system, the distinguished historian just cited, employs the following language: "During this whole century (the 17th,) the Lutheran church was *greatly agitated;* partly by controversies among the principal doctors, to the great injury of the whole community; and partly by the extravagant zeal and plans of certain persons, who disseminated new and strange opinions, uttered prophecies, and attempted to change all our doctrines and institutions. The controversies which drew the doctors into parties, may be fitly divided into the greater and the less; the former such as disturbed the whole church, and the latter such as disquieted only some parts of it."[1] False as is the charge of the Romish Stanislaus Rescius, that the Lutheran church had, in less than a century, given birth to two hundred and seventy sects,[2] there is but too much truth in the gloomy picture drawn by that master of ecclesiastical history, Dr. Mosheim. Of similar import is the testimony of Dr. Henke: "The Form of Concord," says he, "much rather gave rise to new cases of discord. Papal divines rejoiced, and ridiculed as well this peace measure, as the contentions which it was designed to settle, but which it only aggravated." Indeed, the bare enumeration of these controversies, the *Melancthonian,* or *Crypto-Calvinistic,* the *Zwinglian,* the *Calixtine,* the *Synergistic,* the *Helmstadian,* the *Pietistic* controversies, together with those concerning the *Ubiquity* or *omnipresence of Christ's body,* and the *Hypostatic union* of the two natures in Christ, and many others, will suffice to establish the position we affirm, whilst they stand as lasting monuments of the futility of extended creeds, either to prevent controversy or to promote unity of sentiment. Yea, instead of casting oil upon the troubled waters, this extended symbolic system did but agitate the church more, and divert her attention alike from her spiritual growth within, and from efforts to continue

(1) Mosheim, vol. III p. 157 of Murdock's ed.

(2) In his Tractatus de Atheismis and Phalarismis Evangelicorum, p. 327. Kocher, p. 213.

ner extension without. The extent and engrossing character of these intellectual conflicts, may be read in the fact, that on a single one of these disputes, the hypostatic or personal union of the two natures in Christ, about two thousand works were published;[1] and that distinguished servant of Christ, Augustus Hermann Francke, was formally charged with thirty heresies!! Numerous other testimonies might be adduced, to prove the augmented intensity given to these controversies by the adoption of these symbolic books; but it is self-evident to every intelligent mind, that when a controverted topic is made the subject of symbolic decision, and the divines holding one opinion are in danger of losing their living, and of seeing their families robbed of bread, the discussions will acquire a double violence from the self-interest necessarily involved in the result.

Finally, the inaptitude of this extended symbolic system is loudly proclaimed by the fact, that even in those countries which did receive all these books, not only the neologians, but *the great majority of those who adhere to the fundamental doctrines of the Bible, have renounced the symbolic authority of these writings, and regard them as in many points defective exhibitions of divine truth.* In not a single kingdom or principality of Germany, is unqualified assent to them any longer required. On this subject, let us again listen to the testimony of Dr. Kollner, Professor of Theology in Leipsic, an author whose statement of historical facts cannot be successfully impugned. In his recent work on Symbolics, he says:[2] "That these symbolical books actually teach the doctrines of the Scriptures, is confessedly a point disputed not only by many, but by a majority of the ministers of the church." "The truth seems to be, that the prominent doctrines of Christianity are undoubtedly taught in these symbols, such as the depravity of man, the necessity of Redemption through Christ, and of pardon and justification solely by the grace of God. But these fundamental truths are expressed in a manner, which, whilst it may perhaps accord with individual passages of Scripture, is inconsistent with its general tenor, and fails to distinguish the outward

(1) Atqui hinc sexcenti, quid dico sexcenti, bis mille libri conscripti sunt de communicatione idiomatum, de unione hypostatica, &c. Elementa Theol Dog Vol. II. p 93.

(2) Vol. 1, p. 146

form of the Revelation from its inward kernel." And again, "It may as well be openly acknowledged, and affirmed for the benefit of the church, that *there are but few divines* who yet believe and teach the views of the symbolical books; and of these some are *prejudiced fanatics, and others, however orthodox they profess to be, give their own interpretation to these books.*"[1] "Under these circumstances it is evident, that these books can no longer serve as a rule of doctrine:"[2] "For not only have the rationalists abandoned them, the leading champions of orthodoxy have also deviated from them, such as Doederlein, Morus, Michaelis, the venerable Reinhard, Knapp, Storr, Schott, Schwartz, Augusti, Marheinecke, Hahn, Olshausen, Tholuck and Hengstenberg."[3] That our prominent divines in this country, within the same period have done the same, such as Drs. Endress, Lochman, H. A. Muhlenberg, and the great mass of our divines now living, and of our church during the last quarter of a century, we fully established in our *Vindication of American Lutheranism,* in the Lutheran Observer during the past year. It was, therefore, natural that the Synod of Pennsylvania many years ago ceased to require a pledge of conformity to any of these symbols; as we also proved in the vindication referred to, by the testimony of two highly respectable divines still spared to the church, and as we know personally since thirty years, when we were licensed by that body. Still, to be without any other symbol than the Bible, was manifestly a defect, and how did the General Synod, believing it such, and feeling herself called to furnish a remedy, fulfil her vocation? She did it, we reply, in a manner, evincing alike her consciousness of the progress of theological science, and the scriptural development of the church, as well as her respect for her ecclesiastical ancestry; in a manner, we venture to affirm, that has commanded the respect of all enlightened divines of other churches, and has been signally blessed of God for her own enlargement and improvement. She required unqalified assent to the Bible, and an assent to the Augsburg Confession, as a substantially correct exhibition of the fundamental doctrines of the Bible. She did it by

(1) Vol. I., p. 148.
(2) Kollner, p. 147.
(3) Idem, p. 121.

establishing her Theological Seminary on the same doctrinal basis, not for the purpose of teaching the symbolic system of the sixteenth century, for her leading members had all relinquished some of its features; but as her Constitution, adopted in 1825, just a quarter of a century ago, explicitly declares, to prepare men to teach, not all the doctrines or aspects of doctrine in the Augsburg Confession, but the "*fundamental doctrines;*" and not those aspects of doctrine which might be considered fundamental peculiarities of that Confession, but "the fundamental doctrines of *the Scriptures;*" those aspects of doctrine which Christians generally regard as fundamental truths of *the word of God.* Or, as the same idea is expressed in another clause of that Constitution, the design of the General Synod in establishing her Seminary at Gettysburg, was, "to furnish the church with pastors, who sincerely believe, and cordially approve of the doctrines of the Holy Scriptures, as they are *fundamentally* taught in the Augsburg Confession."

Such is the enlightened position of the General Synod of our church. After ages will, we doubt not, bestow upon her that tribute of admiration, which leading spirits in all denominations now concede to her; but which some of her own beloved and esteemed sons seem unable to appreciate. And here it may not be amiss to utter a few words in reply to some strictures on Theological Seminaries by a recent writer on *Church-Feeling.* If, as his previous mention of Pennsylvania College renders probable, he refers to the Theological Seminary in the same place, we reply that undoubtedly the symbolical books of any institution and church, should be taught by those connected with them; and this we are happy to know is faithfully done in our Institution. We would also remind that writer of what he seems to have forgotten, that the symbolical books of any institution, Synod, or General Synod, are those books which they have adopted, and avowed as their rule of faith; and that the symbolical books of the General Synod and the Seminary at Gettysburg are the *Bible,* and the *Augsburg Confession, as a substantially correct exhibition of the fundamental truths of the Bible.* To this the professorial oath of office in the Seminary adds a similar *fundamental* assent to the two Catechisms of Luther. This doctrinal basis of the Seminary is secured from change by legislative charter, and by provision for appeal to the Supreme Judiciary of the State. Now, these doctrines always have been and still are fully and faithfully taught in this Institution. The Professors believe and teach the same doctrines now which they have taught for thirty years, and for the purpose of teaching which they were elected to their present important stations; and we may add, the very same doctrines, which that writer himself has preached for twenty years and still preaches! For them to inculcate on their students the obsolete views of the old Lutherans, contained in the former symbols of the church in some parts of Germany, such as exorcism, the real presence of the body and blood of Christ in the eucharist, private confession, baptismal regeneration, immersion in baptism, as taught in Luthers Larger Catechism, &c., would be to betray the confidence of those who elected them to office, and to defeat the design of the Institution, not one dollar of whose funds was contributed by Synods or individuals professing these views. Nor is it correct, if our institution be intended that the views of individuals and not of the church are taught in it. The doctrines taught are substantially those presented in the Popular Theology, and that these are the prevailing views of our church in America, we clearly established in different articles on American Lutheranism,[1] during the last year. We now merely add the testimony of two respectable divines, then omitted. The first is the *Rev. Dr. Morris*, who is extensively acquainted with the views of our church, and in his Introduction to Dr. Kurtz's "Why are you a Lutheran," affirms: "Dr. Schmucker's valuable Popular Theology has contributed much to remove wrong impressions from the minds of many intelligent readers, and the Lutheran Observer with its extensive circulation still continues to exhibit us in a true light." The other is *Rev. Dr. Baugher*, President of Pennsylvania College. With the exception of several minor shades of doctrine, in which we are more symbolic than he, we could not ourselves, in so few words, give a better description of the views taught in the Seminary than that contained in his "Abstract of the Doctrines and Practice of the Evangelical Lutheran Synod of Maryland," presented to his Synod, in which the points of symbolic differences are disposed of in these words: "We believe the scriptures

(1) See Lutheran Observer for 1850.

teach, that there are but two sacraments, viz.: Baptism and the Lord's Supper, in each of which truths essential to salvation are *symbolically represented.* We do not believe that they exert any influence *ex opere operato. Neither do the scriptures warrant the belief,* that Christ is present in the Lord's Supper in any other than a *spiritual* manner." And again, "Luther's Larger and Smaller Catechisms, the Formula Concordiæ, Augsburg Confession, Apology, and Smalkald Articles, are called, *in Germany,* symbolical books of the church. *We* regard them as good and useful exhibitions of truth, but *do not receive them as binding*[1] on the conscience, except so far as they agree with the word of God." "We believe in the reality of revivals of religion, and regard them as a source of the richest blessings to the church." There seems, therefore, to be no ground of apprehension as to our Seminary, since the doctrines of *our* symbols, and the *prevailing* doctrines of our *American church,* are here faithfully taught.

With brethren entertaining the views of scripture doctrine, and the symbolic position here attributed to our church, we delight to co-operate. It is true several respectable divines of our church have, within the last few years, devoted more attention to these symbolical books, and urged others to do so. To this we make no objection. We have spent probably more time in their perusal than these brethren; yet we shall be very slow to believe, that after having studied and preached the Bible for fifteen or twenty years, they will now suffer themselves to receive, under the guidance of these symbolical books, doctrines, which, after so long a search, they had failed to find in the word of God. Yet should they even change their views of doctrine, we can still live in harmony with them, if they are willing to let us continue to teach in peace what they themselves formerly inculcated, and what we have always taught, and what we were appointed to teach.

In view of what has been advanced, the symbolic position which the General Synod has adopted, in fulfilling her vocation, may be reduced to three features, viz.: 1. She has declared against the extended symbolic system of the for-

---

(2) The italics in this quotation are ours, to show more clearly the points of agreement.

mer ages of our church. 2. She has avowed the necessity of a brief creed, to exclude fundamental errorists from her pale; and, 3. She has adopted the Augsburg Confession, as to fundamentals, for this purpose, as well on account of its intrinsic excellence, as its important historical associations. With this, we for ourselves, are fully satisfied. We believe this position, so signally blessed of God, to be truly apostolic, and well calculated to extend the borders and improve the doctrinal purity and spiritual character of our church. Yet there seem to be some few ministers even in the General Synod, who appear not to trust either themselves or others, with so much apostolic liberty, though it is much less than the church enjoyed for four centuries, yea, so far as doctrine is concerned, for a thousand years after the apostolic age! If it is deemed advisable to gratify this yearning after human creeds, we would propose the adoption of the following system:

1. *The so-called Apostles' Creed.*
2. *The Nicene Creed.*
3. *The Augsburg Confession*, so far as its doctrinal articles are concerned: with one single clause annexed, stating that its teachings on the following doctrines shall not be regarded as binding, but belief or rejection of them be left to the conscience of each individual, viz: the real presence, baptismal regeneration, private confession and absolution, "Ceremonies of the mass," the personal and condemning guilt of natural depravity, prior to moral action.

This arrangement would cover the differences existing in our church, and allow a rational liberty in investigating the scriptures on these controverted topics whilst it would exclude all errors, and sufficiently distinguish us as a denomination. It would unite in harmony all portions of our church, except those who not only implicitly adopt all the errors and obsolete views of the symbolical books, but are also unwilling to co-operate with such as cannot conscientiously follow their example. Even the Scandinavian churches, recently established in our North-western States, could probably unite with us, as some of them, at least, whilst adhering to the Augsburg Confession in general, propose to reject some of its povisions, such as private confession and absolution, as also some of the usages of their fatherland, the wearing of the gown, the burning of candles on the altar by day, and the churching of women.[1] "In short, they propose to restore the *church system to the simple, pure and evangelical position, that it undoubtedly occupied in the times of the apostles and the first christians.*" This is exactly the truly enlightened, the exalted position of our General Synod. We hail with delight the co-operation of these noble Northmen, and of all others who labor in the same spirit, and bid them a hearty God speed ; assured that in that great day the inquiry of the Master will be, whether we have conformed our doctrines not to the writings of Luther, but *to the tuition of his own inspired word.*

(1) See Mr. Langland's political and religious paper, termed *The Democrat,* issued at Racine, Wisconsin.

INDEX.

www.ingramcontent.com/pod-product-compliance
Lightning Source LLC
LaVergne TN
LVHW010220110826
845151LV00004B/1161

* 9 7 8 1 4 2 5 5 2 6 4 9 8 *